Study Guide

English

AQA English

GCSE Success

GCSE Success

AQA
English
Language & Literature

Steven Croft

Contents

This book and your GCSE course 4

Controlled Assessment and functional skills 6

Preparing for the examination 7

Five ways to improve your grade 8

1 Writing for audience and purpose

1.1 Understanding the importance of audience and purpose ... 9

1.2 Context and topic 12

Sample GCSE question 15

Practice questions 16

2 Analysing written and spoken language

2.1 Analysing written texts 17

2.2 Analysing spoken language 23

Sample GCSE question 29

Practice questions 31

3 Exploring non-fiction texts

3.1 Approaching non-fiction texts 32

3.2 Magazine articles 33

3.3 Biographies and autobiographies 36

3.4 Travel writing 38

3.5 Documentary writing 40

3.6 Literary non-fiction 42

Sample GCSE question 45

Practice questions 46

4 Studying media texts

4.1 Examining newspapers 47

4.2 Looking at advertising 52

4.3 Film and television 57

Sample GCSE question 62

Practice questions 63

5 Presenting views, ideas and information

5.1 Presenting an argument 64

5.2 Persuasive writing 71

5.3 Presenting advice 77

5.4 Presenting information 80

Sample GCSE question 84

Practice questions 85

6 Imaginative and creative writing

6.1 Types of imaginative and creative writing 86

6.2 Aspects of story writing 89

6.3 Descriptive writing 93

Sample GCSE question 96

Practice questions 97

7 Studying Shakespeare

7.1 Types of Shakespearean play	98
7.2 Plot and structure	100
7.3 Opening scenes	102
7.4 Presenting characters	106
7.5 Shakespeare's language	109
7.6 Endings	113
Sample GCSE question	115
Practice question	116

8 Studying drama

8.1 Approaching the text	117
8.2 Opening scenes	119
8.3 Presenting characters	121
8.4 Setting, stage directions and themes	123
Sample GCSE question	126
Practice questions	127

9 Exploring prose texts (contemporary prose and Literary Heritage prose)

9.1 Novels and short stories	128
9.2 Openings	130
9.3 Developing characters	135
9.4 Setting and context	140
9.5 Exploring themes	143
Sample GCSE question	145
Practice questions	146

10 Studying poetry

10.1 Reading poetry	147
10.2 Features of poetry	149
10.3 Poetry in context	155
10.4 Comparing poems	160
Sample GCSE question	163
Practice questions	165

11 Speaking and Listening

11.1 What Speaking and Listening involves	166
11.2 Presenting	167
11.3 Discussing and listening	169
11.4 Role playing	170
Controlled Assessment Speaking and Listening practice tasks	172

Practice questions answers	173
External exam practice papers	176
Answers	194
Acknowledgements	199
Index	200

This book and

AQA English Language

Scheme of Assessment	Covered in Chapters...
Unit 1 Understanding and producing non-fiction texts (external exam) **Section A Reading** At Higher Tier, you must answer four questions based on three non-fiction texts. At Foundation Tier, you must answer five questions, including those requiring shorter responses, based on three non-fiction texts. Texts will be drawn from a range of non-fiction genres including media sources (including texts with images and / or other presentational devices) and literary non-fiction such as travelogues and biographies. **Section B Writing** At both Higher and Foundation Tiers, you must do two writing tasks. The writing tasks will also be based on a range of non-fiction genres and all tasks will ask you to write for specific audiences and purposes, adapting your style so that it is fit for purpose. *The functional elements of English are embedded within this unit, allowing you to show that you are a competent reader and writer in your daily life.* **This unit will count for 40% of the total GCSE marks (20% for Section A and 20% for Section B).**	1, 2, 3, 4, 5
Unit 2 Speaking and Listening (Controlled Assessment) You will be assessed on **three** speaking and listening tasks although you may well do more than one performance of each activity during the unit. You will be assessed on one activity in each of the following categories: • Presenting • Discussing and listening • Role playing **This unit will count for 20% of the total GCSE marks.**	11
Unit 3 Understanding spoken and written texts and writing creatively (Controlled Assessment) • **Part A Extended reading** You will need to submit **one** task from a bank of tasks set by AQA. The tasks you will be set will draw on your study of one extended text from any genre, including non-fiction. This may include a collection of poems, short stories or non-fiction. You could use any of the collections from the Anthologies *Moon on the Tides* and *Sunlight on the Grass*. You can use any of the texts being studied for GCSE English Literature, but you must submit a separate task that meets the requirements of the GCSE English Language course. • **Part B Creative writing** You will submit **two** pieces of writing prepared under controlled conditions chosen from two of the topics given in this unit. • **Part C Spoken language study** You will need to submit **one** study of spoken language, in either an oral or written response, prepared under controlled conditions and chosen from the topics given for this unit. **This unit will count for 40% of the total GCSE mark (15% for part A, 15% for part B and 10% for part C).**	1, 2, 3, 6, 7, 8, 9, 10

your GCSE course

AQA English Literature

There are two routes you can take through your GCSE English Literature course.

Route 1

Scheme of Assessment	Covered in Chapters...
Unit 1 Exploring modern texts (external exam) • **Section A Modern prose or drama** You answer **one** question, from a choice of two, given on a modern set text you have studied (prose or drama). • **Section B Exploring cultures** You answer **one** question on the set text you have studied (texts that explore different cultures). **This unit will count for 40% of the total GCSE mark (20% for Section A and 20% for Section B).**	2, 6, 8, 9

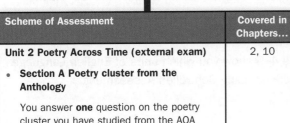

PLUS

Scheme of Assessment	Covered in Chapters...
Unit 2 Poetry Across Time (external exam) • **Section A Poetry cluster from the Anthology** You answer **one** question on the poetry cluster you have studied from the AQA Anthology *Moon on the Tides*. The question will be in two parts. • **Section B: Responding to an unseen poem** You answer **one** question on an unseen poem. **This unit will count for 35% of the total GCSE mark (23% for Section A and 12% for Section B).**	2, 10
Unit 3 The significance of Shakespeare and the English Literary Heritage (Controlled Assessment) You complete **one** Controlled Assessment task, which asks you to make links between a play from Shakespeare and any other text, of any genre from the English Literary Heritage. **This unit will count for 25% of the total GCSE mark.**	2, 7, 8, 9, 10

Route 2

Scheme of Assessment	Covered in Chapters...
Unit 1 Exploring modern texts (external exam) • **Section A Modern prose or drama** You answer **one** question, from a choice of two, given on a modern set text you have studied (prose or drama). • **Section B Exploring cultures** You answer **one** question on the set text you have studied (texts that explore different cultures). **This unit will count for 40% of the total GCSE mark (20% for Section A and 20% for Section B).**	2, 6, 8, 9

PLUS

Scheme of Assessment	Covered in Chapters...
Unit 4 Approaching Shakespeare and the English Literary Heritage (external exam) • **Section A Shakespeare** You answer **one** question, from a choice of two, on the Shakespearean text you have studied. The question will be in two parts and asks you to consider a short extract from the play. • **Section B Prose from the English Literary Heritage** You answer **one** question, from a choice of two, on the set text you have studied (a prose text from the English Literary Heritage). **This unit will count for 35% of the total GCSE mark (20% for Section A and 15% for Section B).**	7, 9
Unit 5 Exploring poetry (Controlled Assessment) You complete **one** Controlled Assessment task, which asks you to make links between a range of poems that must cover contemporary poetry and poetry from the English Literary Heritage. You may use poems from the Anthology *Moon on the Tides* for this unit. **This unit will count for 25% of the total GCSE mark.**	10

Controlled Assessment and functional skills

Controlled Assessment

Controlled Assessment is a form of internal assessment in which you work under controlled conditions, but in a different way to that of an externally set exam. Controlled Assessment replaces traditional coursework in all GCSE English, English Language and English Literature specifications.

Basically, it is used:
- To assess Speaking and Listening tasks.
- To allow coursework-type tasks to be undertaken in the classroom or other environment under supervision.

Three different levels of supervision are used, depending on the task and the way it is being assessed:
- **Formal supervision (high level of control)** – the tasks are set by AQA and students must be directly supervised at all times. Under these circumstances there will be no contact with other students.
- **Informal supervision (medium level of control)** – students are given outlines of questions or tasks and it is likely that you will have access to resources. It may be that your work is assessed through participation in group work of some kind. The person supervising you can give you limited guidance.
- **Limited supervision (low level of control)** – students work under clearly specified conditions. However, some work may be completed without direct supervision and will not contribute directly to your assessment.

The course overviews on pages 4–5 show you which units of English Language and English Literature are assessed using Controlled Assessment.

Functional skills

Functional skills in English are concerned with developing the skills to enable you to use English effectively in everyday life. They are the practical skills that help you to get the most out of your work, your education and everyday life. Possessing sound functional skills helps you to deal with a whole range of situations, tasks and activities that you can be faced with in your day-to-day life. For example, being able to deliver a presentation on a particular topic, summarise the key points in a text, work out the best deal on various adverts for mobile phones or write a letter of application for a job.

In order to show effective functional skills, you will need to:
- Write documents of various kinds and on various subjects.
- Make effective presentations in a range of contexts.
- Read and summarise effectively information from different sources.
- Use spelling, punctuation and grammar accurately so that your meaning is clear.

Opportunities to develop your functional skills are embedded in the AQA GCSE English Language course you are studying.

Preparing for the examination

Planning your revision

Effective revision is very important in achieving a good grade in GCSE English Language and English Literature and you should make sure that you prepare yourself well for the examination. Here are some points to bear in mind:

- Begin your revision in good time.
- Make sure that you know exactly what to expect on each of your exam papers and what they will require you to do. A good way to do this is to look carefully at specimen or past exam papers.
- Look at the mark schemes for your exam papers – these will show you what the examiners are looking for. (You can find specimen papers and mark schemes on the AQA website.)
- Organise your revision carefully and devise a revision programme or timetable to ensure that you know you can cover all the material in the time you have available.

Preparing a revision programme

Here are some ideas to think about when drawing up your revision programme:

- Identify all the areas you need to revise and manage your revision time effectively – draw up a plan fitting in all the topics / activities you will cover.
- Make sure you know all the texts that you are studying very well. Read them again at least once before the exam.
- Make notes on key points as you revise and test yourself on them.
- If you are studying a drama text, if possible, watch a performance (perhaps on DVD) of it again as part of your revision.
- Make sure that you are able to write accurately and fluently. If you have problems with any areas (e.g. spelling, punctuation), work on them to improve your knowledge before you sit the exam.

How this book will help you

This *Revise GCSE AQA English Language and Literature Study Guide* will help you because:

- It contains all the **essential content** for your AQA GCSE English Language and English Literature courses.
- **Examiner's tips** in the margin and highlighted **key points** throughout the book will draw you to important points you might otherwise miss.
- **Progress checks** are included in each chapter to help test your skills and confirm your understanding.
- **Sample GCSE questions with answers** can be found at the end of each chapter to give you an idea of what the examiners want to see.
- **Practice GCSE questions** are provided at the end of each chapter with summary answers to guide you on the points you should be covering.
- **Example practice exam papers** for both AQA English Language and AQA English Literature are provided at the back of the book to give you valuable practice in answering the type of questions you will get in the exam. Summary answers are also provided to guide you on the points you should be covering. Note that the extracts used in these practice exam papers are shorter than the extracts you will be provided with in the actual exam.

Five ways to improve your grade

❶ Practise the kinds of questions you will need to answer

As part of your preparation for the exams, you should **make sure you are completely clear about the kinds of questions you will need to answer**. You should have practised writing answers to these kinds of questions, both throughout the course and as part of your revision programme. Examples are given at the end of each chapter in this book, as well as in the practice papers on pages 176–193.

❷ Read the question carefully

Many students fail to answer the actual question set. Perhaps they misread the question, or answer a similar one they have studied during revision. To avoid doing this, **read the question once right through**, then **re-read it more slowly**. Some students <u>underline</u> or **highlight** key words as they read through the question. Questions set for GCSE English Language and English Literature often ask you to give your own views on a topic. **Make sure you express your ideas clearly** and, where necessary, **support your ideas with appropriate references and evidence**.

❸ Plan your answer

Planning what you are going to write is a very important part of answering the question. Essays written without any form of planning are usually poorly structured and rambling and, consequently, score low marks. Don't think that time spent planning your work is wasted – **careful planning will mean that you produce a much better answer**.

❹ Write accurately

The quality of your written communication is very important. Make sure your responses are written as clearly and as accurately as possible and make good use of spelling, punctuation and grammar. Poor spelling, punctuation and grammar will mean that you will not score as highly as you might and can interfere with the clarity of what you want to say. Try to **leave time to check through your work** before the end of the exam.

❺ Keep a check on the time

Time is a major factor in writing an examination answer. In order to ensure you say all you want to say in the time allowed and do not have to leave the essay unfinished, **you need to time yourself carefully**.

1 Writing for audience and purpose

The following topics are covered in this chapter:

- Understanding the importance of audience and purpose
- Context and topic

1.1 Understanding the importance of audience and purpose

LEARNING SUMMARY

After studying this section, you should be able to understand:

- what is meant by purpose in speech and writing
- the importance of audience

In the work that you study and produce for your GCSE course (both in written and spoken English) you should always be aware that the ideas of **audience** and **purpose** lie at the centre of any piece of writing, or spoken communication.

These two words are key terms that you need to be constantly aware of both in studying the writing of others and in producing your own writing.

Purpose

AQA	E Lang	E Lit
	✓	✓

Writing and speech can have many purposes and each purpose can itself take many forms. Here are some possible purposes:

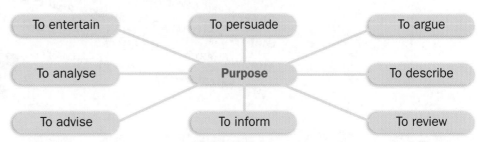

These are just some of the possible purposes that speech and writing can have. Obviously, sometimes there may be more than one purpose and sometimes a variety of purposes might overlap.

Look at these two texts. What do you think is the main purpose of each?

Text 1

What are biofuels?

Biofuel is the name given to any kind of fuel that is made out of living things or from the waste that they produce.

For example:
- wood, straw, etc.
- methane (called biogas) from animal waste
- liquid fuels such as diesel or ethanol made from processed plant material or oil from plants

Nowadays the term 'biofuel' has mainly come to mean liquid fuels of some kind made from crops that have been farmed such as rape, maize or sugarcane.

Text 2

The scene was changing rapidly. What, a few minutes earlier, had been a tranquil landscape basking in the warm sunlight of an early autumn afternoon had now assumed a darker and more ominous atmosphere. The trees that had glowed a soft golden shade now were dark and their branches began to sway and creak as the light breeze gathered force and became an increasingly strong wind. The sun had now disappeared completely behind the black clouds that were piling up in the sky and it was then that we heard, still way in the distance, the first threatening growl of thunder.

The purpose of text 1 is **to inform**. The purpose of text 2 is **to describe**.

Audience

AQA	E Lang	E Lit
	✓	✓

The audience to which a piece of writing or speech is addressed can be very varied. Here are some examples of broad audience groups:

- **Different age groups**, e.g. a fairy story might be aimed at very young children; an advert advertising special offers for pensioners might be aimed at the over 60s.
- **Special interest groups**, e.g. an advert for a history book club would be aimed at those interested in reading about history; a report of a football match is likely to be aimed at those interested in football or, maybe even more specifically, one of the teams that the report features.
- **Professional groups**, e.g. an article in *The Times Educational Supplement* is likely to be aimed at those involved in the teaching profession; an article on the latest advances in keyhole surgery published in a medical journal is likely to be aimed at doctors and surgeons.
- **Different social groups**, e.g. a leaflet explaining the benefits available to those who do not have much money is likely to be aimed at people in a lower income group; a university prospectus is aimed primarily at students.
- **General audience**, e.g. a popular newspaper is aimed at a broad general readership.

You will see from this that audiences can vary greatly in both type and size. For example, a note to your newsagent cancelling a magazine will have an audience of one person – your newsagent, whilst a popular newspaper can have an audience of millions.

> **KEY POINT**
>
> Audiences and purposes can vary greatly. Make sure that you think carefully about the purpose and audience of any writing or speech that you are asked to write about.

Here are two extracts from different texts. The first is the opening of a novel and the second is an advertisement. Read each extract carefully.

Text 1

> When Farmer Oak smiled, the corners of his mouth spread till they were within an unimportant distance of his ears, his eyes were reduced to chinks, and diverging wrinkles appeared round them, extending upon his countenance like the rays in a rudimentary sketch of the rising sun.
>
> His Christian name was Gabriel, and on working days he was a young man of sound judgment, easy motions, proper dress, and general good character.
>
> From *Far From the Madding Crowd* by Thomas Hardy

Text 2

Pip 12.08.09

Pip 02.03.10

PGFCA

Scrappy was starving when we found her and Pip had been wandering the streets for weeks surviving any way she could.

Many animals do not have anyone to love them. Could that person be you? For only £2 per month you could say 'I love you' to an abandoned animal.

I want to sponsor a dog! Call **06057 888 555** or fill in your name and address below.

Mr/Mrs/Miss/Ms/Other ....

Address ....

.... Postcode ....

Telephone: .... Date of birth ....

The writer of text 1 aims to entertain the reader. This is the primary purpose. This text is the opening of a novel and the writer concentrates on describing one of the main characters in order to introduce him and give the reader a sense of what he is like. As a novel, its purpose is also to entertain the reader.

As a novel this text is also aimed at those who enjoy reading fiction for pleasure.

> **PROGRESS CHECK**
>
> 1 What does the writer of text 2 aim to do (i.e. what is its purpose)?
> 2 Who is text 2 aimed at (i.e. who is its audience)?
>
> 1. This text is an advertisement, which is trying to persuade the reader to donate money to help look after abandoned dogs.
> 2. The text is aimed at a general readership, but obviously focuses on those who like dogs and are concerned about their welfare. This is the audience who are most likely to want to donate money to help look after abandoned dogs.

1.2 Context and topic

LEARNING SUMMARY	After studying this section, you should be able to understand:
	• what is meant by context
	• what is meant by topic

Context

AQA	E Lang	E Lit
	✓	✓

As you have seen, any text has a purpose or a combination of purposes. However, the purpose of a text is not something that you should see in isolation. You have already seen that purpose is closely linked to the idea of audience, but it is also closely linked to **context** and **topic**. All texts are written within a certain context and are concerned with a certain subject or topic.

The **context** is to do with the situation in which the text takes place. For example, a historical context may be concerned with the period in time that a text is set and the effect this has on the way it is written; or in looking at a poem written during the First World War, the war-time context is likely to have an important part to play in the way the poem has been written. The way in which a letter of complaint is written will be dependent on the context of the particular complaint that is being made.

Topic

AQA	E Lang	E Lit
	✓	✓

The **topic** refers to what the text is about – its subject matter. Obviously, this is closely linked to the context.

Here are three short texts. Read them carefully.

Text 1

Text 2

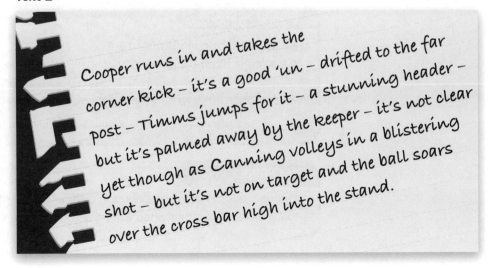

Text 3

2 Shaw Street
Hipwall
Lancaster
L12 6AB

Mr Atkinson
Light House Apartments
Thistle Road
Brighton
BN4 16J

10th April

Dear Mr Atkinson

Further to my recent enquiry about accommodation for August, I would like to confirm my booking for Flat B with a sea view, arriving 3 August and departing 10 August.

There will be four of us in the party – two adults and two children.

I enclose a cheque for £50 as a deposit.

Yours sincerely,
D. Smith

The **context** of text 1 is a 'Situations Vacant' section of a local newspaper. Within the context of that section of the newspaper it is completely in context, but if you found it in the middle of the TV guide section it would appear out of context.

The **context** of text 2 is part of a commentary on a football match and set within the context of a commentator watching and describing the match.

The **topic** of text 1 is the job – the details of the job are given – note the use of language connected to the topic, e.g. assistant, required, experience, training.

The **topic** of text 2 is a particular football match and the kind of language used reflects that topic, e.g. corner kick, ball, header, keeper.

PROGRESS CHECK

1. What is the context of text 3?
2. What is the topic of text 3?

1. It is a letter booking accommodation and has been produced within the context of booking a suitable holiday flat.
2. The topic is a letter to book a holiday flat. The language used reflects the nature of the topic, e.g. accommodation, arriving, departing, deposit.

KEY POINT

Purpose, audience, context and topic are all closely linked and should be thought about together when writing or looking at texts.

Sample GCSE question

Write a review of a book that you have read recently for your local reading group's monthly magazine.

Book Review: Of Mice and Men

John Steinbeck's novel 'Of Mice and Men' is set in America during the Depression and tells a moving story of two itinerant workers, George and Lennie. The novel opens as the two men are making their way across country to a ranch where they gain employment, and it is in this opening scene where we learn a great deal about their relationship.

The two men are portrayed as being very different. George is described as being "small and quick" whereas Lennie, who has the mentality of a small child, is "huge" and "bear"-like. However, it soon becomes clear that, despite the stark contrast of their physical appearances and mental capacities, they share a deep and well-established friendship. George is seen to act as a kind of 'parent' figure to Lennie who, because of his actions whilst in their previous place of employment, is the cause of them having to 'move on'.

In addition to them sharing a deep friendship, they also share a dream – one of owning their own farm. We learn of the dream early on in the novel where we see George reassuring Lennie by painting a wonderful picture of how, one day, they will have the security of owning and working on their own farm and being able to settle down and "live off the fatta the lan'". Lennie is seen to draw a great deal of comfort from being told what could be seen as a 'bedtime' story, especially as it is promised that he will "tend the rabbits".

'Dreams' is just one of the themes that Steinbeck explores in 'Of Mice and Men' and they seem to be born out of loneliness, another major theme of the novel. Although the story is mainly set on the ranch, Steinbeck introduces a variety of characters through which he explores the effects of loneliness and isolation. For example, Crooks is a man hired to look after the horses on the ranch. Not only is he seen to be socially isolated through a physical disability but he bears the added burden of being discriminated against because he is black. Crooks lives and works separately from the rest of the men, which highlights the sense of his isolation, and is seen to have developed very little self-worth: "Crooks had reduced himself to nothing".

Other characters are seen to live a lonely existence too. For example, Candy, an old ranch hand, has only his dog for companionship and the only woman on the farm also suffers in her loneliness due to her unhappy marriage to the ranch owner's son, Curley. The fact that Steinbeck doesn't give her a name emphasises her apparent 'insignificance' and the flirtatious behaviour she demonstrates seems to be how her loneliness manifests itself. However, even she has a dream.

Steinbeck's success in portraying believable characters, along with his ability to use language effectively to describe both characters and setting, make this novel extremely entertaining and, although the sense of foreboding which can be detected throughout the novel makes the ending somewhat expected, it doesn't affect the level of suspense that Steinbeck achieves.

Good opening – brief outline of plot gives the reader a clear idea of the context of the novel.

Clear initial impression of characters supported by references to the text. These give the reader specific examples of the language used.

Moves on to mention a key theme of the novel. Again the comments are firmly rooted in the text. These help the reader to form an overview of the focus of the novel.

Discusses other themes and how they relate to the other characters and the setting of the story.

Discusses other characters, again fulfilling the purpose of giving the reader a clear overview.

Gives a judgement on the novel and the effectiveness of the ending, which gives the reader an impression of the reviewer's overall opinion of the novel.

Practice questions

1. Write an article for your school magazine in which you express your views on the contribution that the Internet has made to education.

   (External exam question: English Language, Unit 1)

2. Your school magazine has invited students in your school or college to write about their most memorable experiences. The students whose writing is selected for publication will receive a prize.

   Write about your most memorable experience to send in as your entry.

   (External exam question: English Language, Unit 1)

3. A group of students from your school or college is going on a camping trip to Scotland. Write an advice leaflet for them, giving them advice on what to take with them and essential 'dos' and don'ts' when camping.

   (External exam question: English Language, Unit 1)

4. Write a letter to your local newspaper arguing either for or against plans for a wind farm, the site for which has been proposed near where you live.

   (External exam question: English Language, Unit 1)

2 Analysing written and spoken language

The following topics are covered in this chapter:

- **Analysing written texts**
- **Analysing spoken language**

2.1 Analysing written texts

LEARNING SUMMARY

After studying this section, you should be able to understand:

- the kinds of texts you might be asked to analyse
- how to approach your analysis
- how to analyse a text
- how to approach your own analytical writing

The kinds of text you might analyse

	E Lang	E Lit
AQA	✓	✓

One of the keys to success in studying English is developing your ability to analyse the ways in which writers use language in different forms and explore the effects of the language choices they make in creating images in the reader's mind.

Throughout the course you will need to analyse various kinds of written texts.

Here are some examples of the kinds of texts you might encounter:

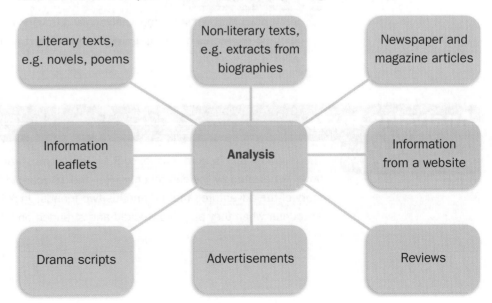

Literary texts, e.g. novels, poems

Non-literary texts, e.g. extracts from biographies

Newspaper and magazine articles

Information leaflets

Analysis

Information from a website

Drama scripts

Advertisements

Reviews

Approaching analysis

	E Lang	E Lit
AQA	✓	✓

When you analyse a piece of writing of any kind, you need to approach the task in an organised way and have some kind of plan.

We have already looked at the importance of thinking about purpose, audience, context and topic when looking at a piece of writing. Your analysis will look at other features too.

Your analysis may include:
- **what** is being said in the text
- **how** it is being said – how the **language** is used
- the **effects** created by the particular use of language

You must support your ideas with specific **references** from the text, drawing **conclusions** about the effectiveness of the writing.

Here are the key elements you need to think about when approaching your textual analysis.

Audience, purpose, topic, context and content	What is the text for or what is it doing? (purpose)
	Who is the text addressing or aimed at? (audience)
	Where, or under what circumstances, does the text appear? (context)
	What is the text about? (topic)
	What does the text say? (content)
How language is used	How does the writer use specific words or phrases?
	How does the writer use particular kinds of words?
	How does the writer use and structure sentences?
	How is the text laid out?
The effects created	What effect does the text create overall?
	What specific features of language are used?
	What effect is created by the structure or layout of the text?

KEY POINT

Remember that when writing analytically it is very important that you give **specific examples** of **language use** from the text and comment on the **effects** they create.

Analysing texts

	E Lang	E Lit
AQA	✓	✓

The following text is from a novel by R.M. Ballantyne, first published in 1857. The novel is narrated by the central character, the 15-year-old Ralph Rover, and tells the story of the adventures that he and his two friends, Jack Martin and Peterkin Gay, encounter when they are shipwrecked and stranded on a tropical island.

Read the extract through carefully.

"It's all over with us now, lads," said the captain to the men; "get the boat ready to launch; we shall be on the rocks in less than half an hour."

The men obeyed in gloomy silence, for they felt that there was little hope of so small a boat living in such a sea.

"Come boys," said Jack Martin, in a grave tone, to me and Peterkin, as we stood on the quarterdeck awaiting our fate;--"Come boys, we three shall stick together. You see it is impossible that the little boat can reach the shore, crowded with men. It will be sure to upset, so I mean rather to trust myself to a large oar, I see through the telescope that the ship will strike at the tail of the reef, where the waves break into the quiet water inside; so, if we manage to cling to the oar till it is driven over the breakers, we may perhaps gain the shore. What say you; will you join me?"

We gladly agreed to follow Jack, for he inspired us with confidence, although I could perceive, by the sad tone of his voice, that he had little hope; and, indeed, when I looked at the white waves that lashed the reef and boiled against the rocks as if in fury, I felt that there was but a step between us and death. My heart sank within me; but at that moment my thoughts turned to my beloved mother, and I remembered those words, which were among the last that she said to me--"Ralph, my dearest child, always remember in the hour of danger to look to your Lord and Saviour Jesus Christ. He alone is both able and willing to save your body and your soul." So I felt much comforted when I thought thereon.

From *The Coral Island* by R.M. Ballantyne

Now think about what kind of text this is and how language is used to create effects.

Here are some ideas you might have noted:

- **Purpose and audience:**
  The extract is from a novel and so the primary purpose is to **entertain**. The audience is likely to consist of those who enjoy reading adventure novels, particularly ones dealing with the sea and people fending for themselves in a strange environment.

- **Context, topic and content:**
  You might have noted that the novel was first published in 1857 and that might have some bearing on the ways in which language is used and the ways in which the content of the story is handled.

- **Language and effects:**
  - The use of adjectives creates the sense that there is little hope for those on board the ship, e.g. '**gloomy** silence', '**little** hope', '**sad** tone', '**heart sank**'. This impression is further emphasised by Ralph's phrase, 'I felt that there was but a step between us and death' and that he remembers his mother's last words to him.
  - Adjectives and adverbs are also used to create a sense of the violence of the storm, e.g. '**white** waves', '**lashed** the reef'.
  - A **simile** is used to create a sense of the violence of the storm, 'the white waves that lashed the reef and boiled against the rocks as if in fury'.
  - The **personification** gives a feel of the violence of the storm.

You might have noticed too that some of the words and phrases used sound a little unusual, reflecting the fact that this novel was written about 150 years ago, e.g. phrases such as 'What say you; will you join me?' and 'So I felt much comforted when I thought thereon'.

Writers use language in different ways to achieve different effects.

Approaching a text

AQA   E Lang ✓   E Lit ✓

When preparing to write analytically about a text, you need to adopt a **structured** approach to examining **what** the text has to say and **how** it says it.

Here is one possible approach you could use.

Stage 1

1 A preliminary read of the material to get a general idea of what the text is about.
2 Re-read the text, this time making a note of the key points.

Carry out this stage on the following text, an article on Fairtrade from the RSPB magazine, *Wingbeat*.

good for the environment?
Phoenix member Rosanna Pound-Woods tests its green ethics.

What is Fairtrade?
Fairtrade ensures that farmers in developing countries receive a fair price for their produce. This not only means that they are making a decent living, but that they have a sustainable source of income, allowing them access to vital healthcare, education and nutrition: in many cases, lifting them out of poverty entirely.

What's more, Fairtrade products are affordable and by buying them, we're doing our bit to help others. In 2008, it is estimated that at least 7.5 million people benefited as a result.

Fairtrade products are all around us these days; go to your local supermarket and you'll find Fairtrade bananas, chocolate, coffee, tea, sugar... and even clothes! Spending that little extra on Fairtrade products is helping to improve the lives of thousands of farmers in poorer countries. But what is it doing for the environment?

Pros and cons
Whilst Fairtrade products make a real difference to the lives of people, they come at a cost. Because Fairtrade goods are produced in distant developing countries and exported to developed countries, they clock up thousands of food miles. This leads to increased carbon emissions, contributing to the problem of global warming.

However, to be certified as Fairtrade, products do have to meet strict environmental criteria. These include guidelines on agrochemicals, waste, soil and water, use of synthetic fertilisers, herbicides, pesticides and the use of non-renewable energy. Fairtrade farmers are frequently encouraged to produce organic crops where economically and socially practical. Furthermore, all local ecosystems are protected during the growing of the crops.

Most Fairtrade products being imported into the UK are transported by ship, not air – a more environmentally-friendly way of transporting them. In 2005, global transportation of Fairtrade-certified products was responsible for just 0.03% of food mile emissions in the UK and only 0.001% of the country's total carbon emissions.

Fair played
The following examples show Fairtrade helping producers to become more environmentally-friendly:

• Some of the Fairtrade premium received by tea workers in India has been used to purchase a solar-panelled system to replace the traditional wood-burning heater used by the workers.

• Cotton farmers in the Gujarat province of India are now growing organic Fairtrade cotton. This helps to improve their health and livelihood and may also help the environment. This 3-year project has enabled farmers to sell cotton to big manufacturers such as Marks & Spencer.

• Costa Rican coffee farmers are replanting trees to prevent soil erosion. They have also invested in environmentally-friendly ovens which are fuelled by recycled coffee hulls and dried macadamia nut shells.

The verdict
It is true that buying products from far away countries is not generally the most environmentally friendly thing to do: many environmentalists are now urging people to "buy local" instead.

With regard to products such as apples and plums, which can be grown locally, it is perhaps wiser to "buy local" rather than to "buy Fairtrade". However, many products can only be grown in warmer climates, so surely in this case it is better for us to pay the extra price to get a Fairtrade-certified product, which we know has met environmental criteria and is therefore hopefully as eco-friendly as possible.

Is it a question of whether we value human beings above the environment? Some believe that the chance to help poor farmers out of poverty far outweighs the environmental cost. However, others believe that it is more important for us to preserve the earth for future generations.

So, is Fairtrade good for the environment?
Well, considering the food miles associated with importing products from thousands of miles away, I initially presumed that the answer would be no. However, having found out that Fairtrade products are the most environmentally friendly option in many cases, I must say that this has persuaded me to buy more Fairtrade products in the future: not only will I be helping small farmers in poor countries, but I will be helping the environment too!

Fairtrade cotton farm by Joerg Boethling (Still Pictures).

WB 8

Here are some key ideas you might have noted:
- An explanation of what 'Fairtrade' means is given.
- It poses the question 'what is Fairtrade doing for the environment?'
- It examines the pros and cons of the Fairtrade scheme – e.g. the produce clocks up thousands of food miles but, on the other hand, Fairtrade farming helps to protect local ecosystems.
- It give examples of how Fairtrade is helping producers to become more environmentally friendly.
- A verdict is given, but it is not clear-cut and two views are offered based on whether we value human beings above the environment.
- On balance, the writer is in favour of Fairtrade on the grounds that she feels it is the most environmentally friendly option.

Stage 2

Having established the **topic** and **content** of the text, now think about its **purpose** (what the writer wants to achieve) and its **audience** (who the writer wants to read it.)

Here are some ideas about the purpose and audience of the Fairtrade article on page 20.

Purpose:
- To inform the reader about the Fairtrade scheme.
- To examine the pros and cons of the scheme with regard to Fairtrade and the environment.
- To give examples of the scheme in action.
- To answer the question as to whether Fairtrade is good for the environment.

Audience:
- A general readership.
- Those interested in environmental issues.
- Those interested in finding out more about the Fairtrade scheme.
- Those wanting to make an informed choice about buying Fairtrade products.

> **KEY POINT**
>
> Adopt a logical approach to your analysis.
> Think about and answer:
>
> | PURPOSE | – | AUDIENCE | – | CONTENT |
> |---------|---|----------|---|---------|
> | WHAT? | | WHO? | | HOW? |

Stage 3

Having established the links between content, audience and purpose, the next stage is to look at how language is used to suit the particular audience and achieve the particular purpose.

When you are analysing a text, it is important to support your points with evidence and then comment on it.

Use the **PEE technique** (also known as the 'PEC technique' (Point, Evidence, Comment) or the '123 technique'):

- **P**oint – make a point.
- **E**vidence – provide evidence / an example from the text.
- **E**xplanation – give an explanation about how the evidence backs up your point.

For example, look at how one student began her analysis of the Fairtrade article on page 20.

Makes a point	The writer begins the article by reminding us how
	Fairtrade products are all around us these days, not just
Quotes evidence to support the point	coffee, tea and chocolate but "… even clothes." This
	suggests that Fairtrade covers a much wider range of
	products than the reader might be aware of and she wants
Gives an explanation	to emphasise that. She comments how Fairtrade is helping
	to improve the lives of thousands of farmers in poorer
	countries. She ends her opening section with the key
	question that she will address in the article – what effect is
	Fairtrade having on the environment?
Makes a point	The writer goes on then to look at the pros and cons of the
	issue, making the point that Fairtrade products do have a
Quotes evidence to support the point	down-side too and "come at a cost". This cost comes in the
Gives an explanation	form of the number of food miles transporting the goods
	from their countries of origin to other countries, often
	thousands of miles away, and obviously this does not help
	in controlling global warming.

Remember to use PEE in your analyses:

POINT – state the point you are making clearly.

EVIDENCE – give an example or quotation to support your point.

EXPLANATION – explain or comment on your point or idea.

> **KEY POINT**
>
> It is **essential** that you support the points you make with specific examples and evidence from the text, and explain or comment on the meaning or significance of the examples you have given.

2.2 Analysing spoken language

Different kinds of speech

AQA	E Lang	E Lit
	✓	✗

Speech can take many forms and different kinds of speech can have different characteristics. Like writing, all speech acts have a **purpose** and address a particular **audience**, and are set within a particular **context**.

What the purpose and audience are, and what context the speech takes place in, will be major determining influences on the form that the speech takes, the kind of language that is used and the kind of effect that it achieves.

These factors also determine the **level of formality** of the speech. Basically, speech can be **formal** or **informal** to varying degrees.

For example, during a chat with a friend:
- The purpose might simply be to inform or entertain, for example, if you were telling each other what you did last night; or it might be to persuade, for example, if you were trying to convince your friend to go shopping with you.
- The audience would be your friend.
- It would take place in an informal context.

On the other hand, if you attended an interview for a job:
- The purpose would be to try to persuade the interviewer that you are the person for the job.
- Your audience would be your interviewer.
- It would take place in a formal context.

It is highly likely that you would speak and use language differently when talking with your friend to the way you would use language in a formal interview situation.

Spontaneous speech

AQA	E Lang	E Lit
	✓	✗

In basic terms, speech can be classed as either **spontaneous** or **planned**.

Spontaneous speech (sometimes called **unplanned** speech) is speech which is not thought out beforehand. The vast majority of the speech that we use on a day-to-day basis is unplanned. Because this kind of speech is not planned or thought-out before we speak, it has a range of features that are typical of it.

Features of spontaneous speech

The first thing to note about spontaneous speech is that, unlike written language, we do not speak in carefully constructed, grammatically correct sentences. The bulk of spontaneous speech consists of ungrammatical units called **utterances**. These express what we say or 'utter'.

Here are some features to look out for in spontaneous speech:
- **Turn-taking** – most conversations between two or more people involve the people taking turns to speak (although not in a regular pattern).
- **Adjacency pairs** – we use these all the time in conversation: one utterance leads to another – one speaker says something and another speaker says something in response. For example, if speaker A asks a question and speaker B answers, that is an adjacency pair.
- **Pauses** – these happen a lot in spontaneous speech. Some are very short, but some can be quite long.
- **Voice-filled pauses** – these are gaps in the conversation that are filled by some kind of non-verbal sound, e.g. 'erm', 'er', 'um', etc.
- **Fillers** – these fill gaps in the conversation too but they are words rather than sounds. However, they are words that do not have a real meaning, e.g. 'you know', 'I mean', 'well'.
- **Overlaps** – these occur where one speaker begins speaking before the other speaker has finished, or they both speak at the same time.
- **Repetitions** – these often occur when the speaker is not sure what they are saying or when they are searching for the right word.
- **False starts** – these happen when a speaker begins to speak and then corrects himself / herself by beginning the utterance again.
- **End clipping** – when letters are dropped from the ends of words, for example, 'happenin' instead of 'happening'.
- **Contractions** – when words are shortened by running them together, for example, 'don't' instead of 'do not'.
- **Slang** or **colloquial** language – this is frequently used in informal spontaneous speech.

Abbreviations are used in transcripts to indicate certain features:

Symbol	Meaning
(.)	micropause
(0.5)	pause of 0.5 seconds
<u>underlining</u>	emphasis of a particular word
[	overlap
bold or *italic*	shouting

KEY POINT

When analysing spontaneous speech, as well as identifying features, you should also explain what they show about the speakers, and their attitudes and relationships to each other.

Transcript of spontaneous speech

When spontaneous speech is represented in written form, it is written in the form of a **transcript** in which the speech is presented so as to give as good an indication as possible of how it was spoken.

Look at this transcript of three Year 10 students speaking about their favourite texts from their GCSE English Literature course.

Kat	well (.) which were your favourite then?
Ed	I really liked (.) like er Lord of the Flies
Sam	yeah (.) I might a known (.) typical boys stuff that (.) rubbish (.) it were pants (.) dont know how I managed to get to the end of it
Ed	well I thought it was <u>good</u> and I
Sam	[gi it a rest (.) not even gonna talk about it (.) bad enough havin to read it
Kat	I thought An Inspector Calls were <u>fantastic</u> and erm I think (.) I thought that the char(.) characters were (0.5) really vivid.
Sam	yeah I'd go along wi that (.) better than Lord of the Flies anyway (0.5) not that that's sayin much
Ed	yer not keen on lit are you Sam

Some of the features of spontaneous speech that appear in this transcript include:

- Pauses, e.g 'well (.) which'.
- False starts, e.g. 'I really liked (.) like'.
- Voice-filled pauses, e.g. 'er', 'erm'.
- Emphasis of words, e.g. '<u>fantastic</u>'.
- End-clipping, e.g. 'sayin', 'havin'.
- Contractions, e.g. 'don't', 'I'd', 'that's'.
- Fillers, e.g. 'well'.
- Overlaps, e.g. 'and I
                 [gi it a rest'.
- Turn-taking and adjacency pairs occur throughout.
- Non-standard grammar, e.g. 'it were' (instead of 'it was').
- Slang, e.g. 'pants'.

Planned speech

AQA   E Lang ✓   E Lit ✗

Planned speech differs from spontaneous speech in one very obvious way – it has been thought-out and planned in advance. Sometimes it might have been written out (or **scripted**) before it is delivered.

For example, many speeches, such as one given by a politician or one given by the Best Man at a wedding, will probably have been written down in some form. Other kinds of planned speech, such as that given by a teacher to a class, is likely to have been planned, but may not have been written down.

The main purpose of many speeches is that the speaker wants to affect the feelings, views, emotions or ideas of the listener in a certain kind of way. The art of speech-making of this kind is called **rhetoric**. To make their speeches effective in putting across their message and persuading their listeners, speakers often use a range of **rhetorical features**.

Features of planned speech

Here are some of the rhetorical features that you might find in planned speech:

- **Emotive language** – language that is specially chosen to appeal to the emotions of the listener.
- **Exclamations** – these can add emphasis and impact to particular points (they can lose their effectiveness, though, if over-used).
- **Guarantees or pledges** – e.g. in political speeches, politicians often give guarantees that they will do things that others have failed to do.
- **Repetition** – repeating key words, phrases or ideas can highlight key points and give added impact for the listener.
- **Patterns of three** (**use of three**) – this is a very common technique in which the speaker uses three words or phrases, often creating a strong rhythmic effect, which adds impact to the words, for example, 'I came, I saw, I conquered.'
- **Lists** – speakers use lists of points or ideas to build up the effect of what they are saying and, again, to add emphasis to the words.
- **Questions** – speakers often use questions directed at their listeners. These are called **rhetorical questions** and are not questions that require an answer – they are used for effect and to add weight to the speaker's point or argument, for example, 'why should we tolerate this?'.
- **Personal pronouns** – speakers often use personal pronouns, e.g. 'we' to include the listener and give the impression that they are all on the same side.
- **Literary techniques** – often literary techniques, such as the use of metaphors and similes, are used to add effect to the speech.
- **Phonological techniques** – these are to do with the sound effects created by the words. Speakers can use features such as **alliteration**, **assonance** and **rhyme** to create effects. For example, soft 'm' sounds might imply sympathy or respect, while harsh 't' sounds could convey strength, anger or frustration.

The following is an extract from a speech given by Tony Blair (British Prime Minister from 1997 to 2007), which he gave following the start of the US and British military strikes on targets in Afghanistan on Sunday, 7th October 2001.

Read the speech through carefully.

As you all know from the announcement by President Bush, military action against targets inside Afghanistan has begun. I can confirm that UK forces are engaged in this action. I want to pay tribute at the outset to Britain's armed forces. There is no greater strength for a British prime minister and the British nation at a time like this to know that the forces we are calling upon are amongst the best in the world.

They and their families are of course carrying an immense burden at this moment and will be feeling deep anxiety, as will the British people, but we can take great pride in their courage, their sense of duty, and the esteem with which they are held throughout the world. No country lightly commits forces to military action and the inevitable risks involved. We made clear following the attacks upon the US on 11 September that we would take action once it was clear who was responsible. There is no doubt in my mind, nor in the mind of anyone who has been through all the available evidence, including intelligence material, that these attacks were carried out by the al-Qaeda network headed by Osama Bin Laden.

Equally it is clear that they are harboured and supported by the Taliban regime inside Afghanistan. It is now almost a month since the atrocity occurred. It is more than two weeks since an ultimatum was delivered to the Taliban to yield up the terrorists or face the consequences. It is clear beyond doubt that the Taliban will not do this. They were given the choice of siding with justice, or siding with terror. They chose terror.

There are three parts, all equally important, to the operation in which we are engaged - military, diplomatic and humanitarian. The military action we are taking will be targeted against places we know to be involved in the al-Qaeda network of terror or against the military apparatus of the Taliban. The military plan has been put together mindful of our determination to do all we humanly can to avoid civilian casualties. I cannot disclose how long this wave of action will last. But we will act with reason and resolve.

The following features have been highlighted in the speech:

- Personal pronouns are used. They create a sense that the speaker is addressing the listener directly.
- The speaker gives a personal promise. This creates the sense that he is sincere and that the listeners can rely on him to do the right thing.
- Superlatives are used to highlight the speaker's beliefs and opinions.
- The speaker uses patterns of three, which link together key ideas and create a strong sense of rhythm, and adds effects to his words.
- The plural personal pronoun is used, coupled with the collective term 'the British people', which again adds weight and emphasis to the key point – in this case they are 'one' people who have the same interests and need to work together to achieve them.
- Emotive language is used to pay tribute to the armed forces.
- The speaker gives a personal assurance that no one who has seen the evidence that he has could doubt the people responsible for the attacks.
- The plural personal pronoun used refers to himself and the government / American government.

In analysing planned speech you should think about:
- How the speech is structured.
- Key features of the speech.
- How speakers establish a rapport with the audience.
- How language is used to create impact (and what that impact is), e.g. vocabulary, rhetorical devices, tone, etc.
- The use and impact of timing, pace, pauses and movement (if speech is presented in a visual form).

> **KEY POINT**
>
> When analysing planned speech, look for a range of features, understand how they are used in the speech and explain the effects that they create.

Sample GCSE question

Read the following extract from 'The Perfect Storm'. Here, Reeves, a Canadian observer on a Japanese fishing boat, the Eishin Maru, contacts the US Coast guard as her ship is hit by the storm.

While she's talking, Coast Guard New York breaks in; they've been listening in on the conversation and want to know if the Eishin Maru needs help. Reeves says they've lost most of their electronics and are in serious trouble. New York patches her through to the Coast Guard in Halifax, and while they're discussing how to get people off the boat, the radio operator interrupts her. He's pointing to a sentence in an English phrase book. Reeves leans in close to read it: "We are helpless and drifting. Please render all assistance." (Unknown to Reeves, the steering linkage has just failed, although the radio operator doesn't know how to explain that to her.) It's at this moment that Reeves realizes she's going down at sea.

"We had no steerage and we were right in the eye of the storm", she says. "It was a confused sea, all the waves were coming from different directions. The wind was picking up the tops of the waves and slinging them so far that when the search-and-rescue plane arrived, we couldn't even see it. The whole vessel would get shoved over on its side, so that we were completely upside-down. If you get hit by one wave and then hit by another, you can drive the vessel completely down into the water. And so that second before the vessel starts to come up you're just holding your breath, waiting."

They're dead in the water, taking the huge waves broad-side. According to Reeves, they are doing 360-degree barrel rolls and coming back up. Four boats try to respond to her mayday, but three of them have to stand down because of the weather. They cannot continue without risking their own lives. The ocean-going tug Triumph C leaves Sable Island and claws her way southward, and the Coast Guard cutter Edward Cornwallis is on her way from Halifax. The crew of the Eishin Maru, impassive, are sure they're going to die. Reeves is too busy to think about it; she has to look for the life jackets, work the radio and satellite phone, flip through the Japanese phrase book. Eventually she has a moment to consider her options.

"Either I jump ship, or I go down with the ship. As for the first possibility, I thought about it for a while until I realized that they'd hammered all the hatches down. I thought, 'God, I'll never get off this friggin' boat, it will be my tomb.' So I figured I'd do whatever I had to do at the time, and there was no point in really thinking about it because it was just too frightening. I was just gripped by this feeling that I was going to have to do something very unpleasant. And it wasn't until the moment we lost steerage that I actually thought we were going to die. I mean, I knew there was a real possibility, and I was going to have to face that."

From The Perfect Storm by Sebastian Junger

Sample GCSE question

1 **a)** What is the purpose of this extract?

> The main purpose of this extract is to put across to the reader the severity of the storm and the serious position that the people on the boat are in. The writer wants the reader to understand the tension that Reeves felt and get an idea of just how frightening the situation was. The writer also wants to give the reader an idea of the attempts that were being made to rescue the crew.

Clear focus on purpose of writing and the effects the writer wishes to create.

b) How does the writer use language to achieve his effects here?

> The writer uses a number of techniques to make the description have more impact on the reader. The focus is on the character, Reeves, and the writer uses her experiences to give an account to the reader. We are told what she is doing and what she says to the Coast Guard. The writer uses both reported and direct speech to tell us what she said, and this makes the piece more interesting by giving us the feeling that this is a real person's experience. Reeves describes the wild state of the sea in direct speech and this again gives a sense of immediacy and the impression that we are getting a first-hand account from someone who was there. The description of boats setting out to rescue them but having to turn back emphasises the desperate nature of the situation. This desperation is echoed by Reeves's words when she finds all the hatches hammered down: "God, I'll never get off this friggin' boat, it will be my tomb." In addition, descriptive phrases, such as "taking huge waves broad-side", "doing 360-degree barrel rolls", and the description of the tug as she "claws her way" through the sea emphasise the severity of the weather conditions.

A number of techniques identified here, supported well by references and quotations from the text, together with explanations of the effects created. Some perceptive points.

Practice questions

1 Choose a newspaper article for yourself.

Write about the views the writer expresses in the article and the manner by which he / she sustains the reader's interest.

You should comment on and analyse how the writer has:
- used a style and tone appropriate to the subject
- made use of fact and opinion
- selected words and phrases for effect
- used sentence structuring and paragraphing to support his intention of sustaining the reader's interest

(Controlled Assessment task: English Language, Unit 3, Part A)

2 Research the ways in which politicians convey their views and ideas in their speeches. You should focus on two or three specific speeches and comment on:
- the techniques that the speakers use
- the ways in which the speeches are structured
- how they use language to create specific effects
- the overall impact and effectiveness of the speeches

(Controlled Assessment task: English Language, Unit 3, Part C)

3 Discuss the features of spoken language in at least two interviews you have listened to.

You may wish to discuss some or all of the following, as appropriate:
- register
- humour
- slang
- intonation
- context
- vocabulary

You may also wish to discuss other features that you have considered.

(Controlled Assessment task: English Language, Unit 3, Part C)

3 Exploring non-fiction texts

The following topics are covered in this chapter:

- Approaching non-fiction texts
- Magazine articles
- Biographies and autobiographies
- Travel writing
- Documentary writing
- Literary non-fiction

3.1 Approaching non-fiction texts

LEARNING SUMMARY

After studying this section, you should be able to understand:

- what non-fiction texts are
- how to approach non-fiction texts

What are non-fiction texts?

AQA	E Lang ✓	E Lit ✗

The term 'non-fiction texts' is a very broad one, covering a wide range of very different kinds of writing, including:

- reviews
- newspaper articles
- magazine articles
- information leaflets
- advertisements
- diary entries
- biographies and autobiographies
- letters
- travel writing

You might note that some of the kinds of texts listed here can also come under the heading 'media texts' as well as 'non-fiction' texts. Whatever the sources, all non-fiction texts have one or more of the following purposes:

- to inform
- to persuade
- to describe
- to advise
- to argue
- to explain
- to review
- to entertain

In order to develop your understanding of non-fiction texts, read as widely and as frequently as possible.

In reading and writing about non-fiction texts, you need to be able to do a number of things:

● **Understand** what the text is saying.
● **Distinguish** between **fact** and **opinion.**
● Follow an argument.
● **Select** material from the text to **suit** your task.
● Be **aware** of how the material is **presented.**
● **Understand** the effects created by the **ways** in which the material is written or presented.

How to approach non-fiction texts

	E Lang	E Lit
AQA	✓	✗

Whether you are writing about non-fiction texts as part of your exam or for Controlled Assessment, you will understand the text more effectively if you approach it in a **systematic** manner.

Here is one way you could do this:

> Read the question or task carefully.

> Underline any key words or important words.

> Read the text through to get a general idea of what it is about – don't worry if you don't understand everything on the first read.

> Read the text again, this time looking for information that you will need in order to answer your question or complete your task.

Look at a range of non-fiction texts as you progress through your course and build up your knowledge of the ways in which different kinds of texts are written and presented.

In addition to reading and analysing non-fiction texts, you might also be asked to write your own texts. In order to do this effectively you need to have developed a clear understanding of the form, language and style of a wide variety of non-fiction texts. For example, you might be asked to write a newspaper or magazine article, your own review of something or an information leaflet of some kind.

3.2 Magazine articles

LEARNING SUMMARY

After studying this section, you should be able to understand:

● how to follow an argument
● the difference between fact and opinion
● how illustrations and layout can contribute to the effect of an article
● the language techniques used to shape reader response

Following the argument

	E Lang	E Lit
AQA	✓	✗

Read the article on page 34 from the RSPB magazine *Wingbeat*, which is aimed at teenagers.

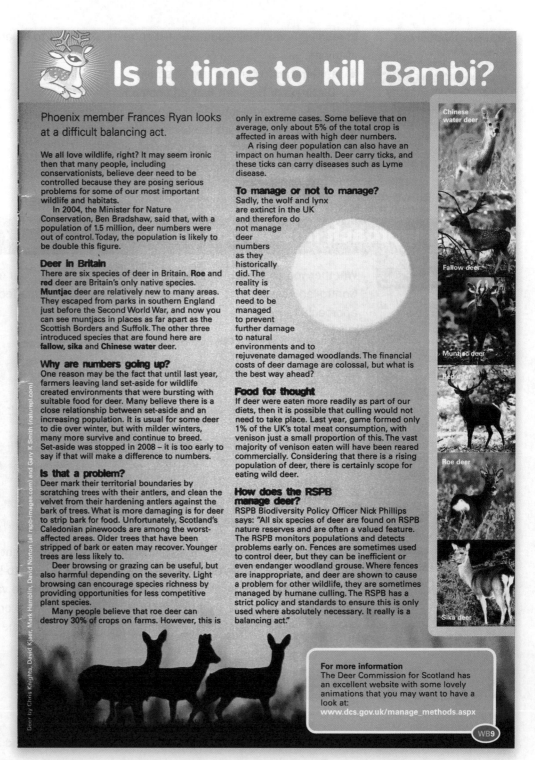

Is it time to kill Bambi?

Phoenix member Frances Ryan looks at a difficult balancing act.

We all love wildlife, right? It may seem ironic then that many people, including conservationists, believe deer need to be controlled because they are posing serious problems for some of our most important wildlife and habitats.

In 2004, the Minister for Nature Conservation, Ben Bradshaw, said that, with a population of 1.5 million, deer numbers were out of control. Today, the population is likely to be double this figure.

Deer in Britain
There are six species of deer in Britain. **Roe** and **red** deer are Britain's only native species. **Muntjac** deer are relatively new to many areas. They escaped from parks in southern England just before the Second World War, and now you can see muntjacs in places as far apart as the Scottish Borders and Suffolk. The other three introduced species that are found here are **fallow**, **sika** and **Chinese water** deer.

Why are numbers going up?
One reason may be the fact that until last year, farmers leaving land set-aside for wildlife created environments that were bursting with suitable food for deer. Many believe there is a close relationship between set-aside and an increasing population. It is usual for some deer to die over winter, but with milder winters, many more survive and continue to breed. Set-aside was stopped in 2008 – it is too early to say if that will make a difference to numbers.

Is that a problem?
Deer mark their territorial boundaries by scratching trees with their antlers, and clean the velvet from their hardening antlers against the bark of trees. What is more damaging is for deer to strip bark for food. Unfortunately, Scotland's Caledonian pinewoods are among the worst-affected areas. Older trees that have been stripped of bark or eaten may recover. Younger trees are less likely to.

Deer browsing or grazing can be useful, but also harmful depending on the severity. Light browsing can encourage species richness by providing opportunities for less competitive plant species.

Many people believe that roe deer can destroy 30% of crops on farms. However, this is only in extreme cases. Some believe that on average, only about 5% of the total crop is affected in areas with high deer numbers.

A rising deer population can also have an impact on human health. Deer carry ticks, and these ticks can carry diseases such as Lyme disease.

To manage or not to manage?
Sadly, the wolf and lynx are extinct in the UK and therefore do not manage deer numbers as they historically did. The reality is that deer need to be managed to prevent further damage to natural environments and to rejuvenate damaged woodlands. The financial costs of deer damage are colossal, but what is the best way ahead?

Food for thought
If deer were eaten more readily as part of our diets, then it is possible that culling would not need to take place. Last year, game formed only 1% of the UK's total meat consumption, with venison just a small proportion of this. The vast majority of venison eaten will have been reared commercially. Considering that there is a rising population of deer, there is certainly scope for eating wild deer.

How does the RSPB manage deer?
RSPB Biodiversity Policy Officer Nick Phillips says: "All six species of deer are found on RSPB nature reserves and are often a valued feature. The RSPB monitors populations and detects problems early on. Fences are sometimes used to control deer, but they can be inefficient or even endanger woodland grouse. Where fences are inappropriate, and deer are shown to cause a problem for other wildlife, they are sometimes managed by humane culling. The RSPB has a strict policy and standards to ensure this is only used where absolutely necessary. It really is a balancing act."

Chinese water deer

Fallow deer

Muntjac deer

Red deer

Roe deer

Sika deer

For more information
The Deer Commission for Scotland has an excellent website with some lovely animations that you may want to have a look at:
www.dcs.gov.uk/manage_methods.aspx

WB9

Deer by Chris Knights, David Kjaer, Mark Hamblin, David Norton (all rspb-images.com) and Gary K Smith (naturepl.com)

Having read the article, the first stage is to identify the main point of the argument.

Argument: The deer population of Britain has grown so much that they are causing a problem to some wildlife habitats, and the question of their management needs examining.

Now look carefully at how the writer develops her ideas:

Section 1: The writer outlines the basic problem – the deer population in Britain has grown so much that they are creating a problem for other wildlife.

Section 2: The point is made that although there are six species of deer in Britain, only two of them are native species.

Section 3: Reasons are given for the rising deer population.

Section 4: The problems being caused by these increasing numbers are outlined.

Section 5: The question of managing the deer population is discussed.

Section 6: The question of eating wild deer is raised.

Section 7: Details are given on how the Royal Society for the Protection of Birds manages the deer populations on its reserves.

Fact and opinion

AQA   E Lang ✓   E Lit ✗

In the article on page 34 you are given quite a lot of factual information, but there are also some opinions given too. When reading articles it is important to distinguish between **fact** and **opinion**.

Facts in the article include:
- There are six species of deer in Britain.
- The wolf and lynx are extinct in the UK.
- Last year, game formed only 1% of the UK's total meat consumption.

Opinions in the article include:
- The deer population today is likely to be 3 million.
- Some people believe that roe deer can destroy 30% of crops on farms.
- Setting aside farmland for wildlife may have led to an increase in the deer population.

Illustration and layout

AQA   E Lang ✓   E Lit ✗

Illustration and layout are very important features of non-fiction texts. Look again at the article on page 34.

The headings

The main heading poses a question which immediately captures the reader's attention. The use of the term 'Bambi' puts the cartoon image of the young deer into the reader's mind and indicates straight away the emotive issues that the article is bound to raise. The sub-headings give the article a clear structure and make it clear to the reader what information each section contains.

The illustrations

The image of the cartoon character 'Bambi' links directly with the title of the article and emphasises that the article is going to deal with an emotive and contentious issue. The large sun and the images in silhouette of the deer give a sense, perhaps, of a natural environment.

The photographs

These allow the reader to see what the different kinds of deer look like – perhaps acting as a kind of mini identification guide. They also add colour and interest to the page, which makes it more appealing.

The further information

The box at the bottom of the page gives the reader information about where they can find out more about this issue. The use of the term 'lovely animations' again suggests a cartoon link and makes the website sound interesting, which may help to encourage the reader to look at it.

> **KEY POINT**
>
> All these features combine to add effect to the words of the article and so make it have greater impact on the reader.

Language techniques

AQA · E Lang ✓ · E Lit ✗

A number of techniques are used to make the language have more impact on the reader. In the article on page 34, the following techniques are used:

The use of questions: The title itself poses the key question and questions are also used in the sub-headings and in the text. The questions used as sub-headings raise key issues and then the writer suggests answers to them in the section that follows. The questions used in the text have the effect of making the reader think about what has been said, e.g. 'The financial cost of deer damage is colossal, but what is the best way ahead?'

> Look at all the aspects of an article when you are writing about it.

Vocabulary: Words are used to give a sense that the deer pose a real problem, e.g. 'they are posing serious problems', 'roe deer can destroy 30% of crops', 'the cost of deer damage is colossal'.

Use of quotations and sources: The deer population figures given by the Minister for Nature Conservation quote possible figures on the extent of the damage to crops (notice that the writer does not present these figures as 'facts' – she uses terms like 'some people believe'.). The long quotation at the end from the RSPB's Biodiversity Officer gives some detail on how one organisation handles the problem.

3.3 Biographies and autobiographies

LEARNING SUMMARY

After studying this section, you should be able to understand:
- the features of biographies
- the features of autobiographies

Features of biographies and autobiographies

AQA · E Lang ✓ · E Lit ✓

Biographies are texts that tell us about the lives of other people by writers who have usually studied the **life** of the person they are writing about in some detail. When reading a biography, though, you should always remember that the biography presents that particular **writer's view** of their subject. There may be other views too and a different writer may present quite a different picture.

Autobiographies are written by the subjects themselves. This means that the views we get of a person's life and actions are very much those of that person. Of course, their views may also be **coloured** by the writer wanting to give a particular impression or the fact that they see things in a particular way.

One of the most immediate **differences** between these two forms is that biographies are written in the **third person** while autobiographies are written in the **first person**.

KEY POINT

Biographies and autobiographies, although having a common general function, are different in their approach and style. As a result, different effects are created.

Look at the following extract. It is from a **biography** of Abraham Lincoln, President of the USA from 1861 to 1865.

The miserable log cabin in which Abraham Lincoln was born was a floorless, doorless, windowless shanty, situated in one of the most barren and desolate spots of Hardin County, Kentucky. His father made it his home simply because he was too poor to own a better one. Nor was his an exceptional case of penury and want. For the people of that section were generally poor and unlettered, barely able to scrape enough together to keep the wolf of hunger from their abodes.

Here Abraham Lincoln was born February 12th, 1809. His father's name was Thomas Lincoln; his mother's maiden name was Nancy Hanks... They had been married three years when Abraham was born. Their cabin was in that part of Hardin County which is now embraced in La Rue County, a few miles from Hodgensville - on the south fork of Nolin Creek. A perennial spring of water, gushing in silvery brightness from beneath a rock near by, relieved the barrenness of the location, and won for it the somewhat ambitious name - "Rock Spring Farm."

From *Abraham Lincoln* by William M. Thayer

Now read this extract from Peter Kay's **autobiography**, *The Sound of Laughter*. Here, as he takes his first driving lesson, he recalls his childhood passion for cars.

I'd spent my whole life dreaming of this moment. Ever since I'd played with toy cars as a child. Pushing them round on the floor in the back room at home, in and out of table legs, over my dad's slippers, making that engine noise, you know the one, the higher the gear, the higher the humming noise. I'd drive it as far as the tips of my fingers would stretch and then with a screech of brakes I'd spin it around and drive it back towards me. Matchbox, Corgi, I had the lot, sports cars, buses, even a London taxi. I'd line them up along the fireplace. Then they'd take part in the biggest race in the world until my mum shouted me for tea.

If I wasn't playing with cars then I'd be lying on the floor in front of the TV drawing them, designing them. I drew supercars, cars that could fly, cars that performed spectacular stunts I'd seen in James Bond films or anything with Burt Reynolds. I drew cars in every colour my bumper pack of felt tips would allow.

From *The Sound of Laughter,* the autobiography of Peter Kay.

Apart from the time period in which the two were written, there are a number of differences in style in the ways these two extracts are written.

Biography:
- It describes Lincoln's family and childhood home.
- It is written in the third person throughout.
- It has a more detached stance.

Autobiography:
- It has a more personal tone, and is written in the first person.
- It explains the writer's inner thoughts and feelings.
- It describes personal memories in detail.

3.4 Travel writing

LEARNING SUMMARY	After studying this section, you should be able to understand:
	• some of the features of travel writing

Features of travel writing

AQA	E Lang	E Lit
	✓	✓

As the name suggests, travel writing is concerned with **describing experiences** of travel in one form or another. However, there is much more to successful travel writing than simply describing journeys or writing about holidays.

The best travel writing can:
- **convey** the experience of a journey or exploration of a new country in a vivid way
- deal with the **inner feelings** and emotions that the experience promotes
- invite us to look at the world in a **different** way
- allow the reader to **participate** in the journey.

The following extract is from Bill Bryson's *Notes from a Small Island,* in which he describes his experience on a tour around the British Isles.

> I went to Milton Keynes, feeling that I ought to at least have a look at a new town. Milton Keynes takes some getting to from Oxford, which is a little odd because it's only just up the road. I selected it as my destination on the basis of a quick look at a road map, assuming that I would, at worst, have to take a train to Bicester or some such place and then another from there. In fact, I had to go all the way back to London, catch an Underground train to Euston and then finally a train to Milton Keynes – an overall journey of perhaps 120 miles in order to travel between two towns about 30 miles apart.
>
> It was costly and time-consuming and left me feeling a tiny bit fractious, not least because the train from Euston was crowded and I ended up sitting facing a bleating woman and her ten-year-old son, who kept knocking my shins with his dangling legs and irritating me by staring

at me with piggy eyes while picking his nose and eating the bogies. He appeared to regard his nose as a kind of mid-faced snack dispenser. I tried to absorb myself in a book, but I found my gaze repeatedly rising against my wishes to find him staring at me with a smug look and a busy finger. It was quite repellent and I was very pleased, when the train finally pulled into Milton Keynes, to get my rucksack down from the overhead rack and drag it across his head as I departed.

I didn't hate Milton Keynes immediately, which I suppose is as much as you could hope for the place. You step out of the station and into a big open square lined on three sides with buildings of reflective glass, and have an instant sense of spaciousness such as you almost never get in English towns.

From *Notes from a Small Island* by Bill Bryson

In this extract, Bryson gives us a range of information about his journey but he goes further than simply cataloguing where he went and what he saw.

Here are some points you might have noted:

- He explains where he is and where he is going to.
- He describes the route he needs to take.
- He describes some of the things that happened on the journey.
- He gives a very personal account of his journey.
- He explains his feelings and thoughts throughout the journey.
- He describes his initial impression of his destination.
- He goes on to give a more detailed description of the place.

PROGRESS CHECK

1. What techniques does Bryson use in the extract above to make his writing more interesting and effective?

1.
- Much of the effect of his writing comes from the humour he creates, such as the description of the boy on the train.
- He reveals his view of the place indirectly and with irony – "I didn't hate Milton Keynes immediately, which I suppose is as much as you could hope for the place".
- He uses quite detailed descriptions so readers can clearly picture the scene in their minds.
- He compares the town with other places he has visited.

KEY POINT

Travel writing consists of more than just a description of a journey or place and often uses a variety of techniques and approaches to convey its information to the reader.

3.5 Documentary writing

After studying this section, you should be able to understand:

- the features of documentary writing

Features of documentary writing

AQA	E Lang ✓	E Lit ✓

You might be more used to hearing the term 'documentary' in connection with film or television but it is also a genre that has been used for many years in writing.

Documentary writing often has a strong social or political purpose and is used to:

- **expose** things that the public should know about
- **educate** people in some way
- bring about **reforms**.

Writers **observe** and **present**, through their writing, **aspects** of the world they see around them or report on certain issues or situations.

Read the following extract from *A Walk in a Workhouse* in which the writer, Charles Dickens, describes a visit to a London Workhouse in 1850 and gives an impression of what he found there.

> When the service was over, I walked with the humane and conscientious gentleman whose duty it was to take that walk, that Sunday morning, through the little world of poverty enclosed within the workhouse walls. It was inhabited by a population of some fifteen hundred or two thousand paupers, ranging from the infant newly born or not yet come into the pauper world to the old man dying on his bed.
>
> In a room opening from a squalid yard, where a number of listless women were lounging to and fro, trying to get warm in the ineffectual sunshine of the tardy May morning, — in the "Itch-Ward," not to compromise the truth, — a woman, such as Hogarth has often drawn, was hurriedly getting on her gown before a dusty fire. She was the nurse, or wardswoman, of that insalubrious department — herself a pauper — flabby, raw-boned, untidy — unpromising and coarse of aspect as need be. But on being spoken to about the patients whom she had in charge, she turned round, with her shabby gown half on, half off, and fell a-crying with all her might. Not for show, not querulously, not in any mawkish sentiment, but in the deep grief and affliction of her heart; turning away her dishevelled head; sobbing most bitterly, wringing her hands, and letting fall abundance of great tears, that choked her utterance. What was the matter with the nurse of the itch-ward? Oh, "the dropped child" was dead! Oh, the child that was found in the street, and she had brought up ever since, had died an hour ago, and see where the little creature lay, beneath this cloth! The dear, the pretty dear!

The dropped child seemed too small and poor a thing for Death to be in earnest with, but Death had taken it; and already its diminutive form was neatly washed, composed, and stretched as if in sleep upon a box. I thought I heard a voice from Heaven saying, It shall be well for thee, O nurse of the itch-ward, when some less gentle pauper does those offices to thy cold form, that such as the dropped child are the angels who behold my Father's face!

From *A Walk in a Workhouse* by Charles Dickens

In this extract, Dickens emphasises the number of people in the workhouse and the wide age range that the inhabitants consisted of. He also creates a sense of the sadness and grief that people in the workhouse experienced.

Dickens conveys to us an impression of what he experienced on his visit through his use of language.

For example:

- The sense that the people in the workhouse are cut off from the outside world, and the world that they inhabit is one of poverty, e.g. 'the little world of poverty enclosed within the workhouse walls'.
- The age range is described vividly from the 'infant newly born or not yet come' to the 'old man dying on his bed'.
- His use of adjectives creates a sense of mood, e.g. 'squalid', 'listless', 'lounging', 'ineffectual', 'coarse', 'shabby'.
- The impact of the description of the dead child and the woman's reaction.
- His use of personification in relation to 'Death' creates a very sad, even futile tone.
- He uses alliteration to highlight the way in which the people live, e.g. 'listless women were lounging to and fro.'
- Religious diction is used, perhaps to emphasise the innocence of the people, e.g. 'I heard a voice from Heaven'; 'the angels who behold my Father's face'.
- The use of rhetorical language, e.g. the repeated 'Oh' to capture a sense of the woman's grief and Dickens's recreation of her voice.

3.6 Literary non-fiction

What is literary non-fiction?

AQA	E Lang	E Lit
	✓	✓

Literary non-fiction is a genre of writing that can encompass a number of the types of writing already discussed and there are no hard and fast boundaries between them.

Essentially, literary non-fiction is a term used to describe texts that are written in a style that applies the techniques of 'literary' writing to topics that are non-fiction.

An example of this kind of writing is the book *Fever Pitch* by Nick Hornby. Below is an extract from it.

Fever Pitch is about the author's relationship with football, particularly Arsenal Football Club, and this extract describes Hornby's feelings about the upcoming Arsenal versus Liverpool game at Anfield, in the last game of the 1988–1989 season. Arsenal needed to win by two clear goals in order to win the Championship. Read the extract through carefully.

I went to work in the afternoon, and felt sick with nerves despite myself; afterwards I went straight round to an Arsenal-supporting friend's house, just a street away from the North Bank, to watch the game. Everything about the night was memorable, right from the moment when the teams came on to the pitch and the Arsenal players ran over to the Kop and presented individuals in the crowd with bunches of flowers. And as the game progressed, and it became obvious that Arsenal were going to go down fighting, it occurred to me just how well I knew my team, their faces and their mannerisms, and how fond I was of each individual member of it. Merson's gap-toothed smile and tatty soul-boy haircut, Adams's manful and endearing attempts to come to terms with his own inadequacies, Rocastle's pumped-up elegance, Smith's lovable diligence… I could find it in me to forgive them for coming so close and blowing it: they were young, and they'd had a fantastic season and as a supporter you cannot really ask for more than that.

I got excited when we scored right at the beginning of the second half, and I got excited again about ten minutes from time, when Thomas had a clear chance and hit it straight at Grobbelaar, but Liverpool seemed to be growing stronger and to be creating chances at the end, and finally, with the clock in the corner of the TV screen showing that the ninety minutes had passed, I got ready to muster a brave smile for a brave team. 'If

Arsenal are to lose the Championship, having had such a lead at one time, it's somewhat poetic justice that they have got a result on the last day, even though they're not to win it,' said the commentator David Pleat as Kevin Richardson received treatment for an injury with the Kop already celebrating. 'They will see that as scant consolation, I should think, David,' replied Brian Moore. Scant consolation indeed, for all of us.

From *Fever Pitch* by Nick Hornby

Think about the ways in which this extract combines the features of literary writing with those of non-fiction writing. Here are some ideas:

- The topic is clearly a factual account describing how Hornby felt as the crucial game approached.
- A good deal of factual information is included.
- Information about the players, the football ground and the game itself is provided in detail.
- Literary techniques are used to make the description more vivid, for example, 'I got ready to muster a brave smile for a brave team'. Note the use of repetition here.
- The players are described almost as 'characters', identified by key features, for example, 'Merson's gap-toothed smile', 'Rocastle's pumped-up elegance', 'Smith's lovable diligence'. Note the use of carefully selected nouns and adjectives here.
- Direct speech is used to convey a sense of the commentary.
- The varied sentence structure helps to heighten the sense of excitement and tension by varying the pace and tempo of the writing.

KEY POINT

Many of the techniques found in literary non-fiction texts are exactly the same as those that novelists or short story writers might use to create their effects.

Another example of literary non-fiction is the book *Pole to Pole* by Michael Palin, in which he describes his journey from the North Pole to the South Pole. This is an example of travel writing too. In the following passage, he describes his journey across Norway.

The mountains climb quite steeply to 2000 feet and we have to stop a lot in the first hour, partly to free snowmobiles bogged down by their heavy loads, but mainly to photograph the spectacular views out across King's Fiord, fed by three glaciers and rimmed with sweeping mountain peaks. As soon as the motors are turned off and the natural silence restored, the size and scale and majesty of the landscape is indescribable. There are no trees on Spitsbergen, and therefore few birds except around the coast, and with unbroken snow shrouding the valley below us there is an atmosphere of magnificent peacefulness.

Soon we are across the pass and putting the snowmobiles down a snow-slope so steep that we are warned not to use the brake. This is to prevent the trailers from swinging round and pulling the vehicles over – and presumably sending the driver hurtling downhill in a mass of wreckage, though they don't tell you the last bit. We twist and turn through some perilous gullies which Roger refers to with a certain relish as Walls of Death, as in 'Michael, we'd like to do another Wall of Death sequence'. The whole adventure seems to have gone to his head since he chose the codeword 'Raving Queen' for his end of the two-way radio. Fraser, at the other end, is 'Intrepid One', and I suppose it does take away some of the terror to hear, floating across a glacier, the immortal words: 'Raving Queen to Intrepid One, Michael's on the Wall of Death…Now!'

On the other side of the pass another epic wintry panorama is revealed on the shores of Engelsbukta – 'English Bay' – where an English whaling fleet under Henry Hudson took refuge in 1607 while in search of the north-east passage. Much of the bay is still frozen, and we see our first seals – nothing more than tiny black blobs – waiting beside their holes in the ice. A ptarmigan, in its white winter coat, peers curiously down at us from a pinnacle of rock, and a pair of eider ducks turn low over the bay.

From *Pole to Pole* by Michael Palin

Many literary techniques have been used in this writing. For example:

- Vivid description, e.g. 'to free snowmobiles bogged down by their heavy loads'; 'fed by three glaciers and rimmed with sweeping mountain peaks'; 'an atmosphere of magnificent peacefulness'.
- The use of imagery, e.g. 'hurtling downhill in a mass of wreckage'; 'Wall of Death'; 'nothing more than tiny black blobs', which creates a picture in the reader's mind.
- The use of alliteration, e.g. 'twist and turn'; 'size and scale'; 'white winter coat'.
- The use of direct speech (in the second paragraph), which makes the story realistic and adds a sense of voice and immediacy.

PROGRESS CHECK

1 What other literary techniques do you find in this writing?

1. • The creation of atmosphere, e.g. 'the size and scale and majesty of the landscape is indescribable'; 'another epic wintry panorama is revealed'.
   • The creation of tension, e.g. 'We twist and turn through some perilous gullies'; 'putting the snowmobiles down a snow-slope so steep that we are warned not to use the brake'.

Sample GCSE question

Write a review of your favourite television programme for a TV programme guide.

On first appearances, `The Wire' may just seem like another cop show. First appearances are deceiving. `The Wire' is far more than that. This is a programme not only about the police; it goes much deeper than that. It is about the modern American city, specifically Baltimore.

Good introduction gives the reader an indication of the kind of programme and the reviewer's view of it.

Each series of `The Wire' incorporates a different facet of the city, from the dealers in the impoverished East Side to the police that hunt them, the struggling dockers in an industry that is falling, the trials and tribulations of City Hall and the deals and double crossings of a mayoral campaign, a crippled state education system failing its future, and the role the media has to play in all of these elements.

A broad overview of the focus of the different elements that various programmes have and the issues they deal with, made interesting through use of alliteration.

The show has been described as a modern day Shakespeare, and in many ways it could be considered in this light what with the plot twists and turns, the overarching storylines playing out over the entire series and the sheer amount of plotting, scheming, and backstabbing that characters from all walks of life become embroiled in.

Gives ideas on the complexities of the plotting and the ways the programmes link together.

Co-created by David Simon and Ed Burns, the series prides itself on its realism and attention to detail. Before creating `The Wire', Simon was a journalist for the `Baltimore Sun' (featured in the show) where he spent a year working alongside the city's homicide department whilst Burns was a homicide detective turned school teacher. It was the collective experiences of the programme's creators that helped create the air of gritty realism that surrounds the programme. The show is shot entirely in Baltimore, in its streets and its buildings, and the creators were keen to show the real Baltimore; the run down and derelict townhouses, the dilapidated project towers, and the people who inhabit these places, much to the dismay of the councillors of the city.

Background of the series creators and the influence this has had on them.

Information given on the settings used for filming.

The essence of the city is captured by Robert Coleman, director of photography, who insisted on using wide angle camera techniques wherever possible, thereby incorporating as much as possible into his scenes, not just the characters who happen to be on-screen at that particular moment. There are even characters played by real-life criminals who had been put away by Ed Burns, the best of which has to be a man of the cloth who was actually one of Baltimore's biggest drug kingpins in the late seventies / early eighties.

Comment on camerawork and effects.

What makes this possibly the best TV programme to have ever been created is that it actually demands its audience's attention. Incredibly tightly written and expertly crafted, the audience is often required to read between the lines and as the tagline suggests, `All the pieces matter...'

Effective concluding paragraph with ideas on effects on audience.

Practice questions

1 Write a fact sheet giving advice on how to look after a pet of your choice.

(External exam question: English Language, Unit 1)

2 Write an article explaining what you think is the greatest threat to continued human life on the planet and explain what you think should be done to try to solve the problems.

(External exam question: English Language, Unit 1)

3 Write a leaflet aimed at 11 to 13 year olds, in which you give them advice about how to write a good piece of imaginative writing.

(External exam question: English Language, Unit 1)

4 Write a review of a film of your choice for a film review website.

(Controlled Assessment task: English Language, Unit 3)

5 Write the script of an interview with an actor from one of your favourite films.

(Controlled Assessment task: English Language, Unit 3)

4 Studying media texts

The following topics are covered in this chapter:

- **Examining newspapers**
- **Looking at advertising**
- **Film and television**

4.1 Examining newspapers

LEARNING SUMMARY

After studying this section, you should be able to understand:

- how to look at a newspaper report
- the difference between fact and opinion
- how to compare newspaper reports

Looking at a newspaper report

AQA	E Lang	E Lit
	✓	✗

The main function of a newspaper is to **report** news of all kinds to the reader. This covers a very wide area and can range from informing the reader about very serious issues to entertaining them with amusing or trivial news items.

Apart from being available to buy in hard copy, newspapers are also available to read online on the Internet. Although the online versions contain the same kind of news items as the paper copy, the layout often differs to suit the electronic format.

Some of the different kinds of news items that might be found in a newspaper include news of world events, national news, political news, local news, sports news, entertainment news (film, TV, theatre, etc.), minor news items and gossip.

In addition to presenting news, newspapers often do something else too, including:
- commenting on events
- making judgements
- giving opinions.

When analysing the effect of a newspaper article, there are a number of features to take into account, all of which add something to the effect of the piece.
For example:
- **The headline** – this is the first thing you notice and read when looking at an article.
- **The photographs or illustrations** (if used) – again, the reader's eye is drawn to these, often before reading the content.
- **Captions** that go with the photographs and illustrations.
- **Content** – this is very important because it contains the main body of information to be communicated to the reader.

All these elements combine to create the effect of the article.

Look at the article below and read it carefully. Think about what it has to say and the effect that it creates.

The Lonsdale News, Sunday, June 27 2010   + 15

Flash Floods Devastate Local Villages

Homes, businesses and lives ruined as flood water rises

Flash floods devastated villages in Derbyshire overnight on Friday.

The full extent of the destruction is not yet known, but one thing is for certain: repairing the damaged property and getting people's lives back to normal could take months, if not years.

Destruction

The floods came after days of persistent rain and gale force winds, not encountered in this part of the country for years.

The situation could not be worse for many residents, whose lives have been washed way in the disruption of the last few days.

One victim of the floods was Charlie Turner, 54, from Leafdale. He awoke on Saturday morning to find his home swamped under a metre of water.

But there was more terrible news waiting for him in nearby Greenham when he went to open up the family

business, Charlie's Chippie.

He found flood water halfway up the walls and his deep-fat fryers completely submerged. Says Charlie, 'My grandfather Charlie opened this chippie in 1960 and we've been open 6 days a week ever since. I feel like I'm letting down the family name by having to close up'.

Charlie's life has been devastated by the flood and it will take him many months to repair the damage.

Widespread damage

Every villager in Leafdale has a similar story to tell, and although the weather is due to ease this week, this is no consolation to the many whose homes and businesses have already been ruined.

Single mum-of-two Anna Grayson said, 'I just don't know where to start. We're going to have to stay at my mum's until the repair work can be done on the house. It's just a dreadful situation'.

The **headline** immediately indicates to the reader that the article is concerned with flooding. It uses **alliteration** in 'flash floods' to highlight the main point of the article. The use of the word 'flash' also implies that it happened so quickly the villagers weren't prepared for it. The **strapline** continues to hold the reader's attention through **use of three** ('Homes, businesses and lives'), which emphasises the damage caused by the flood.

The use of the **present tense** in the headline and strapline makes the story seem more immediate / real.

The **image** in the article adds to its effect by showing at a glance what the article is about, and the extent of the flooding.

Throughout the article, **sensational words** are used for effect, e.g. 'destruction', 'terrible', 'devastated'. **Emotive words** are also used, for example, 'victim'.

Repetition of 'devastate', 'devastated' stresses the problems caused, and **hyperbole** (**exaggeration**), e.g. 'could not be worse' highlights the extent of the situation. In addition, the metaphor 'lives washed away' creates an upsetting image in the reader's mind.

The fact that the article uses **quotes** from people who have been affected by the flood makes it seem more real, and allows the reader to identify with the situation the people face. The article focuses in particular on one 'victim of the floods' whose home and business have been damaged. This highlights the extent of the flood damage. A quote from this man is used, which talks about how long his business has been going and how it was founded by his grandfather. This gains sympathy from the reader by stressing the family connection. In addition, the inclusion of 'single mum-of-two' lets readers identify and sympathise with the woman's situation.

Throughout the article, **opinion** is used by the writer to sound like fact, e.g. 'repairing the damaged property... could take months'. This again highlights the extent of the damage, suggesting that residents will suffer for a long time, and ending the article on rather a bleak note.

The difference between fact and opinion

AQA | E Lang ✓ | E Lit ✗

When reading articles, it is important to be able to distinguish between fact and opinion.

Facts are statements that can be proven. Opinions are personal points of view – some people will agree with them, whereas others will not.

Comparing newspaper reports

AQA | E Lang ✓ | E Lit ✗

The effect that a story has on the reader depends very much on the way the story is written and presented. Sometimes different newspapers treat the same story in quite different ways to create different effects.

Writers can influence the effects that their stories create in various ways. Here are some of the main ones:
- The headlines and sub-headings they use.
- The way they use language to present the story.
- The particular ideas they choose to include.
- The way they present the facts.
- The use of comments and opinions.
- The tone they create in their writing.
- The way they use photographs and illustrations.

> **KEY POINT**
>
> When analysing newspaper articles and reports, be specific – give examples and comment on them. Remember to look at all the features, not just the text.

The following two reports are about the same story. They give details about the sighting on Google Earth of an object that some think might be an image of the Loch Ness Monster.

Article 1 is an example of an online article and Article 2 is an example of an article from a newspaper.

Article 1

NEWS HOME

Search   Explore News

- News Home
- Top stories

- Business & Money
- Sport
- Travel
- Weather
- Entertainment
- Music
- Food

- Have your say
- FAQs
- Contact Us
- Like this page?

Is it Nessie?

By Joe Johnson

This supposedly extinct marine dinosaur's flippers and tail seem to be similar to those of the shape spotted in the satellite image.

A satellite image of what looks like the notorious Loch Ness Monster has been captured by Google Earth.

The amazing photo seems to show a huge dinosaur-type shape, with flippers and a tail, swimming in the depths of Loch Ness.

Loch Ness is 23 miles long and 230 metres deep at its deepest point. There have been claims of sightings of the famed Loch Ness Monster for centuries, with the first sighting recorded as long ago as 565AD.

Whether the photo will be the one that solves the mystery remains to be seen, but scientists certainly seem interested in it and are willing to carry out further research.

Go to Google Earth and see for yourself.

Article 2

22   *The Lonsdale News, Sunday, June 27 2010*

Who's lurking in the loch?

Victoria Smith

She's been spotted again – the Monster of Loch Ness. Apparently.

Last week, another sighting of the famous Loch Ness monster was reported, this time via a particularly observant Internet user who spotted the mysterious shape on Google Earth.

The legendary Loch Ness monster is said to represent the plesiosaur, a marine reptile that lived during the Mesozoic era. The Google Earth image appears to show a very large object with what some say look like fins and a tail, which represents the plesiosaur. It certainly creates an intriguing picture.

Sceptics insist that this is simply an image of a large boat cruising on the loch, which does seem a far more likely story. Indeed, scientists have yet to produce any evidence of the existence of the Loch Ness monster, despite a long history of the myth. Tales and sightings of the Loch Ness monster are thought to have been in existence for more than 1000 years. The famous black and white photograph of a long-necked dinosaur-type creature, which bore a striking resemblance to the plesiosaur, happily bobbing about in the loch, was uncovered as a fake, but a great many more hoaxes followed.

Perhaps the object is in fact the elusive Nessie – a great big, solitary, 1000-year-old monster. Or perhaps it is simply a boat. I know which one my money will be on.

The most famous 'photo' of Nessie was exposed as a hoax

Another sighting of Nessie?

Jupiterimages, / Photos.com / Thinkstock

Look carefully at each of these articles and think about the things that they have in common and the ways in which they differ. Here are some points you might have noted:

Similarities between the two reports:

- The same news item provides the starting point for each report.
- They report the same basic information regarding the Google Earth sighting.
- Neither article shows the actual Google Earth image of what could be the Loch Ness Monster.

Although both reports draw on the same information as the starting point for their stories, there are significant differences in how they treat that material.

Differences between the two reports:

Article 1	Article 2
The Headline	
• The headline 'Is it Nessie?' gives an initial impression that the image may well be the Loch Ness Monster. Note the use of the term 'Nessie', which is a popular nickname for the Loch Ness Monster and creates a slightly light-hearted tone.	• The headline 'Who's lurking in the loch?' creates a light-hearted almost jokey tone whilst at the same time addressing the key question – is it the Loch Ness Monster or not? Note the use of the alliterative 'lurking in the loch' to give a catchy feel to the headline.
The Content	
• In terms of text, this article is shorter although it does contain some information that the other article does not and adopts a much less sceptical stance. • The response of the scientists also gives the impression that the image is intriguing and that it needs further study. • The mention of other sightings is summed up in a single sentence – 'There have been claims of sightings of the famed Loch Ness Monster for centuries…' • It contains details such as that experts believe Nessie might be an extinct marine dinosaur, that Loch Ness is 23 miles long and that the object seen appears to have a dinosaur-type shape, a tail and flippers. This shows that some people accept the possibility that there might be some kind of undiscovered creature living in Loch Ness.	• The article begins with the Google Earth story and then goes on to give information about the 'Nessie' legend. • The article moves on to discuss the most famous hoax sighting and then mentions the great many more hoaxes. This seems to suggest a degree of scepticism on the part of the writer as to whether Nessie really exists. • This suggestion is reinforced by the fact that the writer mentions how scientists have yet to produce any evidence of the existence of the creature. • The entire article has a questioning tone, shown through statements such as '…this is simply an image of a large boat cruising on the loch, which does seem a far more likely story'; and through humorous imagery, such as 'happily bobbing about in the loch', which highlights the dubiousness of the story. • The article ends with a very sceptical statement about what the object really is. The adjectives used to suggest that it is Nessie imply a strong sense of doubt, e.g. 'elusive', '1000-year-old'. The fact that the writer ends the article with the statement 'I know which one my money will be on.' sums up her general attitude towards the existence of the Loch Ness Monster.
The Images	
• The image is in colour and shows a representation of what a marine dinosaur might have looked like. This gives an idea of a link between this image and that seen on Google Earth and gives a sense of credibility to the theory that Nessie might possibly be such a creature.	• The old, grainy black and white photograph, which turned out to be one of the most notorious hoaxes, is used as the first picture. Perhaps this was chosen to illustrate the sceptical tone of the article. • The other picture (also in black and white) shows a boat on Loch Ness, perhaps to emphasise the likelihood of the Google Earth image being just this.

Here are some of the key features to look at when comparing newspaper reports or articles:

- The language used in the reports or articles.
- The ideas chosen for inclusion.
- The ways the facts are presented.
- The use of opinion and comment.
- The tone created in the writing.
- The way images and illustrations are used.
- The headlines and sub-headings used.

> **KEY POINT**
>
> Articles about the same story can be very different in the message they put across and the effects they create.

4.2 Looking at advertising

LEARNING SUMMARY

After studying this section, you should be able to understand:

- different kinds of advertising
- some of the features of advertising
- how to analyse advertisements

Different kinds of advertising

AQA	E Lang	E Lit
	✓	✗

Advertising is all around. We encounter it every day in many ways and in many forms. The range of advertising and the techniques used in it is hugely varied but, in the end, all advertising has one thing in common – its purpose. The key purpose of all advertising is to **persuade** us to behave or think in a particular way.

Not surprisingly, advertising is big business and large sums of money are spent on producing advertisements. It has become a very specialised business in the modern world and many companies employ advertising agencies to produce advertisements for their products or services.

Here are some of the kinds of advertising that you will be familiar with:

- Product advertising – this covers a vast range of different kinds of products, e.g. cars, coffee, financial services.
- Holiday advertising – this can cover a wide range of holiday types and locations.
- Charity advertising – e.g. for the RSPCA, Royal National Lifeboat Institution or OXFAM.
- Public services and information – e.g. police warnings about mobile phone theft, fire safety adverts.
- Job advertisements.

Features of advertising

	E Lang	E Lit
AQA	✓	✗

Advertising agencies usually do several things to ensure that their advertisements are effective:

- They carry out market research to make sure that their advertising campaign is correctly targeted and likely to be successful.
- They assess the strengths and qualities of the product they are advertising and sample consumer reactions to it.
- They use their imaginative, artistic and language skills to produce an appropriate advert.

All the adverts we will look at in this section are the product of all these processes.

In designing an advert, the advertiser takes a number of factors into account:

- **The appeal** – all adverts are designed to appeal to something within us. For example, wealth or status, comfort, security, fashion sense, leisure pursuits, health fears, conscience.
- **The headlines or slogans** – these are the key words that catch the eye and draw attention to the advert. They need to be eye-catching and persuasive.
- **The language of the advert** – some adverts rely entirely on photographs or pictures of some kind and contain no words. Some rely entirely on the catchy slogan or headline. Many use text as well in order to create their effects and they use particular techniques to make the language they use as effective as possible.

Here are some features that you will often find in the 'language of advertising':

- **Exaggeration** – words are often used to claim that the product is the best in some way, e.g. 'the fastest', 'most comfortable', 'most advanced'. These words are called **superlatives**.
- **Imperatives** – verbs that issue commands, like 'Buy now!', 'Don't miss this!'.
- Claims that cannot be proved, like 'this will save you money', 'the finest that money can buy'.
- **Repetition** – key words are often repeated to drive the message home.
- **Appealing words** – such as 'bargain', 'beautiful', 'luxurious'.
- Sound appeal – the use of **alliteration**, **assonance** or **rhyme**, e.g. 'silky and super soft'.
- Words that appeal to taste – 'tangy', 'tasty', 'sweet'.
- The use of **imagery** – similes are commonly used, e.g. 'as fresh as morning dew'.
- The use of pseudo-technical or scientific language.
- The use of **humour** and **puns** (plays on words) – words with double meanings are often used.

> **KEY POINT**
>
> The effects of an advert are often the result of a combination of a number of factors.
>
> When analysing advertisements, look for:
> - the visual impact
> - who the advert is designed to appeal to
> - the use of the slogan and pictures
> - the language used
> - the relationship between these features.

Analysing advertisements

AQA — E Lang ✓ — E Lit ✗

Advertisements can take many forms. For example, some use quite a bit of text, whereas others might not use text at all but rely purely on a visual image or images. Sometimes, adverts can look very simple but often there is far more to them and the way that they work than appears at first sight.

To begin with you should think about the audience the advert is aimed at and the purpose that it is designed to achieve, and then go on to analyse it in more detail.

When analysing advertisements, you should consider four basic things:
- **Images / layout** – look carefully at the way in which the images and words are arranged.
- **Slogans or catchwords** – these are often in larger print and catch the reader's attention immediately.
- **Blurb** – the more detailed text, describing the product or subject of the advert, giving information about it, etc. This is often in smaller print.
- **Effect** – the overall effect produced by the advertisement.

The following advertisement uses several techniques. Look at it carefully and begin by thinking about its audience and purpose.

Here are some ideas:

Audience: People interested in animals; those who would like to help Chester Zoo by providing a kind of sponsorship; possibly younger people who are more likely to send text messages.

Purpose: To encourage people to donate money to the zoo through this adoption scheme.

Large lettering with emphasis on 'Adopt Me' to capture the reader's attention and give the sense that the chimpanzee is addressing the reader directly. Note the lettering style.

Information that this advert refers to Chester Zoo chimpanzees.

Sub-heading indicates benefits of adopting – note the use of the word 'Fantastic'.

Bullet-point list tells the reader exactly what they get for adopting one of the animals.

The word 'exclusive' is used twice to emphasise the special benefits.

Details of number to text 'CHIMP' to.

The dominant image is designed to appeal to the readers, whilst the bright green background makes the advert stand out.

Sub-heading captures the attention and interest of the reader.

Question to grab readers' attention, followed by an interesting piece of information, which also points to the fact that chimpanzees are our closest relatives.

Comparing adverts

Look at the following advertisements.

NO ARTIFICIAL COLOURS, FLAVOURINGS OR PRESERVATIVES IN [Mars] OR [Snickers] Raising The Bar

Free

from artificial colours, flavourings, preservatives

VERSATILE, LIGHTWEIGHT AND POWERFUL!

Light but powerful – the CleverClean 10 is our most advanced vacuum cleaner, with twice the cleaning capability of the CleverClean 5!

At **ONLY £39.99*** plus £6.99 P&P
don't miss out on the CleverClean 10!

That's a saving of £15!

"The new CleverClean 10 is perfect for me! I'm confident that it picks up every last crumb – my carpets are spotless!"

Mrs Johnson, Northallerton

With its attractive appearance, super lightweight feel (only 5lbs) and easy-grip handle, the CleverClean 10 is the ideal cleaning solution for your home.

Complete with dusting brush and attachments, the CleverClean 10 is capable of reaching even the deepest-set dust and crumbs! And the new F12 filtration system means your carpets will be almost as good as new!

The vacuum comes with an extra-long 10 metre power cable, giving you extra flexibility.

- Lightweight
- The ultimate cleaning solution
- Easy-grip handle
- Extra-long power cable

Or for £3.50 extra, you can opt for the super-long 15 metre power cable!

* For a limited period only. Usual price £54.99.

To order your CleverClean 10 now, fill in the form overleaf and send off today!

We offer a full refund if you are not completely happy.

FREE hand-held vac with every CleverClean 10

vacuums

The techniques used in each of the adverts and the effects they create are listed below.

Mars bar advert:	V V Vacuums advert:
<ul><li>The striking feature about this advert is the lack of words used. The dominating image is of a Mars bar on a blank white background.</li><li>Note that the product is so well known that it is instantly recognisable even though it is not named. (Only the small bar at the foot of the advert carries the name of the products.)</li><li>The word 'Free' replaces 'Mars' and this is qualified in the smaller lettering beneath, informing the reader that the bar (and others by the same manufacturer) is free from artificial colours, flavourings and preservatives.</li><li>At the foot of the advert, in smaller letters, this message is stressed and accompanied by images of the products that the advert refers to.</li><li>Note the use of the play on words in the phrase 'Raising the Bar' – bar in the obvious sense of a chocolate bar, but the phrase can also mean 'raising standards', suggesting that the standard of the confectionery is raised by being free from artificial ingredients.</li></ul>	<ul><li>This advert is very different in style to the Mars advert in that it uses a great deal of text and a number of images. It is very colourful and a bit cluttered, with a number of different font sizes, styles and colours.</li><li>The main image shows the woman using the vacuum cleaner and she looks very happy with it.</li><li>Technical detail is given, such as weight and the F12 filtration system.</li><li>Language, including superlatives, is used to emphasise its superior qualities, e.g. 'most advanced', 'powerful', 'super lightweight'.</li><li>Lots of exclamatory sentences are used to emphasise the value of the product and perhaps to attract the readers' attention.</li><li>A quote from a happy customer is included, which highlights the quality of the product and the satisfaction customers will have from buying it.</li><li>The text of the advert speaks directly to the reader, using the second person pronoun 'you', which gives a personal touch and may even make the advert seem more trustworthy and reliable.</li><li>The price has been substantially reduced and the saving of £15 is stressed through the use of the yellow box, which immediately catches the eye.</li><li>Free hand-held vac and an optional extra-long power cable are offered, together with a money-back guarantee if the purchaser is not completely happy, which implies that this is a high-quality product.</li></ul>

KEY POINT

When analysing adverts, look at all aspects of them. Give detailed comments and examples to illustrate the techniques used and comment on the effects created by the use of these techniques.

4.3 Film and television

LEARNING SUMMARY	**After studying this section, you should be able to understand:** • the purpose of film and television previews and reviews • the purpose of interviews and features

Previews and reviews

AQA	E Lang ✓	E Lit ✗

Film and television previews and reviews appear every day in a whole range of publications, from newspapers to specialist film and television magazines.

Although previews and reviews are often similar in style and content, they do have different purposes.

The preview

A preview of a film or television programme is written to be read before a film is released or before a television programme is screened. It serves several functions including:

- Giving the reader an idea of what the film or programme is about but without revealing so much as to spoil the later enjoyment of it.
- Giving an idea of who is in it.
- Giving some background about the actors, production, etc.
- Telling the reader when it will be released, screened, etc.

The review

A review is a report on a film or programme that has already been screened. It also has several functions, including:

- Giving an outline of what the film or programme is about for those who haven't seen it.
- Giving information on who is in it.
- Giving views on the strengths and weaknesses of aspects of the film or programme, e.g. the acting, the plot, the setting.
- Commenting on the overall success of the film or programme.

Look at the examples of a preview and a review on the following pages.

Previews

Here is an example of a **preview** of the popular soap opera 'Emmerdale', which could be found in a TV guide.

What features can you identify in this preview?

Who's going to murder Mark?

EMMERDALE

Emmerdale's self-made millionaire Mark Wylde meets his end this week...

This has been a dramatic week for the residents of Emmerdale, with the secrets and lies of wealthy businessman Mark Wylde, played by actor Maxwell Caulfield, finally coming to the fore.

After weeks of build-up, Mark's web of lies and deception is revealed when his wife, Natasha, walks in on Mark's steamy clinch with ex-lover, Faye. But the story doesn't end there.

Drama and Deception

Mark is revealed as a bigamist – he is still married to Faye, as well as Natasha, and has recently discovered that he is the father of Faye's son, Ryan – as well as having three children with Natasha: nasty Nathan, who's already caused trouble in the village; spoilt single girl Maisie, and 10-year-old baby of the family, Will.

The web becomes ever more tangled as it emerges that Maisie has secretly been seeing Ryan, unaware that he is actually her half-brother!

Having ruined so many lives, Mark is about to become a figure of hatred, and this week, after years of drama and deception, viewers will see his tangled life brutally ended.

The big question is... who dunnit?

Sleepy village or den of iniquity?

Here are some features you might have noted:

- The headline poses the question that followers of the show will want to know the answer to: 'Who's going to murder Mark?'
- The sub-headings indicate the possible motives for the murder.
- The first two paragraphs refer to incidents from recent episodes to recap on where the action was left.
- The text reveals a little of what will happen but does not reveal exactly how, so as not to spoil the storyline for the reader / viewer.
- The text gives a brief insight into the nature and relationships of some of the characters.
- The preview is written in quite an informal style, using some non-standard language, e.g. 'who dunnit', 'steamy clinch' and contractions, e.g. 'doesn't', 'who's'.
- Alliteration is used in the sub-heading and in the main text for emphasis and to keep the text sounding interesting, e.g. 'Drama and Deception', 'nasty Nathan'.
- The colours and images used in the preview give an immediate impression of darkness, suggesting shadowy and wicked events, and the main image contrasts with the two smaller images of the normal, wholesome impression of the village and the countryside.

Reviews

Now look at the following review. It is a review of the Harry Potter film 'Harry Potter and the Half-Blood Prince' written shortly after the film was released in the cinemas. What do you notice about the style, content and structure of the review?

If you're a Harry Potter fan, then you'll probably want to bolt an extra star to my grumpy rating. The film-makers have dusted down their vast Hogwarts set, reunited the cast, and poured a ton of money into magicing-up some impressive effects.

Daniel Radcliffe is maturing into the role of the eponymous wizard with real authority. There's a sweet touch to the romantic interest that develops between Harry's best friends Hermione and Ron. And more established performers are on hand to provide actorly gravitas: Michael Gambon is on lovely, genial form as Hogwarts headmaster Dumbledore, and Alan Rickman brings saturnine elegance as the sinister Professor Snape.

While *The Order Of The Phoenix* worked hard to engage people like me who'd never picked up a JK Rowling book, **Harry Potter And The Half-Blood Prince** lazily assumes our fascination with all things Potter-related from the get-go.

The plot, involving Harry's attempt to find out the identity of the owner of a heavily notated potions exercise book he finds, is all set-up, no pay-off. Overloaded with exposition and dark references to Harry and Voldemort's past, it feels like a prelude to the franchise climax of the final film.

There are a few decent set-pieces: a creepy battle between Harry and a hoard of slimy and fanged amphibian thingamajigs in a huge cave flickers with excitement; and I loved the moment when London's Millennium Bridge – notorious for its wobble when first opened – is turned into CGI jelly by Voldemort's underlings.

But these are few and far between in a relentlessly talky and curiously shapeless film. In one of the few light touches that alleviate the air of faux solemnity, a waitress asks the wizard: "Who's Harry Potter?" The reply: "Oh, no one. A bit of a tosser really." I don't quite agree, but the final instalment has a lot of ground to make up. **EDWARD LAWRENSON**

Here are some points you might have noted:

- The review is written in the first person and so creates a sense that we are hearing the reviewer's views directly.
- The reviewer comments on the development and performance of the central actor.
- The review compares the approach of the film to the earlier Harry Potter film, 'The Order of the Phoenix'.
- It directly addresses the reader by using the personal pronoun 'you'.
- The review uses informal language with contractions (e.g. 'you'll', 'who'd') and colloquial words and phrases (e.g. 'poured a ton of money', 'thingamajigs'), which create a chatty tone.
- The writer has made effective use of adverbs and adjectives to create vivid descriptions, e.g. 'a hoard of slimy and fanged amphibian thingamajigs in a huge cave'; 'a relentlessly talky and curiously shapeless film'.
- Some negative points are made about the way the plot works and some positive comments are made on the 'decent set-pieces'.
- The final paragraph sums up the generally negative view of the film.

Interviews and features

AQA	E Lang	E Lit
	✓	✗

Interviews with stars of film and television are very popular with the public, whether conducted on television chat shows or published in print in magazines, newspapers or on websites. When produced to be read, rather than seen or heard, interviews can be presented in a variety of ways.

The following web page shows one way in which this kind of interview can be presented. It is an interview with the actress who plays the character, Rachel, who is returning to the television show 'Winterberry Park'.

LTV HOME   [Search]   [Explore the LTV]

Accessibility help
Text only

LTV Homepage

» Winterberry Park Home
» Video
» Episodes
» Archive

» Characters & Cast
   Characters A–Z
   Cast A–Z
» Interviews

» Games
» Quizzes
» Pictures

» Places
» Webcam

» News
» Your say
» FAQs

Contact Us

Like this page?
Send it to a friend

Winterberry Park

Katherine Christensen INTERVIEW

Rachel returns to her roots! Katherine Christensen talks to us about her character Rachel's dramatic return to Winterberry Park village this week.

So Rachel's returning to the village. Why?
She's left her husband, Tony. She gave up her entire life in Winterberry Park to go and live with him in Chicago, but she caught him cheating with an old flame and decided enough was enough. So she's back, and ready to cause trouble!

Playing flirty Rachel in the hit show Winterberry Park.

Has the character of Rachel changed at all?
Well, she's older and a little bit wiser, but she's basically the same old Rachel. She's still brassy and flirty, she still wears cheap-looking, revealing clothes, and she still has the potential to cause trouble! Oh, but she has gone back to her natural hair colour and given up smoking and drinking... at least for a while...

Ah, can we detect from that that Rachel might be having her first baby?
You'll have to wait and see! All I can say is that she has a few surprises in store for the locals!

Medioimages / Photodisc / Thinkstock
Rachel's cheating hubby, Tony.

Why did you come back to the show?
I enjoyed every minute of playing Rachel in the show, but I left because I felt it was time to move on and try something new. I've had a few years away now, just spending time with my husband and daughter and doing some stage performances. I feel ready now to go back. Many of the same people are still on the show, and I can't wait to get back to working with them all!

When looking at interviews you should think carefully about the following:
- The format of the interview.
- The content of the interview.
- The use of images.

For example, in the interview on page 60:

1 Format

The way the interview is presented gives a strong sense of being 'live', by using the exact words spoken. It also gives a sense of the personality of the actress Katherine Christensen because it is as if we can 'hear' the words spoken.

2 Content

The interviewer focuses on topics and ideas that readers / viewers might want to know about. The answers give some detail and by the end of the short interview there is a feeling that you have discovered things about the character. This is, of course, exactly what those interested in the programme would want.

3 The use of images

The images used here are related to the interview in that one shows the actress Katherine Christensen; another shows her in character as Rachel in a scene from 'Winterberry Park' and another one shows a portrait shot of the character Tony, who is mentioned in the interview.

Sometimes interviews are presented without any questions or even without a sense that an actual interview has taken place. Instead, the edited comments of the subject of the interview are run together to give the impression that they are speaking without answering specific questions.

Other interviews are presented using direct speech, quoting what the interviewer has said, interspersed with comments inserted by the writer editing the interview.

> **KEY POINT**
>
> Interviews can be presented in various ways and each creates a different effect and serves a different purpose.

Sample GCSE question

Write an article for a magazine promoting a particular interest that you have.

WHOSE WEBSITE IS IT ANYWAY?

Every Saturday night for thirteen weeks, millions of people sit glued to their television screens, to see what trouble their hero will get into. Even more importantly, how will he get out of trouble? When the series ends, in fact even when it's on air, some fans turn to the Internet to talk to other fans and to try to figure out what will happen in the next episode or series. Who is their hero? Exactly!

Opening paragraph captures the reader's attention. Note the use of questions and exclamation.

There are many 'Doctor Who' fan-sites across the Internet, with all the latest news from the 'Doctor Who' world: episode guides, information about monsters and villains, details of characters, competitions, planets featured in 'Doctor Who', and spin-off shows' websites like 'Torchwood' and 'Sarah Jane Adventures'. There is one official 'Doctor Who' website. All the others have been created by fans of the show.

Gives an overview of Dr Who fan-sites.

A number of fan-sites have additional pages with topics such as episode guides, monsters and villains, the TARDIS, characters, photos from filming, rumours, spoilers, and gadgets. A few websites even have competition pages, such as Caption Competitions, and Guess the Episode. There are no prizes, it is all just for fun, and your 'name' goes onto the leaderboard, stating how many competitions you have won.

More detailed information given on what the fan-sites contain.

Some people enjoy using Cboxes, the shortened name for Chat Boxes, which are featured on most of the 'Doctor Who', 'Torchwood' and 'Sarah Jane Adventures' fan-sites. The Cbox is just a box on the side of a page (although some people have whole pages of their sites dedicated to them) where fans can discuss subjects related to the show. On the odd occasion, arguments and debates begin, but these don't happen often on most of the 'Doctor Who' fan-sites' Cboxes because the same people tend to go on the websites and Cboxes, so a friendly atmosphere is formed.

Explanation of Chat Boxes and how fans use them.

In addition, there are a few online magazines for 'Doctor Who' which, as the name suggests, have the layout of a real magazine showing two pages on the screen and all the page numbers at the side. The online magazines are made in the style of real magazines, with a front cover, contents, articles, comics, reviews and other features that real magazines tend to have. Both of the spin-offs, 'Torchwood' and 'Sarah Jane Adventures', also have some fan fiction on various websites, as well as 'Doctor Who'.

Discussion of format of online magazines.

To me, however, the most enjoyable and interesting aspect of fan-sites is in creating one myself. To begin, some people use templates, which you choose when making an account on the 'website-host'. Other people create their website from scratch with HTML ('Hyper Text Markup Language), the raw programming language that forms everything on any website. I have tried both options and now use a mixture. I've had my own website on different hosts since January 2007, but have had my website on its current host since late June 2008 and try to update it as often as possible.

Personal interest in creating website explained with some use of technical language (explanation given of abbreviation to help the reader understand).

Part of the excitement lies in watching the hit counter, which records the numbers of visitors in total; as I write this the hit counter on my website is over 25,000 visitors. Even more satisfying is getting an award from other fan-sites, which people tend to hand out at specific events such as a new year. I discovered out of curiosity that, on typing "Doctor Who fan-sites" in the Google search engine, my website appeared third on the first page, alongside two of the most professional and well-known fan-made 'Doctor Who' websites on the Internet!

Personal comments on satisfaction gained from website.

Consequently I, and many others, do not suffer withdrawal symptoms when the latest television series has ended. Instead, I work on my own website or do a bit of 'surfing' to see what other websites have to offer. Why don't you dip your toe in too?

Effective conclusion.

Practice questions

1 Write an article for a local newspaper presenting the case for the development of more computer/Internet facilities for young people at the library in your town.

(External exam question: English Language, Unit 1)

2 Many people feel strongly about the amount of violence and bad language that is used on television. You are the editor of a newspaper. Write an editorial for your paper expressing your feelings about this issue.

You should state clearly:
- what your view is
- the effects of violence / bad language on television
- what you think should be done to address the issue

(External exam question: English Language, Unit 1)

3 You have to give a talk to your class about the advantages and disadvantages of the Internet.

Write what you would say.

(Controlled Assessment task: English Language, Unit 3, Part C)

5 Presenting views, ideas and information

The following topics are covered in this chapter:

- **Presenting an argument**
- **Persuasive writing**
- **Presenting advice**
- **Presenting information**

5.1 Presenting an argument

LEARNING SUMMARY

After studying this section, you should be able to understand:

- how to plan an argument
- how to begin your argument
- how to develop your argument
- how to end your argument
- different approaches and techniques

How to plan an argument

AQA	E Lang	E Lit
	✓	✗

There are many types of arguments and they can be about almost anything. They can be formal or informal, written or spoken, and structured in all kinds of ways.

For the purposes of studying GCSE English Language, though, it is likely that you will be given the topic on which to construct your argument and you will be assessed on your ability to write this argument effectively.

When presented with the topic on which to base your argument, your aim is to present and develop your point of view as clearly and effectively as possible.

In order to do this, you must first establish what your ideas on the given topic are and what your view is. To establish this, it can help to 'brainstorm' your ideas. Try to think not only about points to support your view but also about those that do not agree with it.

From this, you need to decide what particular points you want to make and in what order you want to make them. It is important that you support your ideas with evidence to add weight to your case. When you have developed your case, you then need to draw your argument to a close with an effective conclusion.

Here is one way in which you can plan your argument:

1. Think about the topic you have been given.
2. Work out what you think.
3. Brainstorm ideas both **for** and **against** the view you have taken.
4. Decide which points you want to make and the order in which you want to make them.
5. Develop your ideas on each point.
6. Decide on the evidence that you will give to support your ideas.
7. End your argument with an effective conclusion.

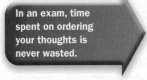

In an exam, time spent on ordering your thoughts is never wasted.

> **KEY POINT**
>
> Careful planning is the secret to writing an effective argument.

Now let's look at each of these stages in more detail.

Beginning your argument

AQA	E Lang	E Lit
	✓	✗

Here is an example of a question that requires you to write an argument as a response.

'Write an argument either supporting or opposing the view that skateboarding should be banned in town and city centres.'

Having decided on what view you wish to take, you would now brainstorm your ideas.

Here are some points that a student made in response to this question.

For skateboarding:
- Town centres are for the use of all groups.
- It is good exercise.
- It develops skills.
- Skateboarders use the architecture for a purpose.
- Some cities encourage skateboarders.
- Skateboarding can be viewed as a 'performance art'.
- It gives youngsters something to do.
- There are few areas provided by councils where skateboarders can go.
- Support for local businesses selling skateboarding equipment.

Against skateboarding:
- Damage to architecture.
- Danger to the public.
- Nuisance to shoppers.
- Elderly people feel intimidated.
- Irritating for nearby shopkeepers.
- Skateboarders are hooligans.
- There are other places for them to go.

There are quite a few points here both for and against the view that skateboarding should be banned in town and city centres.

Fact and opinion

Some of the points the student made are **facts** and some of them are **opinions**. Most arguments are a mixture of fact and opinion and it is important to bear this in mind when planning your argument.

For example, 'Skateboarders are hooligans' is an opinion and not a fact. On the other hand, 'Skateboarding provides exercise' is a fact as it is a strenuous activity.

Some points may be partially true, for example, 'Skateboarding is irritating for nearby shopkeepers'. It may well be that some nearby shopkeepers are irritated by skateboarders but others may not be.

You may think there are too many points here to develop fully and use in your response (particularly if you are working under the time constraints of an exam) so you may choose not to use some of them. You will need to decide which points you consider important enough to use in your argument.

The opening paragraph

The **opening paragraph** of your argument is very important. This is where you have the chance to capture your reader's interest and make clear which point of view you will argue from.

Here is how the student begins his argument on skateboarding:

> In recent years, skateboarders have become a familiar sight in our towns and cities but their presence has provoked a good deal of criticism from various members of the public. However, I would argue that much of this criticism is unjustified and that we should show more tolerance towards their use of the town and city centre environment to pursue their hobby.

Discourse marker / connective used to link paragraphs.

Notice how the student begins the argument with a **statement of fact** that cannot be disputed. He then uses the connective 'however' to change the direction of his writing and allow him to state clearly the view he takes and the line that his argument will follow.

The student uses typical language features of writing to argue. His language is quite formal, with some long, interesting words used (e.g. 'provoked', 'tolerance') and complex sentences.

KEY POINT

Your opening paragraph should capture the reader's interest and state your viewpoint.

Developing your argument

AQA	E Lang	E Lit
	✓	✗

Having written your opening paragraph, you then need to develop your argument in more detail. This is where the **key points** that you identified earlier come in.

There are a number of ways that you can develop the main part of your argument. Here are two possible approaches:

- You can **develop** your response by initially stating the view that you are opposing and outlining why people might hold this view, and then countering this view by putting forward the arguments that you support.
- You can write your argument totally from one viewpoint but, throughout the response, you make reference to alternative views where appropriate.

> Avoid the type of approach where you impartially put all the points in favour of a view, then all the points against and then end with a brief 'What I think' type of paragraph.

The student who wrote about skateboarding chose the second kind of approach.

Here's how he began to develop his ideas:

> Discourse markers / connectives used to link sentences / paragraphs.

At a time when we hear a lot in the news about young people today taking less exercise and being less fit than in the past, skateboarding offers an enjoyable and demanding way of taking exercise. The problem for some is that this exercise often takes place in the pedestrian precinct of a town centre.

Some people believe that groups such as skateboarders should be kept out of town centres but it can be argued that town centres should be able to cope with the demands of different groups of people.

In contrast to this view that skateboarders are simply a nuisance, some towns and cities in other countries actually welcome them as just one element that makes up the varied life of a town or city. Barcelona, for example, takes the view that skateboarders and different groups, such as shoppers and tourists, can co-exist in harmony.

Notice how the student is clearly arguing the case for skateboarding being allowed in town and city centres. He also brings in other commonly held **opposing views** so that he can counter them with his own arguments.

Later, the student brings in other ideas.

Using opposing views – a useful technique to add impact to the view you want to express.

Personal experience – used to add weight to the argument. Ideas are based on actual experiences.

Use of three – listing three details is an effective way to get your point across.

Rhetorical question – used for effect.

Presents an example of a different attitude – another technique to give support to the argument.

> Many say that there are plenty of other places that skateboarders can go to skate but this is simply not true. Skateboard parks are few and far between and very often they are situated in out-of-the-way places. In my own town there is one very small area in a large park on the outskirts of town for skateboarders to use. Surely this is not good enough? The facilities are poor, the park has no lighting and it is situated in a secluded area. This is certainly not a safe or attractive environment even in daytime and after dark it is virtually a 'no-go' zone. Is this the kind of facility that we want to encourage our young people to go to?
> On the other hand, in some countries such as the USA and some continental countries, excellent facilities are provided in safe and central locations.

Notice again how the student uses a commonly held view in order to present the **counter-argument**. It is also worth noting how he supports his ideas with examples from his **own experience** and **factual information** about the contrasting situation in other countries.

The various techniques used here are all designed to add weight to the argument and, therefore, strengthen and give impact to the views that the student is putting forward.

You can make your writing more effective by:
- Making sure your opening sentences create maximum impact.
- Structuring your paragraphs effectively in a logical way to develop your points.
- Making sure that your sentences are structured correctly and that you use a variety of sentence types to make your writing more interesting.

KEY POINT

A range of techniques and approaches, such as rhetorical questions and personal anecdotes, should be employed to present the argument as effectively as possible.

Ending the argument

AQA — E Lang ✓ — E Lit ✗

The ending of the argument is just as important as the beginning and so you should make your final paragraph as convincing as possible. Here is how the student ended his essay on skateboarding:

Signals that the argument is being drawn to a close.

Emphasises the key point being made.

> In conclusion, then, while some of the concerns raised by those who oppose skateboarding in town centres are legitimate, I do not believe that the answer is a blanket ban. Perhaps the most important point is that our towns and cities are there to serve the needs of many different groups of people, and there must be a way of co-operating and living together with tolerance and accommodating the needs of all – including those of the skateboarders.

Note how **reasonable in tone** this conclusion is. The student recognises the validity of some of the concerns, which actually gives strength to his view that skateboarding should not be banned. The appeal at the end for tolerance and co-operation again helps to convince the reader of the reasonable position of the writer, as well as re-stating the position taken.

Using different approaches and techniques

AQA — E Lang ✓ — E Lit ✗

You can make your argument more effective by using **different techniques**. For example, there are various words and phrases that you can use when discussing different points of view and ideas. These words and phrases are called **discourse markers** or **connectives** and they help you to develop ideas and relate them to others. Some of these have been used by the student writing about skateboarding and have been highlighted. They include:

- However…
- On the other hand…
- The problem for some…
- In conclusion…
- Some people believe that…
- Perhaps the most important point is…
- In contrast to this…

Here are some other useful words and phrases that you might use:

- Alternatively…
- Similarly…
- Nevertheless…
- This suggests that…

Using key words and phrases can help you to make your argument
more effective.

As well as using particular words and phrases to add power to your argument,
there are also other techniques you can use. Here are some ideas:

Rhetorical questions

Rhetorical questions are questions that are used to create an effect, as opposed
to those that require an answer. They raise questions in the reader's mind and
perhaps appeal to the **emotions** and **involve** the reader in the argument.

The student uses this technique when he says, 'Is this the kind of facility that
we want to encourage our young people to go to?' It is designed to make the
reader feel, 'No it isn't – this isn't good enough'.

Personal experience and anecdotes

It can add weight to your argument if you include some reference to your
own experience.

The student does this to some extent when he mentions the situation in his own
town: 'In my own town there is one very small area...'. Such references based
on personal experience, or short personal stories or accounts, can help to prove
your points and give your writing an air of authority.

Using opposing views

Predicting or anticipating what someone who does not hold the same view as
you might say, and then answering it, can also be an effective technique.

Hyperbole

Hyperbole is the use of exaggeration to create particular emphasis or effect, e.g.
'People have been warned millions of times of the dangers of taking drugs'.

KEY POINT

There is a variety of techniques that you can use to make your argument
more effective in presenting, developing and convincing the reader that
your view is right.

PROGRESS CHECK

1 What key stages would you go through in preparing to write an
argument on a given topic?

1. • Decide on your view on the topic.
• 'Brainstorm' your ideas – write a list of all your ideas on the topic, both for and against.
• Distinguish between fact and opinion.
• Decide on the points you want to make.
• Develop your ideas on the points.
• Decide on the evidence you are going to use to support your case.
• Decide on your opening paragraph.
• Develop your ideas through the main section of your essay.
• End your argument with an effective conclusion.

5.2 Persuasive writing

LEARNING SUMMARY	After studying this section, you should be able to understand:
	• the purpose of persuasive writing
	• the different question types
	• effective openings
	• effective endings
	• techniques in persuasive writing

The purpose of persuasive writing

	E Lang	E Lit
AQA	✓	✗

In your examination or as part of your Controlled Assessment, you might be asked to write a response in which you **persuade** your reader of something.

When you are writing to persuade, your aim is to try to make your reader do something or believe something. In many ways, this can be very similar to writing to argue a point but there can be some differences too.

When writing to persuade you might:
• Be more **subjective** in giving your personal view.
• Try to **appeal** to your reader's **emotions** as much as their reason.

In our everyday lives, we constantly see language used in various ways to try to persuade us to do something, believe something, buy something or act in a particular way. For example:
• Advertisements use persuasive language all the time to try to persuade us to buy the products they are selling.
• Charity appeals use persuasive language to try to persuade us to give donations to good causes.
• Public service information uses persuasive language to try to persuade us to behave in particular ways – for example, to stop smoking, to eat lower fat foods, not to drink and drive.

On pages 72–73 is an article from the *Connect* magazine by Greenpeace. It uses persuasive language and techniques to try to persuade us to support a campaign to change the way we fish, and for substantial parts of the world's oceans to be protected. Look carefully at it and make a note of any points you notice about how it uses **language and other techniques** to persuade the reader.

Here are some ideas:
• **Rhetorical questions** are used to form sub-headings and to make the reader think about the issue of problems caused by fishing and the things that can be done to try to help solve the problems.
• Note that the **question** 'What's the catch?' makes use of a **play on words** and the double meaning.
• The phrase 'industrial scale' gives a sense that the writers are talking about fishing on a huge scale.
• The phrase '...the biggest culprits' suggests that fishing in the ways described is causing harm in some way.
• The **quotation** from Charles Clover and the fact that it is in bold type and

quotation marks draws attention to the scale of the issue by using a reference to a popular animated film.

- Vocabulary is used that reflects the view that damage is being done, e.g. 'destruction', 'devastation', 'damaged'.
- The use of specific details of the damage that various kinds of fishing causes gives the reader essential information.
- The **diagrams** of the various fishing methods allow the reader to visualise what each entails.
- The **photograph** shows Greenpeace campaigners in action and adds a dramatic and eye-catching element to the piece.
- Clear **bullet points** indicate how the problem can be solved.
- The use of the first person plural pronoun 'we' in the sub-heading 'How we can make it happen' gives the sense that we all need to work together to solve the problem and that everyone can do something to help save the oceans.

6

GLOBAL: DESTRUCTIVE FISHING

What's the catch?
There are many ways that fish are caught on an industrial scale. Here are three of the biggest culprits.

Beam trawling
Beam trawlers target fish that dwell on the sea bottom. A large, open-mouthed net is attached to a heavy metal beam about the length of a double-decker bus. This is then dragged across the seabed behind a trawler, strip-mining everything in its path.

Long-lines
These are seriously long: a main fishing line up to 150 km in length, with thousands of shorter lines attached along it, each carrying a baited hook. These hooks snare much more than the the fishermen want, killing thousands of sharks and marine creatures each year.

Purse seining and FADs
Purse-seining involves encircling fish with a vast wall of net which is then gathered together at the bottom with a line and closed, like a purse, trapping everything inside. The big problems start when these nets are used with Fish Aggregation Devices ('FADs'). These simulate natural floating objects and attract not only the target fish, like tuna for example, but also turtles, sharks, marlins, rays and many other species. Once a large catch is spotted it's netted and hauled in, and any species that can't be sold are thrown back, dead or dying.

"
Killed alongside the skipjack tuna that finds itself in your tin is almost the entire cast of Finding Nemo.
Charles Clover
Former environment editor
of the Daily Telegraph
"

What's the solution?
To stop the destruction of the marine environment it's vital that fisheries and governments adopt a more sustainable approach that doesn't waste sea life and empty our oceans.

When it comes to catching tuna, pole-and-line fishing is the least damaging to marine ecosystems as species can be closely targeted. By moving tuna fisheries towards this much more sustainable method, thousands of sea creatures could be saved every year.

As for the indiscriminate destruction that beam trawling causes: we want to see it banned completely. We also want to save the world's oceans from further devastation by ensuring that 40% are protected as marine reserves. These underwater 'national parks' will give depleted fish stocks and damaged ecosystems a chance to recover and be safe from destructive fishing practices like beam trawling.

How we can make it happen
Thanks to your support we're tackling the problems in four main ways.

– We are pushing for an end to FADs on tuna purse-seining vessels and we want to see observers onboard to minimise bycatch.

7

Below:
As well as changing the way we catch our fish, we are demanding that 40% of the world's oceans be protected as marine reserves. ©Hilton/Greenpeace

www.greenpeace.org.uk

– We are promoting sustainable pole-and-line tuna fishing and encouraging retailers to choose fish that's sourced this way. Sainsbury's has already caught on, with its own-brand tinned tuna and Waitrose and M&S are following suit. We also need to keep the pressure up on other retailers and major brands, too.

– We've produced a scientific report that clearly shows why 40% of the world's oceans need to be protected as marine reserves and where they would best be located. We're using this valuable evidence to lobby internationally for global marine reserves.

– This summer our largest vessel, the Esperanza will be out in the Pacific Ocean to confront and expose tuna fishing boats that are wasting vast amounts of sealife.

What you can do
You're already doing a huge amount. By giving your support to Greenpeace you help us persuade restaurant owners, chefs, food writers, the fishing industry and governments to stop wasteful bycatch. If you'd like to do more, check out **www.greenpeace.org.uk/buy-tuna** and see where to buy sustainably caught fish. And spread the word – the more people who know about this urgent issue the better ●

Question types on writing to persuade

AQA   E Lang ✓   E Lit ✗

Questions that ask you to **persuade** can be either quite **formal**, requiring a formal style of reply, or they can be more **informal**.

Here is an example of a more formal question:

'Write a letter to your MP to persuade him/her of the importance of improving public transport in your region.'

A question requiring a less formal response might be:

'Write a speech aimed at a group of friends whom you wish to persuade to help you organise a 'fun-run' to raise money for charity.'

> **KEY POINT**
>
> Whatever type of question you get, you need to use language in such a way as to persuade the reader or listener to agree with your view.

Approaching the question

As with writing an argument, clear planning of what you are going to write is essential if you are to write persuasively and convince your reader to your way of thinking. In order to do this you should:

● Write down the aim you wish to achieve (how you wish to persuade your audience).
● Write down all the points you want to make.
● Write down the ideas you will use to support your points.
● Organise your points and ideas into a logical order – the order in which you are going to write about them.

Effective openings

AQA	E Lang	E Lit
	✓	✗

An **effective** opening is one that immediately **captures the reader's attention** and this is exactly what you should do when writing persuasively.

The following show how two students began their responses to the following:

'Write an information leaflet designed to persuade people to visit your home town.'

Read each of these opening paragraphs:

Text 1

> Many people still think of Halifax as a grimy, northern town but they are wrong. Halifax is an interesting town with a lot of places to go and things to see. For example, there is the Piece Hall, which is an interesting old building, there is a good museum and the moors are not far away either if you like walking in the countryside.

Text 2

> What picture comes into your mind when you hear the name Halifax? A grimy, boring northern mill-town? You couldn't be more wrong. Halifax is a town steeped in history and culture with a wealth of features to interest any visitor. For example, there is the magnificent Piece Hall, the only example of an eighteenth century cloth market in Europe, there is the nationally famous Eureka science museum for young people and, of course, the awesome beauty of the hills and dales of the nearby Pennine uplands.

Which of these openings do you think is more likely to persuade you to visit Halifax? The answer would seem to be clearly the second one, but why? Think about this and note down your ideas.

Here are some points you might have noted:

Text 1

- The first sentence seems rather **boring** and **uninspiring**.
- The second sentence describing Halifax as an 'interesting' town with '...a lot of places to go' doesn't sound very exciting because of the vocabulary choices made.
- Examples are listed but they do not sound very exciting either – no detail is provided.

Text 2

- The piece opens with two **rhetorical questions** that capture the reader's interest right from the start.
- The third sentence **challenges** the possible assumption that the town has little to offer, again catching the reader's attention.
- The language used to describe the town is designed to **appeal** to the reader's imagination and create a positive effect, for example 'steeped in history', 'a wealth of features'.
- The examples that are given include lots of **positive adjectives** to make the reader want to see the things described, for example, 'magnificent Piece Hall', 'nationally famous Eureka', 'awesome beauty of the hills'.

> **KEY POINT**
>
> To make your writing more persuasive, use:
> - emotive language
> - rhetorical language
> - visual imagery.

Effective endings

AQA   E Lang ✓   E Lit ✗

Having developed your ideas and put them forward as persuasively as you can, just as in writing an argument, you need to find a way to end your piece of persuasive writing effectively. How exactly a piece of persuasive writing should end depends very much on the specific details of the task but there are two basic ways to bring the writing to a close:

- Sum up what you have said or the points you have made.
- Find a final, particularly persuasive, note on which to end.

Here is how two students ended their pieces on promoting their town:

Text 1

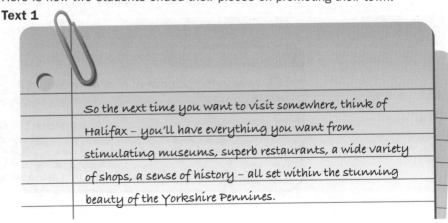

So the next time you want to visit somewhere, think of Halifax – you'll have everything you want from stimulating museums, superb restaurants, a wide variety of shops, a sense of history – all set within the stunning beauty of the Yorkshire Pennines.

Text 2

> And if all this has not managed to persuade you, then this
> might – anyone booking a winter break weekend at one of
> our superb hotels any time between January and March
> (inclusive) will be entitled to a further two nights
> (including breakfast and dinner) for two, absolutely free.
> You can take these two nights at any time and the offer is
> valid for 12 months.

The first student concludes his piece by summing up the **key points** of his piece, which is a good way to end a persuasive piece of writing. The second student, however, opts for a different approach by bringing in a completely new, persuasive selling point, which is also effective.

KEY POINT

Make sure that your ending is powerful and persuasive.

Techniques for making your writing more persuasive

AQA	E Lang	E Lit
	✓	✗

Many of the techniques used in persuasive writing are the same as, or similar to, those you might employ in writing an argument.

Here are some ideas:
- Use **emotive language** to influence the reader's feelings, for example, 'stunning beauty', 'superb restaurants'.
- **Rhetorical questions** involve the reader, arouse interest and make them think.
- **Use of three** or **repetition** of words and phrases can make them have more impact.
- **Exaggeration** can be used to make a point more persuasively (be careful not to over-exaggerate though as this can make your points appear silly).
- **Humour** can help to make your points more persuasive.
- **Direct personal address** makes the reader feel more involved, e.g. using the personal pronoun 'you'.
- **Evidence and justification** give structure and reasoning to your opinion.
- Comparative devices like **similes** and **metaphors** can help to emphasise your main points.

PROGRESS CHECK

1. What is the purpose of persuasive writing?
2. What techniques could you use if you were asked to write persuasively?

1. The main purpose of writing persuasively is to persuade your reader to do something or believe something, or think in a particular kind of way.
2. You might write subjectively, giving your own view, or you might appeal to their emotions and use language in a persuasive way, including features such as exaggeration, humour, emotive language, repetition and rhetorical questions.

5.3 Presenting advice

LEARNING SUMMARY	After studying this section, you should be able to understand: • how language and layout can make advice clear and easy to understand • how language is chosen to suit the audience and purpose

Language and layout

AQA E Lang ✓ E Lit ✗

Advice comes in many forms and we are constantly being given, or seeking, advice of one kind or another. It may be advice on diet, fashion, money, what to see at the cinema, career options and so on. The list is almost endless. Advice can also be presented in different ways. There is verbal advice given by a friend or relative or that we hear on the television or radio, but much of the advice that we encounter will be written. It may be in a magazine, a pamphlet, on the Internet, in a newspaper, book, poster or any other form. Whatever kind of advice is being given, though, the writing is likely to have particular features that it is useful to be aware of.

Here is an advice sheet about fire safety in the kitchen.

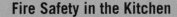

Fire Safety in the Kitchen

Did you know that almost half of all house fires are started in the kitchen? Follow these simple tips to help keep you and your family safe.

Protecting the Family
• Make sure that you have a fire blanket or fire extinguisher close by, and that you know how to use it.

Pans left unattended could boil over

Cooking Safely
• Don't leave children alone in the kitchen whilst you are cooking. Make sure that all saucepan handles and matches are tucked away and out of reach.
• If you leave the kitchen during cooking, turn down the heat under pans, or turn off the heat completely. Never leave your pans unattended for long.
• Take care if you are wearing loose clothing. Keep tea towels and cloths away from the cooker and hob.
• Double check that the cooker and hob have been turned off after you finish cooking.
• Never put anything metal in the microwave!
• Keep all electric leads and appliances away from water.
• Check that the toaster is clean and free from crumbs.
• Keep your oven, hob and grill clean and free from grease and fat.

• Ensure that a smoke alarm is situated just outside the kitchen and that it works. Test it regularly!

Water near electric appliances or sockets can be a fire hazard

What do you notice about the way that this advice is presented?

You might have noted the following points:
- The language is clear and simple.
- It is divided up into clear sections, each dealing with a particular point.
- Bullet points are used to make each specific piece of advice stand out clearly.
- The important advice about the smoke alarm is put in a highlighted box.
- Illustrations are used to help reinforce the point, with ticks and crosses which clearly give information at first glance.
- **Imperatives** (commands) are used to give instructions.

In lots of ways, this example contains many of the key features of effective, written advice bearing in mind that its main purpose is to communicate its ideas clearly and effectively.

KEY POINT

In writing to advise:
- The language is simple and clear.
- The layout helps make the points clear and straightforward.
- The checklist / summary re-emphasises the key ideas.

Language for audience and purpose

AQA E Lang ✓ E Lit ✗

As with most forms of writing, one of the key points to bear in mind when writing to advise is to use language in an appropriate way to address and communicate your ideas to your audience. When writing to advise, it is important that you:
- understand the task set
- understand the **purpose** of the advice
- understand the **audience** it is aimed at
- use language appropriately.

Now look at the example here and the one on the next page.

Text 1

Did you know that thousands of mobile phones are stolen on the street every year?

Young people are most at risk of having their phone stolen, with nearly half of all mobile phone theft victims being under the age of 18. But by taking a few simple steps, you can reduce this risk.

What can you do?
- When you are out and about, keep your phone out of sight in your pocket or in your bag – make sure you keep it with you at all times and out of view.
- When you're using your phone, be aware of what's going on around you and the people who are around you. Don't use it if you feel uneasy about your surroundings.
- Register your mobile phone details with the National Mobile Property Register.

Text 2

Protecting your mobile phone : Directgov – Young people

◄ ► C + http://www.direct.gov.uk/en/YoungPeople/CrimeAndJustice/Keepings Q▾ Google

Cartridge return   Babel Fish   iGoogle   spelling   Photoshop Effects   Check-in   MEDIABANK   »

Directgov

Public services all in one place

Cymraeg | Accessibility | Help | Site index | A A A

Search this site [ ] Go ⊃

Home | Contacts | Do it online | Newsroom

Friday, 23 October 2009

Browse by subject

▸ Crime and justice
▸ Education and learning
▸ Employment
▸ Environment and greener living
▸ Government, citizens and rights
▸ Health and well-being
▸ Home and community
▸ Money, tax and benefits
▸ Motoring
▸ Pensions and retirement planning
▸ Travel and transport

Browse by people

▾ Young people
　▾ Crime and justice
　　▸ **Keeping safe**
▸ Britons living abroad
▸ Caring for someone
▸ Disabled people
▸ Parents

Young people

Protecting your mobile phone

Having your phone stolen is a hassle. It's not just the handset you lose, it's the numbers, messages and photos too. Knowing how to protect your mobile and keep it safe will save you a lot of inconvenience and stress.

Carrying your phone

If you're not making a call, make sure that your phone is hidden away. Keep it in one of your front pockets or inside a bag. Don't attach it to your belt or around your neck.

Thieves are opportunists, so don't make yourself an easy target by showing off the handset you're carrying around.

Lots of people take their phones out of their pockets when they're sitting down. If you're out with your friends, don't put your phone on a table as anyone walking by can easily run off with it.

Making a call

If you're making a call on your mobile in a public area, make sure you always keep an eye on what's going on around you. Thieves go to great lengths to get their hands on the latest handsets, so keep your wits about you.

You should also try to avoid using your mobile phone in public at night. If you do have to use your phone, try to find an area that's well-lit. Also avoid getting out your phone at train stations and bus stops as these are areas that thieves target.

Register, Report, Reunite

Register

You can register the details of your handset with The National Mobile Property Register. This will help the police to return your phone to you if it gets stolen. You should also register the details of your phone with your network provider.

▸ The National Mobile Property Register ⊡

Report

If your phone is lost or stolen, report it immediately to the police.

You should also contact your network provider. When you get through, tell them your phone has been stolen. They'll be able to block both the handset and the SIM card so that they can't be used any more.

Reunite

If the police do recover your stolen handset, it's a lot easier for them to reunite you with your phone if it is registered. They can match up the serial number to your name and address and get it back to you quickly.

Cyberbullying

Laugh at it, and you're part of it...

▸ Find out more about cyberbullying ⊡

Do it online

▸ Find your local police authority

▸ Get more info about knife crime ⊡

▸ Learn more about criminal damage ⊡

Useful contacts

▸ Bullying online

▸ Children and Family Court Advisory and Support Service (CAFCASS)

▸ Citizens Advice Bureau

▸ NSPCC (National Society for the Prevention of Cruelty to Children)

▸ Young people contacts

5.4 Presenting information

LEARNING SUMMARY

After studying this section, you should be able to understand:

- the purpose of writing to inform
- how to write informatively

The purpose of writing to inform

AQA | E Lang ✓ | E Lit ✗

When you are writing to inform, your main **purpose** is to **convey** to your reader certain information as **clearly** and **effectively** as possible. Informative writing, though, can come in many different forms.

Look at these two examples, which tell the reader about the Welsh mountain, Snowdon.

Text 1

Snowdon (Y Widdfa in Welsh). The highest mountain peak in England and Wales (1085m/3560ft), in the Northwest corner of Wales, in Gwynedd. Its top can be reached in one hour from Llanberis on the country's only narrow-gauge rack and pinion railway, opened in 1896 and still using steam engines. The mountain's Welsh name, meaning 'great tomb', derives from the legend that a giant killed by King Arthur is buried at its summit.

Text 2

Mountain Railway, Snowdon
Majestic Snowdon dominates the glorious, ancient landscape of North Wales. At 3,560ft (1085m) it is a true mountain and a place of legend – said to be the burial place of the giant ogre Rhita, vanquished by King Arthur. Some believe that Arthur's knights still sleep beneath. Since 1896, the Snowdon Mountain Railway has been making it easy to claim this mountain peak as one of your lifetime achievements. In a tremendously ambitious feat of engineering, and uniquely in Britain, a rack and pinion railway was built which rises to within 66ft of the summit of the highest mountain in England and Wales.

What do these two informative pieces of writing have in common?

You might have noted that they both:
- use **clear** and **straightforward** language
- base the ideas on facts and legends
- cover the same points
- get straight to the point
- **structure** the ideas **logically**.

Although they have much in common in terms of their content, they do differ in the way they present their information. What differences do you note?

Text 1 is much plainer in style and simply presents the information in a factual way. Text 2, however, uses a much more colourful description in order to put the information across to the reader. For example, instead of the plain *'The highest mountain peak in England and Wales'* we have *'Majestic Snowdon dominates the glorious, ancient landscape of North Wales'*. The *'narrow-gauge rack and pinion railway, opened in 1896 and still using steam engines'* becomes *'...a tremendously ambitious feat of engineering'*, which is described as unique in Britain.

Both of these pieces set out to give the reader information about Snowdon but why do they present it in such different ways? To find the answer to that question we need to think again about those key elements, **audience** and **purpose**. The difference between the two becomes clear when you know that text 1 is the sort of text that would be in an encyclopedia, which sets out to present the **plain facts** as **clearly** as possible. Text 2 is the sort of text that would be in an information leaflet. Although these two share the common purpose of informing their readers about Snowdon, the leaflet would also have the added purpose of attracting potential visitors to the railway. The language that is used to present the information, therefore, is designed to emphasise the dramatic, romantic and unique nature of the place.

Information can be presented to the reader in many forms including advertisements, articles, guide books, leaflets, reports, reference books and web pages.

Read the leaflet on page 82 carefully. It is a pamphlet about the Churchill Museum and Cabinet War Rooms in London. It is an informative leaflet, which tells the reader the following information:
- The leaflet title clearly indicates what the museum consists of and the footer suggests to the reader that they will 'Walk in Churchill's footsteps' by visiting the museum.
- The text informs the reader about the rooms, when they were in operation, what took place there, etc.
- The second part of the text gives details of the Churchill Museum and what the visitor will gain from a visit there.
- Information about booking the venue for corporate events is given.
- Information about supporting the museum is given.

> Note that although both these pieces of informative writing contain mostly facts, some types of informative writing contain not just facts but opinions too.

PROGRESS CHECK

1. What other features do you notice about the leaflet?

1.
   - Photographs give an impression of what the Cabinet War Rooms look like.
   - Information is given about admission prices, etc.
   - Opening times, telephone number, etc. are given and the map gives the location.
   - It is in the form of a standard leaflet: A4 folded into three.

Admission

Tickets

Adults £12.95
Children (under 16 years) FREE
Senior citizens, students £10.40
Disabled £7.75 (carers go FREE)
Special admission rates apply for groups of 10 or more
Please telephone 020 7766 0141

Access

Easy access and reduced admission for disabled visitors and carers.

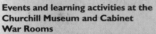

Events and learning activities at the Churchill Museum and Cabinet War Rooms

The Churchill Museum and Cabinet War Rooms is an outstanding place to learn about the civilian experience in the Second World War. Workshops, study sessions and lectures tailored to schools, colleges and adult groups are available in the Clore Learning Centre. To enjoy these exciting activities, booking is essential.

Booking line 020 7766 0130/0132 or email cwr-edu@iwm.org.uk

The Churchill Museum and Cabinet War Rooms also hosts an interesting and varied calendar of activities, events and displays designed for all ages and open to all visitors. Visit our website at **www.iwm.org.uk/cabinet** for details.

Specifically designed for our family visitors, a dedicated family sound guide and interactive trails are available onsite.

How to find us

Find us at

Churchill Museum and Cabinet War Rooms
Clive Steps, King Charles Street, London SW1A 2AQ

Telephone 020 7930 6961

Open daily 9.30am - 6.00pm
Last admission 5.00pm

www.iwm.org.uk/cabinet

Other Imperial War Museum branches

Imperial War Museum London 020 7416 5320
⊖ Lambeth North, Waterloo and Elephant & Castle

HMS Belfast 020 7940 6300
⊖ London Bridge or Tower Hill

Imperial War Museum Duxford 01223 835 000
Junction 10 on M11, south of Cambridge

Imperial War Museum North 0161 836 4000

CHURCHILL MUSEUM and CABINET WAR ROOMS

Walk in Churchill's footsteps

Cabinet War Rooms

The Cabinet War Rooms operated round the clock from the beginning of the war in 1939 to its end in August 1945.

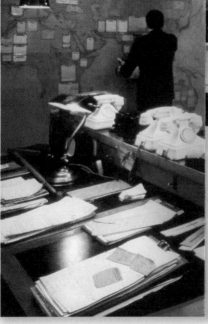

Historic decisions were taken in the Cabinet Room, where Churchill's chair still looks out over the scene of so many crucial meetings. It is where the Prime Minister, his War Cabinet and members of his inner circle survived the Blitz; where they ate and slept; and where his Map Room staff plotted the war.

In 1940, shortly after assuming the office of Prime Minister, Winston Churchill stood in the Cabinet Room and declared, 'This is the room from which I will direct the war'. It was here at the Cabinet War Rooms that Churchill experienced his 'finest hour'.

Step back in time and walk in Churchill's footsteps along the same dimly lit corridors surrounded by the original features of these momentous times.

Churchill Museum

The first major museum in the world dedicated to the life and achievements of Sir Winston Churchill gives you the opportunity to explore the man behind the legend. Discover new and intriguing facts about him and learn how Churchill came to merit the heroic status that he holds to this day.

Writing informatively

	E Lang	E Lit
AQA	✓	✗

Clear planning is essential when writing informatively. If you are answering a question that requires you to write informatively in an exam, it is very important that you plan your ideas carefully before starting to write.

Here's one way of approaching this:

Identify your audience.	Read the question carefully. The exact wording of the question is very important in helping you establish the nature of your audience.
List the key points you want to tell your reader.	Careful identification of the essential information is important.
Put your key points in the order you are going to deal with them.	Structure is always important. Your information should be presented logically and developed in an ordered way.
Decide on the level of detail.	Again this will be closely linked to your purpose.
Plan how you are going to present your information to make it relevant to your audience.	Planning is very important to make sure you don't leave anything out.
Make sure your information can be easily understood.	Use clear language and present your ideas in a straightforward way.

KEY POINT

If you are asked to write to inform, make sure you include all the information needed by your reader.

Sample GCSE question

Write a letter to your headteacher in which you argue that the ICT facilities in the school should be upgraded and increased.

2 Orchard Lane
Topton
Great Standing

1st April 2010

Dear Mrs Maloney,

I am writing to you to express my concern about the poor state of the ICT facilities. It has become clear that we have reached a point where, I believe, students are being educationally disadvantaged by the current facilities provided in school and I ask that you look at the possibility of improving them as a matter of urgency. ← **Purpose of letter is clearly stated, the problem highlighted and a desired outcome mentioned.**

Together with a group of concerned students, I have looked carefully at the situation and several issues have emerged. ← **The first point is explained in some detail.**

Firstly, the machines that we have are very outdated now. They are extremely slow when downloading information and the number of machines out of action is increasing by the week. ← **Discourse markers used to link paragraphs.**

Secondly, the networked systems that we use have become increasingly unreliable and many students have taken to doing work at home on their own equipment because it is not possible for them to do it in school as very often the facilities are not available. ← **The second point is explained and an important issue raised.**

Thirdly, because of the lack of terminals available in the learning centre, access to the research facilities provided by the Internet is very restricted. Again, students are being forced to use their own equipment. Unfortunately, though, not all students are lucky enough to have their own machines at home. ← **A third point is developed.**

I have conducted a survey of all students in Years 10 and 11 and 98% of them feel disadvantaged by the lack of facilities. I would be happy to give you copies of the survey if you feel it would help you argue the case for more funding for this with the governors. ← **The writer provides evidence to support the argument.**

I know that funding is a problem and that you have little available at the moment but I have discussed this with many students and the general feeling is that they would be more than willing to help with fund-raising. Many suggestions have been made, including a sponsored swim, fun-run and sponsored spell. Students also feel that their parents would be willing to help and I am sure that the Parents' Association would help too. ← **Shows an appreciation of the financial constraints on the Head and makes some constructive suggestions that will help the situation.**

It would be useful to discuss these ideas and I would be happy to arrange for a small group of interested students to meet with you. ← **Ends with a constructive suggestion.**

I look forward to hearing your views on this topic.

Yours sincerely,

Tracy Seaton (Form TS11).

Practice questions

① Your local bus company is intending to axe the bus service that serves the area in which you live. You are actively involved in a campaign to save the service.

Write a letter to your local MP putting forward your arguments for why the bus service should be saved and persuading him / her to support your campaign.

(External exam question: English Language, Unit 1)

② Write an article for your local newspaper with the title 'The Internet and education: exciting tool or time-wasting hindrance?'

(External exam question: English Language, Unit 1)

③ You have been asked to help in the organising of a day visit to a place or event in your area. Your job is to prepare an information leaflet for students going on the visit. Write the text of the leaflet, which will inform students of all the details they need to know concerning the visit.

(External exam question: English Language, Unit 1)

6 Imaginative and creative writing

The following topics are covered in this chapter:

- **Types of imaginative and creative writing**
- **Aspects of story writing**
- **Descriptive writing**

6.1 Types of imaginative and creative writing

LEARNING SUMMARY

After studying this section, you should be able to understand:

- the different types of imaginative and creative writing
- the features of stories
- narrative viewpoint

Different types of imaginative and creative writing

AQA	E Lang	E Lit
	✓	✓

Creative writing can take many forms. Here are some examples:

- Narratives that tell a story.
- Narratives in the form of a letter / letters.
- 'Catch-up' narratives on the Internet telling you what has happened on a TV series.
- Dialogues developed through e-mail.
- Different narrative / descriptive tasks based on visual stimulus material that you are given.
- Narratives that are based on a personal experience of some kind.

Some types of creative writing are written specifically for the spoken voice. For example:

- Drama script writing for a stage play
- Scripts for film or television
- Scripts for a radio play

KEY POINT

Imaginative and creative writing can take many forms.

Features of stories

AQA | E Lang ✓ | E Lit ✓

Often, imaginative writing takes the form of some kind of 'story' – this is sometimes called a **narrative**. Although writing a story might sound like quite a simple task, writing an effective and interesting story is not quite so straightforward.

Stories can take various forms. For example, novels are very long stories, often with a number and variety of characters and complex storylines with a lot of things happening.

Short stories are obviously shorter and usually contain fewer characters and events.

The kind of imaginative writing that you will be asked to produce for your course will be relatively short, but no matter what the length, this kind of writing is made up of various features or elements.

> ### PROGRESS CHECK
>
> ① Think carefully about a story you have read and consider all the features that helped to make the story effective or memorable in some way for you. Make a list of them.
>
> 1. Here are some ideas that you might have thought about:
>   • The storyline and the way it is structured.
>   • The characters.
>   • The setting and atmosphere created.
>   • The language the writer uses and the effects created.
>   • The themes or ideas it contains.

> ### KEY POINT
>
> The plot, characters and setting are aspects you need to think about carefully when planning your imaginative writing.

Narrative viewpoint

AQA | E Lang ✓ | E Lit ✓

In imaginative writing, the idea of **viewpoint** refers to whose viewpoint we see the events of the story from or simply who is telling the story – the 'voice' of the story (**narrative voice**).

The most common kinds of narration are **first person** and **third person** narration. You will be familiar with both of these kinds of narrative viewpoint from the novels and stories you have read in the past.

First person narration

In a first person narrative, the narrator is often a character in the story and the story is told directly from this character's point of view – using 'I' to address the reader directly. This kind of narration is found in a wide range of novels and short stories.

For example, Harper Lee uses first person narrative in *To Kill a Mockingbird*, which is told from the point of view and in the voice of the central character, Scout.

> 'Come on round here, son, I got something that'll settle your stomach.'
>
> As Mr Dolphus Raymond was an evil man I accepted his invitation reluctantly, but I followed Dill. Somehow, I didn't think Atticus would like it if we became friendly with Mr Raymond, and I knew Aunt Alexandra wouldn't.
>
> 'Here, he said, offering Dill his paper sack with straws in it. 'Take a good sip, it'll quieten you.' Dill sucked on the straws, smiled, and pulled at length. 'Hee hee,' said Mr Raymond, evidently taking delight in corrupting a child.
>
> 'Dill, you watch out, now,' I warned. Dill released the straws and grinned. 'Scout, it's nothing but Coca-Cola.'
>
> From *To Kill a Mockingbird* by Harper Lee

Third person narration

In a third person narrative, the narrator is outside the story and relates the events, describes the characters, etc. like an outsider looking on. This kind of narrator is sometimes called an **omniscient** narrator meaning that they are 'all seeing and all knowing'.

For example, William Golding uses third person narrative in *Lord of the Flies*.

> Jack was on top of the sow, stabbing downward with his knife. Roger found a lodgement for his point and began to push till he was leaning with his whole weight. The spear moved forward inch by inch and the terrified squealing became a high-pitched scream. Then Jack found the throat and the hot blood spouted over his hands. The sow collapsed under them and they were heavy and fulfilled upon her. The butterflies still danced, preoccupied in the centre of the clearing.
>
> At last the immediacy of the kill subsided. The boys drew back, and Jack stood up, holding out his hands.
>
> "Look."
>
> He giggled and flinked them while the boys laughed at his reeking palms.
>
> From *Lord of the Flies* by William Golding

Differences between first and third person narration

The different kinds of narration create different effects. Here are some of the key differences between the two.

In a first person narrative:
- The writer takes on the role of a character in the narrative.
- The story is told from the 'inside'.
- The narrator seems to speak to the reader directly.
- The narrator can reveal his or her inner thoughts and feelings to the reader.
- This direct voice helps to create a sense that the story is 'real'.
- The viewpoint is limited in that we see everything through the eyes of the narrator and so we do not know what is going on in the minds of other characters.
- The narrator cannot switch so easily from one part of the action to another.

In a third person narrative:
- The narrator is 'god-like' and can see and hear everything that is going on.
- The narrator can tell us things that happen in different places and at different times and can switch to and fro between settings, characters or points in time.
- We are often told what different characters are thinking.
- We are told how characters are feeling.
- The narrator is detached from the action and can make comments on characters or events and influence the reader's reactions to them.

6.2 Aspects of story writing

LEARNING SUMMARY	**After studying this section, you should be able to understand:** - plot and setting - how stories can be opened - how characters can be developed

Plot and setting

AQA	E Lang	E Lit
	✓	✓

In very basic terms, stories usually have a beginning, a middle and an end, and the **plot** consists of the series of events that occur and the experiences the characters go through as the story moves from its beginning, through its middle to its conclusion. The plot, therefore, is concerned with the specific details of the **events that occur** in the story.

> **KEY POINT**
>
> In order to write a successful story you need to:
> - plan your storyline carefully
> - capture and maintain your reader's interest

Careful planning is essential if you are to write an effective story.

The **setting** of a story is closely related to the plot. Obviously, the setting depends on what kind of story it is. Many stories are set against the background of everyday life that we are all familiar with, but even these familiar '**realistic**' backgrounds can be many and varied. For example, a story could be set against a background of home or work, in a town or city or in the countryside, or any combination of the whole range of settings that form the background to our lives.

Other settings may depend more on the writer's imagination. Science fiction stories, for example, are often set against backgrounds that are totally the product of the writer's imagination. Alternatively, the story may be set in a different time period and historical background.

> **KEY POINT**
>
> Whatever the setting of the story, it must remain convincing to the reader.

Openings

	E Lang	E Lit
AQA	✓	✓

The opening of a story or piece of imaginative writing is extremely important because this is where the writer must capture the attention and interest of the reader.

> **KEY POINT**
>
> You must open your story in such a way as to make your reader want to continue reading.

Read the following openings carefully and think about the effects they create in your mind. Do they capture your attention and make you want to read on? Why?

Text 1

Lemona. Lemona. Beautiful woman. Exquisite. She'll be hanged tomorrow. You know that, don't you? And you insist on seeing her? Well, I have no objection personally. But I don't know if she'll agree to see you. That's the problem. That woman is an enigma. In all my thirty years in service, I haven't met a prisoner like her. She doesn't talk to anyone, she's not had a personal visitor that I can remember. It's like she's not of this world. Even at her age, she remains very attractive. A beauty queen. I wish she could be saved. She shouldn't die. But she'll be hanged tomorrow at dawn. The warrant has finally been signed and delivered to me. It's tragic. A real tragedy.

From *Lemona's Tale* by Ken Saro-Wiwa

Text 2

Marley was dead: to begin with. There is no doubt whatever about that. The register of his burial was signed by the clergyman, the clerk, the undertaker, and the chief mourner. Scrooge signed it: and Scrooge's name was good upon change, for anything he chose to put his hand to. Old Marley was as dead as a door-nail.

Mind! I don't mean to say that I know, of my own knowledge, what there is particularly dead about a door-nail. I might have been inclined, myself, to regard a coffin-nail as the deadest piece of ironmongery in the trade. But the wisdom of our ancestors is in the simile; and my unhallowed hands shall not disturb it, or the Country's done for. You will therefore permit me to repeat, emphatically, that Marley was as dead as a door-nail.

From *A Christmas Carol* by Charles Dickens

Here are some points you might have noted:

Text 1

- The repetition of 'Lemona. Lemona' immediately establishes the name of the character and also contains a hint of regret.
- The use of the adjectives 'beautiful' and 'exquisite' creates the sense of there being something special about her, which keeps the reader interested.
- The third sentence comes unexpectedly and creates a kind of shock effect.
- Very short sentences, e.g. 'It's tragic.' and sentence fragments, e.g. 'Beautiful woman.', 'A beauty queen.' are used throughout this opening, which creates a dramatic effect.
- The use of the first person narration creates a sense of the narrator speaking directly to the reader.
- A sense of Lemona's uniqueness is established through words such as 'enigma' and makes the reader want to read on.
- The narrator's regret that she will be hanged is evident and the tragedy of the situation is emphasised.

Text 2

- The opening sentence – 'Marley was dead' immediately captures the reader's attention.
- The addition of 'to begin with' holds the reader's attention as they wonder what this can possibly mean.
- The use of the first person narration creates a sense of the narrator speaking directly to the reader.
- Scrooge is introduced (he is the central character).
- There is an element of humour introduced, e.g. the play on the idea of 'door-nail' / coffin nail, which maintains the reader's attention.

KEY POINT

A variety of techniques can be used to capture the interest of the reader.

PROGRESS CHECK

1. From the examples you have examined, make a list of the ways in which you can make your opening interesting and capture the attention of your reader.

1. - Vivid description.
   - Unusual names or terminology.
   - Intriguing situations.
   - Surprising first sentences.
   - Very short, simple first sentences.
   - The introduction of the central character.
   - Creation of an effective atmosphere.
   - The use of humour.
   - The creation of a sense that something is about to happen.

Developing characters

AQA — E Lang ✓ E Lit ✓

Characters are a very important element in any story. In fact, a story wouldn't be a story without characters of some description and you will need to think carefully about them as the action of your plot will hinge on them. If your story is to be effective, it is essential that your characters are convincing.

Read the following two extracts carefully.

At that moment a young man came into the bunkhouse; a thin young man with a brown face, with brown eyes and a head of tightly curled hair. He wore a work glove on his left hand, and, like the boss, he wore high-heeled boots. "Seen my old man?" he asked.

The swamper said: "He was here jus' a minute ago, Curley. Went over to the cook-house, I think."

"I'll try to catch him," said Curley. His eyes passed over the new men and he stopped. He glanced coldly at George and then at Lennie. His arms gradually bent at the elbows and his hands closed into fists. He stiffened and went into a slight crouch. His glance was at once calculating and pugnacious. Lennie squirmed under the look and shifted his feet nervously. Curley stepped gingerly close to him. "You the new guys the old man was waitin' for?"

"We just come in," said George.

"Let the big guy talk."

Lennie twisted with embarrassment.

George said: "S'pose he don't want to talk?"

Curley lashed his body around. "By Christ, he's gotta talk when he's spoke to. What the hell are you gettin' into it for?"

"We travel together," said George coldly.

"Oh, so it's that way."

From *Of Mice And Men* by John Steinbeck

He was a rich man: banker, merchant, manufacturer, and what not. A big, loud man, with a store and a metallic laugh. A man made out of a coarse material, which seemed to have been stretched to make so much of him. A man with a great puffed head and forehead, swelled veins in his temples, and such a strained skin to his face that it seemed to hold his eyes open and lift his eyebrows up. A man with a pervading appearance on him of being inflated like a balloon, and ready to start. A man who could never sufficiently vaunt himself a self-made man. A man who was always proclaiming, through that brassy speaking-trumpet of a voice of his, his old ignorance and his old poverty. A man who was the Bully of humility.

A year or two younger than his eminently practical friend, Mr Bounderby looked older; his seven or eight and forty might have had the seven or eight added to it again, without surprising anybody. He had not much hair. One might have fancied he had talked it off; and that what was left, all standing up in disorder, was in that condition from being constantly blown about by his windy boastfulness.

From *Hard Times* by Charles Dickens

How do we learn about the characters in these extracts?

You might have noticed that Steinbeck uses several techniques to create an impression of Curley in *Of Mice and Men*:

- He describes his physical appearance in detail – his build, his skin, eyes and hair.
- He describes some of the things he wears.
- We are told how he looks at other characters – 'glanced coldly', 'calculating and pugnacious'. The adverbs and adjectives used suggest that Curley is an aloof person.

Choice of words is very important because it gives the reader clues about the character.

- His arms bending and hands closing into fists further suggest his aggressive nature.
- The way he speaks (he does not greet George and Lennie) and what he says add to this impression.

Now look at how Dickens gives the reader an impression of Mr Bounderby in *Hard Times*:

- He gives us details of Bounderby's occupation and status.
- He describes his physical appearance, using plenty of adjectives (e.g. 'puffed', swelled', 'strained') and a simile ('… like a balloon').
- His nature and attitudes are indicated through descriptions of his voice and opinions.
- Dickens uses imagery and humour to make his description more entertaining and effective, e.g. 'One might have fancied he had talked it off.'

> **KEY POINT**
>
> You can use a variety of techniques to create an impression of your characters.

> **PROGRESS CHECK**
>
> 1 Summarise the ways in which you can show your reader what your characters are like.

1. • What they look like.
   • What they say.
   • How they say it.
   • How they behave.
   • How they feel.

6.3 Descriptive writing

LEARNING SUMMARY

After studying this section, you should be able to understand:
- the purpose of descriptive writing
- how to make your descriptions more vivid and effective

The purpose of descriptive writing

AQA | E Lang ✓ | E Lit ✓

Obviously, effective description is an essential ingredient in writing an effective story. It might be that you are describing characters, a setting, or creating a particular atmosphere. Sometimes, though, as part of your course, you might be set a task that focuses particularly on describing a certain scene, situation or character.

When you are writing descriptively your main aim is to create a **picture** with words so that your reader can imagine **vividly** the scene, person, situation, etc. that you are describing. This means that the words you choose when you write a description are very important and you need to think about them and select them very carefully. However, this does not mean that you should try to cram as many impressive sounding words into your writing as possible. It is just as easy to overdo the description as it is to underdo it.

For example, look at this student's description of a sunset:

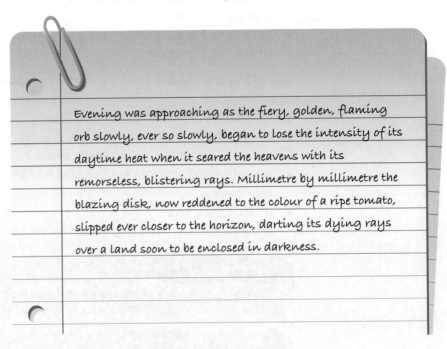

Evening was approaching as the fiery, golden, flaming orb slowly, ever so slowly, began to lose the intensity of its daytime heat when it seared the heavens with its remorseless, blistering rays. Millimetre by millimetre the blazing disk, now reddened to the colour of a ripe tomato, slipped ever closer to the horizon, darting its dying rays over a land soon to be enclosed in darkness.

How effectively do you think the student has described the scene?

Another student took a more straightforward approach:

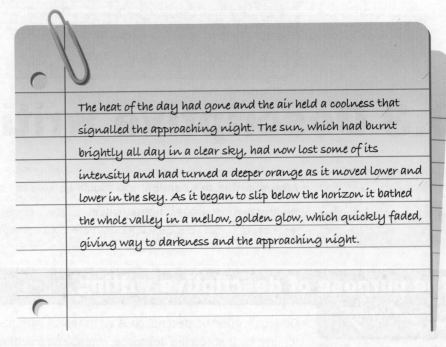

The heat of the day had gone and the air held a coolness that signalled the approaching night. The sun, which had burnt brightly all day in a clear sky, had now lost some of its intensity and had turned a deeper orange as it moved lower and lower in the sky. As it began to slip below the horizon it bathed the whole valley in a mellow, golden glow, which quickly faded, giving way to darkness and the approaching night.

The second student response is more effective than the first student response.

The first description seems a little 'over the top' and uses some overly descriptive words and phrases. The second one is more restrained and because of that is the more effective of the two.

> **KEY POINT**
>
> Effective description involves carefully selecting the right words but make sure you don't over-describe as this can start to be over-elaborate and wordy.

How to make descriptions vivid and effective

AQA	E Lang	E Lit
	✓	✓

In making your writing vivid, you can draw on a number of sources. You could draw ideas from:

- People you have met.
- Situations you have encountered or experiences you have had.
- Sensations you have experienced through your senses (sight, touch, taste, smell and hearing).

You can also use various techniques to make your writing more vivid and effective. You can use:

- **Imagery**, such as **similes** and **metaphors**, to help your readers recreate the scene or experience in their imaginations.
- **Alliteration**, **onomatopoeia** and **assonance** to give particular sound 'effects' to your writing.
- Various **sentence structures** and **rhythm patterns** to build up the desired effect and create a sense of a particular mood or feeling.

Here is an example of a writer creating a description. In this extract Dickens describes the town of Coketown. How does Dickens make his description effective here?

It was a town of red brick, or of brick that would have been red if the smoke and ashes had allowed it; but, as matters stood it was a town of unnatural red and black like the painted face of a savage. It was a town of machinery and tall chimneys, out of which interminable serpents of smoke trailed themselves for ever and ever, and never got uncoiled. It had a black canal in it, and a river that ran purple with ill-smelling dye, and vast piles of buildings full of windows where there was a rattling and a trembling all day long, and where the piston of the steam-engine worked monotonously up and down, like the head of an elephant in a state of melancholy madness. It contained several large streets all very like one another, and many small streets still more like one another, inhabited by people equally like one another, who all went in and out at the same hours, with the same sound upon the pavements, to do the same work, and to whom every day was the same as yesterday and tomorrow, and every year the counterpart of the last and the next.

From *Hard Times* by Charles Dickens

Here are some points you may have noted:

- Dickens uses vocabulary which creates a sense of colour, especially of 'red' and 'black', that he uses to emphasise the 'unnatural' feel of the place.
- He uses metaphors, such as '...tall chimneys, out of which interminable serpents of smoke trailed themselves'.
- He uses similes, such as the one he uses to describe the working of the steam engine which '...worked monotonously up and down, like the head of an elephant in a state of melancholy madness'. Again, this is an unnatural image that emphasises the mechanical, monotonous, industrial nature of the place.
- He uses repetition to give a sense of the streets that all look '...very like one another and many small streets still more like one another, inhabited by people equally like one another'.
- He also uses language that appeals to the senses – '...ill-smelling dye', '...there was a rattling and a trembling all day long'.

> **KEY POINT**
>
> Writers use a range of techniques to make their descriptions more effective. You can use them too in your own writing.

Sample GCSE question

This is part of a longer response to the set task.

Write a description of 'Market Day' in a small town.

The market starts off slowly, the occasional early van arriving bringing traders to gain the favoured spot, set up stall, and put their wares on display. The slow trickle increases in speed and soon the place that used to be a formal, quiet car park is now a bustling marketplace, vibrant colours and noise everywhere.

Good opening paragraph sets the scene and creates a sense of atmosphere as the market begins to gather pace.

Looking from afar you can see small figures, wandering in and out of the stalls, occasionally stopping to peer at the items on display. The whole place is full of colour and people. Smells waft all around the market, the warm smell of fresh doughnuts, cakes, and muffins. The place is very noisy, with people calling and laughing, machines humming and pumping, all with a purpose.

Distant perspective and then homes in on details.

Effective use of description through the senses of sound and smell.

Getting closer to the market, entering the throng of people milling about, the first thing that catches your eye is the fruit and vegetable stall. It's crammed with colourful fruits and lush vegetables. The stall owner is a short Asian woman, cheerfully weighing her fruit and veg out, smiling and chatting to her customers.

More details and establishes a sense of the individual stall holders.

Moving away to the left of the fruit and veg stall, you see the bright reds and pinks of the meat on the butcher's stall. The owner of this stall is a tall, broad-shouldered Welshman, wielding a large meat cleaver. The slabs of meat are succulent, and look full of flavour, while slim white veins of fat ring some of the meat.

More sense of detail.

Coming around the corner you are struck by the amazing variety of colours of the carpet stall. Long, short, round, square, rectangular - all kinds of carpets are on sale. The two African women are scurrying around attending to the desires of multiple people at once. My eye is always caught by the two carpets that are emblazoned with life-like designs. One has a striking wolf, its amber eyes staring out at you, the fur almost seeming real. The second has been woven as a blue / green sea, dolphins leaping out of the waves, showers of water streaming off their backs. Yet, when you touch the carpets, although they look so real, they are soft - velvet-like even - and so very deep.

Effective use of colour and images to create a vivid sense of the carpet stall.

I love following my senses and my nose is one great sense here. Now it leads me to the doughnut store, run by a very small, round man, always with a huge smile on his face as he bags up his doughnuts, cakes and muffins. A few minutes later I retreat from his store, clutching a small bag full of delights for the taste buds.

It takes me about five minutes to walk around the perimeter of the market, the `Maes' as it's known here in Wales. When I get within view of the carpet stall, I perch up on the wall and take a muffin out of my small bag - it's still warm. I hesitate and then take a bite, closing my eyes as the chocolate taste floods through me. I grin. The market on a sunny day like today can get no better.

An effective concluding paragraph using the idea of the muffin to link back to the previous paragraph. Effective use of the sense of taste and the gorgeous flavour of the muffin.

Practice questions

1 Write the script for an interview to be placed on You Tube, in which you are asked questions about how you created the plot and characters of your story.

(You should write 800–1000 words.)

(Controlled Assessment task: English Language, Unit 3, Part B)

2 Write a letter from one of the main characters in a story you have read, in which they reveal their thoughts and feelings at the end of the story.

(You should write 500–800 words.)

(Controlled Assessment task: English Language, Unit 3, Part A)

3 Write a review of a book that you have read or studied.

You should decide what type of publication your review would be in (for example a popular magazine or a magazine aimed at teenagers) and make sure you write in a suitable style.

(You should write 800–1000 words.)

(Controlled Assessment task: English Language, Unit 3, Part A)

7 Studying Shakespeare

The following topics are covered in this chapter:

- Types of Shakespearean play
- Plot and structure
- Opening scenes
- Presenting characters
- Shakespeare's language
- Endings

7.1 Types of Shakespearean play

LEARNING SUMMARY	After studying this section, you should be able to understand: • what the Elizabethan theatre was like • what types of plays Shakespeare wrote

The Elizabethan theatre

AQA	E Lang	E Lit
	✓	✓

Shakespeare's plays, just like any other kind of play, were not written to be read; they were written to be seen on the stage. If you get the chance to see the plays you are studying **performed**, this will help you to appreciate them much more than simply reading them. If you cannot see them live on the stage, then at least try to see a film version or other kind of recording of them. This will really bring the action to life and make them mean much more to you.

> **KEY POINT**
>
> It is really important to see the plays you are studying performed. It will help enormously with your understanding of them.

However, it is worth bearing in mind that in Shakespeare's time the theatres were very different from the ones we have today, and the way the plays were performed was different too.

Here are some of the features of theatres in Shakespeare's time:
- There was no lighting in the theatres and so the plays were performed in daylight. This meant that there were no lighting effects, although sometimes music and songs were used to create a particular atmosphere.
- The actors used very few props and costumes.
- There were no female actors and so the female roles were played by boys.
- The theatre was a much rowdier place than it is now. Many members of the audience watched the play standing in a crowd in front of the stage and they often drank beer and ate while watching the play.

If you want to get a real flavour of the Elizabethan theatre, visit the Globe Theatre in London, which is a working reconstruction of the Globe Theatre of Shakespeare's time.

This is what Shakespeare's Globe Theatre would have looked like:

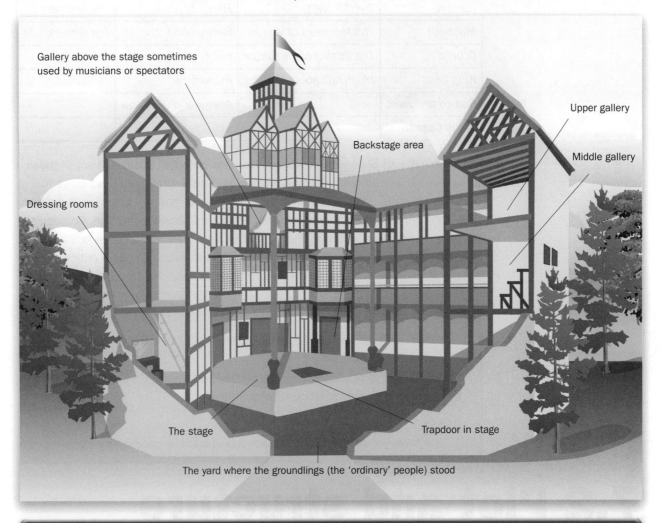

Gallery above the stage sometimes used by musicians or spectators

Upper gallery

Backstage area

Middle gallery

Dressing rooms

The stage

Trapdoor in stage

The yard where the groundlings (the 'ordinary' people) stood

Types of play

AQA	E Lang	E Lit
	✓	✓

Shakespeare wrote nearly 40 plays during his life. These plays can be divided into four main types:

- **Tragedies** – these plays focus on a tragic hero (or couple, as in *Romeo and Juliet*) whose downfall is brought about through weakness or misfortune of some kind. These kinds of play end with the death of the central character(s) but also involve the deaths of a number of other characters. The plays based on characters from Roman History, such as *Julius Caesar*, are also included in this category.

- **Comedies** – these plays involve humour and often confusion, disguise, mistaken identity, etc. Unlike our modern idea of comedy, some of Shakespeare's comedies can be quite 'dark' (as in *Much Ado About Nothing*) but the main thing is that they end happily and there are no deaths at the end.

- **Histories** – these plays are based on historical events and the characters are based on the lives of English kings. These plays contain tragic elements too and are similar in many respects to the Tragedies.

- **Romances** – Shakespeare wrote these plays towards the end of his life (they are sometimes called the 'Last Plays') and they involve magical worlds and happenings, mysterious events and moral lessons contained within a 'happy ending'.

Here are some examples of the various kinds of plays that Shakespeare wrote:

Tragedies	Comedies	Histories	Romances
Hamlet	Twelfth Night	Henry IV (Pt 1)	The Tempest
Macbeth	The Merchant of Venice	Henry IV (Pt 2)	The Winter's Tale
Othello	The Taming of the Shrew	Henry V	
King Lear	Much Ado About Nothing	Richard III	
Romeo and Juliet		Antony and Cleopatra	
Julius Caesar			

A small number of Shakespeare's plays, however, do not fit easily into any of these categories. These are plays that fall somewhere between tragedy and comedy. They contain dark, unsettling elements, but they end 'happily' in so far as no one dies. They are known as 'Problem Plays', 'Problem Comedies' or 'Dark Comedies'. *Measure for Measure*, *All's Well That Ends Well*, and *Troilus and Cressida* are the three plays generally accepted as being of this kind, although some critics also include other plays such as *The Merchant of Venice* and *The Winter's Tale*.

PROGRESS CHECK

1. What is the key difference between the ending of a tragedy and the ending of a comedy?
2. What kind of plays are *Macbeth* and *Julius Caesar*?
3. What kind of play is *Much Ado About Nothing*?

1. A tragedy ends with death of main character (and others); a comedy has no deaths at the end.
2. Tragedies.
3. Comedy.

7.2 Plot and structure

LEARNING SUMMARY	After studying this section, you should be able to understand:
	• what is meant by plot and structure

What are plot and structure?

AQA — E Lang ✓ E Lit ✓

All plays, including those of Shakespeare, have a plot and some kind of structure. Put simply, the **plot** of a play is the 'story' that the play tells and the **structure** is the way that the story is organised and put together.

Plot and structure are important because they make up the whole 'storyline' of the play and so, before you can begin to study the other aspects of the play, you really need to be familiar with these. You cannot begin to study a play properly until you know what happens in it.

There are a number of things you can do:
- **Read** the play thoroughly so that you get a basic idea of who the characters are and what is happening.

- **See** the play in performance – on the stage if possible but, if not, then try to watch it on DVD (your school, college, local library or a DVD store might be able to help you get a copy).
- **Imagine** how the action might take place as you read the play.
- **Act out** some of the scenes to see how they could be performed.
- **Make notes** on each scene to build up a picture of how the plot develops.

As you are studying the plot of your play, you will begin to notice things about how the plot is put together and how the action develops – these are things to do with structure.

KEY POINT

An understanding of this general structure can help you to follow the storyline of the play.

Most plays follow a basic structure similar to this:

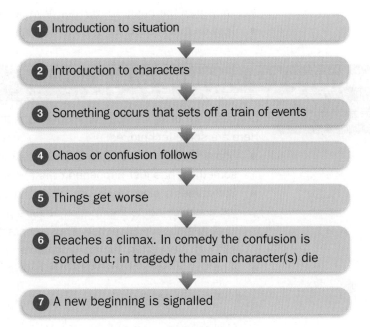

1 Introduction to situation

2 Introduction to characters

3 Something occurs that sets off a train of events

4 Chaos or confusion follows

5 Things get worse

6 Reaches a climax. In comedy the confusion is sorted out; in tragedy the main character(s) die

7 A new beginning is signalled

Here is an example showing a plan of the basic structure of *Romeo and Juliet*:
1 Introduction to the situation – the feud between the Montagues and Capulets.
2 Introduction to the characters – first Romeo, and later Juliet.
3 Incident that provides starting point to play – Romeo meets Juliet.
4 Chaos and confusion – Romeo and Juliet have to keep their love and marriage a secret from everyone. Romeo kills Tybalt.
5 Things get worse – Juliet's parents try to force her to marry Paris. The Friar's plan with the potion. His message to Romeo fails to get through.
6 The climax of the play – Romeo kills Paris, then himself, and Juliet kills herself.
7 The feuding Montagues and Capulets are brought together and the play ends in a spirit of harmony.

PROGRESS CHECK

1 What does the term 'plot' refer to?
2 What is the main thing you can do to help you visualise the action of a play?
3 What is the point in the play called where all the action comes to a head?

1. The storyline. 2. See a performance of it. 3. The climax.

7.3 Opening scenes

LEARNING SUMMARY

After studying this section, you should be able to understand:
- why the opening of the play is so important
- the techniques that Shakespeare uses to open his plays

Why the opening of a play is important

	E Lang	E Lit
AQA	✓	✓

Opening any play at the right point of the action and in the right way is very important because it is vital to capture the audience's attention and interest right from the start. It is important for other reasons as well:
- Most of Shakespeare's openings **set the scene** in some way.
- They form the basis for **further developments** in the play.
- They do this in such a way as to **capture** the audience's **attention** and **interest**.

Techniques for opening plays

	E Lang	E Lit
AQA	✓	✓

Shakespeare uses various techniques to make the openings of his plays effective. Here are some techniques:
- Shakespeare's plays often open in the middle of some kind of action – something has just happened or is about to happen.
- Sometimes a play opens with minor characters talking. Their conversation gives the audience some information about a particular situation or character, or about what has already happened. These characters often refer to a major character although, very often, the main character does not appear until a bit later.
- A particular mood or atmosphere is always established at the beginning of the play.

> **KEY POINT**
>
> Shakespeare uses a variety of techniques to make the openings of his plays more effective. Think about the play(s) that you are studying and see if you can recognise any of these techniques used in the opening of the play(s).

Read the following opening scene from *Macbeth*. Think about the effect that this opening scene has and what you learn from it.

SCENE 1 – An Open place

Thunder and lightning. Enter three WITCHES.

FIRST WITCH	When shall we three meet again?
	In thunder, lightning, or in rain?
SECOND WITCH	When the hurlyburly's done,
	When the battle's lost and won.
THIRD WITCH	That will be ere the set of sun.
FIRST WITCH	Where the place?
SECOND WITCH	Upon the heath.
THIRD WITCH	There to meet with Macbeth.

FIRST WITCH	I come, Graymalkin!
SECOND WITCH	Paddock calls.
THIRD WITCH	Anon!
ALL	Fair is foul, and foul is fair:
	Hover through the fog and filthy air.

WITCHES *vanish.*

Here are some points you might have noted:

- The stage directions '*Thunder and lightning*' suggest a sense of menace and violence.
- Witches are often associated with evil and this helps to raise tension and the expectation that something is about to happen.
- We learn that a battle has taken place – this captures the audience's interest.
- The witches intend to meet Macbeth, which creates a sense of expectation as the audience waits to see what will happen.
- To an Elizabethan audience, the tension would have been further increased as they believed firmly in the evil powers of witchcraft.

Here is part of a student's response to the question, '**Examine the ways in which Shakespeare opens the play *Macbeth*.**'

> The scene opens with thunder and lightning, which on stage would open the play in a dramatic way with loud noises and flashes of light. This would immediately capture the audience's attention and they would be focusing on the stage as the witches appear. The thunder and lightning create a frightening and menacing atmosphere and this sets the tone for the frightening, menacing and evil events that are about to unfold on the stage. The mood and atmosphere are set in this way, but the effect of the scene is wider than simply the setting of mood and atmosphere. It also gives us information that is an important introduction to the events of the play. It seems that the play opens while a battle is raging and the three witches will meet again when it is all over. They seem to have fore-knowledge that this will be before the end of the day. The name of Macbeth is introduced and a connection is therefore established between themselves and Macbeth. Their closing lines:
> "Fair is foul, and foul is fair:
> Hover through the fog and filthy air."
> give us a major clue to what the witches' objectives are. Whatever is good, they find ugly, and whatever is bad and ugly, they find good. They seek, therefore, to turn goodness into evil and this directly links to the events concerning Macbeth that develop in the play.

Annotations:
- The student pays attention to the stage directions, visualises what the effect on the stage would be and evaluates the dramatic effect of these.
- Comments on the creation of mood and atmosphere and connects this to the events that are about to happen.
- Focuses on the information that the scene conveys about what is happening.
- Identifies the significance of the mention of Macbeth and how this links him to the witches.
- Shows an appreciation of the significance of the witches in terms of the thematic development of good/evil in the play and creates a springboard to link the opening scene to later developments in the play.

Now look at the following opening from *Romeo and Juliet*. This play begins with a prologue, which is spoken before the opening scene.

Prologues were sometimes used by dramatists to give the audience an idea of what to expect in the drama they were about to see. Most of Shakespeare's plays do not begin with a prologue, but *Romeo and Juliet* does. What do you learn from this prologue?

> *ACT 1*
>
> *PROLOGUE*
>
> *CHORUS*
>
> Two households, both alike in dignity,
> In fair Verona, where we lay our scene,
> From ancient grudge break to new mutiny,
> Where civil blood makes civil hands unclean.
> From forth the fatal loins of these two foes
> A pair of star-crossed lovers take their life;
> Whose misadventured piteous overthrows
> Doth with their death bury their parents' strife.
> The fearful passage of their death-marked love,
> And the continuance of their parents' rage,
> Which, but their children's end, nought could remove,
> Is now the two hours' traffic of our stage;
> The which if you with patient ears attend,
> What here shall miss, our toil shall strive to mend.

> When looking at the opening scene of the play you are studying, be aware of all its aspects – the giving of information, the introduction of characters, the atmosphere and mood created, and the thematic ideas that are established.

Here are some points you might have noted:

● The play is set in Verona.
● An ancient quarrel exists between two families.
● Two young people, one from each family, fall in love.
● Their love is ill-fated and ends in their deaths.
● The tragedy brings an end to the feud between the families.

Here is the opening scene of *Romeo and Juliet*, which follows the prologue. Read it through carefully.

> *SCENE 1 – Verona. A public place.*
>
> *Enter* SAMPSON *and* GREGORY, *of the house of Capulet, armed with swords and bucklers*
>
> | SAMPSON | Gregory, o' my word, we'll not carry coals. |
> | GREGORY | No, for then we should be colliers. |
> | SAMPSON | I mean, an we be in choler, we'll draw. |
> | GREGORY | Ay, while you live, draw your neck out o' the collar. |
> | SAMPSON | I strike quickly, being moved. |
> | GREGORY | But thou art not quickly moved to strike. |
> | SAMPSON | A dog of the house of Montague moves me. |
> | GREGORY | To move is to stir; and to be valiant is to stand. Therefore, if thou art moved, thou runn'st away. |

SAMPSON	A dog of that house shall move me to stand. I will take the wall of any man or maid of Montague's.
GREGORY	That shows thee a weak slave; for the weakest goes to the wall.
SAMPSON	True; and therefore women, being the weaker vessels, are ever thrust to the wall. Therefore I will push Montague's men from the wall, and thrust his maids to the wall.
GREGORY	The quarrel is between our masters and us their men.
SAMPSON	'Tis all one, I will show myself a tyrant. When I have fought with the men, I will be cruel with the maids, and cut off their heads.
GREGORY	The heads of the maids?
SAMPSON	Ay, the heads of the maids, or their maidenheads - take it in what sense thou wilt.
GREGORY	They must take it in sense that feel it.
SAMPSON	Me they shall feel while I am able to stand, and 'tis known I am a pretty piece of flesh.
GREGORY	'Tis well thou art not fish; if thou hadst, thou hadst been poor John. Draw thy tool, here comes two of the house of the Montagues

Enter two other serving men, ABRAHAM *and* BALTHASAR

SAMPSON	My naked weapon is out. Quarrel, I will back thee.
GREGORY	How, turn thy back and run?
SAMPSON	Fear me not.
GREGORY	No, marry, I fear thee!
SAMPSON	Let us take the law of our side, let them begin.
GREGORY	I will frown as I pass by, and let them take it as they list.
SAMPSON	Nay, as they dare. I will bite my thumb at them; which is a disgrace to them, if they bear it.

PROGRESS CHECK

① Think about the ways in which this scene opens the play, and make a note of the key points.

1. • Two servants from the Capulet family are out in Verona and are looking for trouble.
   • Gregory teases Sampson that he will run away if they see anyone from the Montague household.
   • Sampson says he will take on any man from the Montague family and then he will turn his attention (note the sexual innuendo) to the Montague women.
   • Two servants of the Montagues enter and Sampson wants to start an argument with them. He says he will 'bite his thumb' at them (an insulting gesture).

7.4 Presenting characters

LEARNING SUMMARY	After studying this section, you should be able to understand: • how Shakespeare creates characters • asides and soliloquies

The creation of characters

AQA	E Lang ✓	E Lit ✓

Characters are central to any play. An essential part of your study will be to see how Shakespeare presents his characters and how they function in the play.

Shakespeare gives the audience an impression of the characters in various ways.

Here are some of the ways we get a picture of a character:
- What the character **looks** like (physical appearance, clothing, etc.). When a play is seen on the stage then much of this will be visual, although characters sometimes comment on another character's appearance in the dialogue. Remember to look at the stage directions too when studying your play. These often give information that would be seen if you were watching a performance of the play.
- What a character **says** and **how** it is said.
- What the character **thinks** (often we learn about this from a character's soliloquies).
- How the character **acts** – watch out for reactions to different situations.
- How the character's words **match** their actual **deeds** or their underlying **motives**.
- What other characters **say about a character**.
- How a character **changes** as the play goes on.

> There are several ways that we formulate impressions of characters. Make sure that you take them all into account when considering and making your assessment of a character.

Asides and soliloquies

AQA	E Lang ✓	E Lit ✓

In his plays, Shakespeare makes full use of the dramatic devices of **asides** and **soliloquies**, as a means of revealing to the audience what is in the mind of a character. It is as if the character is speaking aloud to the audience, sharing their thoughts with them or giving them information, and no one on the stage can hear them.

Asides

Asides are comments from a character and are often spoken whilst other characters are on stage.

For example, in *Macbeth* the witches have foretold that Macbeth will become Thane of Cawdor and then King of Scotland. Read the following extract from Act 1 scene 2 (lines 120–143). Macbeth, with his fellow nobleman, Banquo, who witnessed the witches words, has just heard that he has been made Thane of Cawdor, thus partly fulfilling the witches' prophesy.

BANQUO	That trusted home
	Might yet enkindle you unto the crown,
	Besides the thane of Cawdor. But 'tis strange:
	And oftentimes, to win us to our harm,
	The instruments of darkness tell us truths,
	Win us with honest trifles, to betray's
	In deepest consequence.
	Cousins, a word, I pray you.
MACBETH	[Aside] Two truths are told,
	As happy prologues to the swelling act
	Of the imperial theme.--I thank you, gentlemen.
	[Aside] Cannot be ill, cannot be good: if ill,
	Why hath it given me earnest of success,
	Commencing in a truth? I am thane of Cawdor:
	If good, why do I yield to that suggestion
	Whose horrid image doth unfix my hair
	And make my seated heart knock at my ribs,
	Against the use of nature? Present fears
	Are less than horrible imaginings:
	My thought, whose murder yet is but fantastical,
	Shakes so my single state of man that function
	Is smother'd in surmise, and nothing is
	But what is not.
BANQUO	Look, how our partner's rapt.
MACBETH	[Aside] If chance will have me king, why, chance may crown me,
	Without my stir.

Think about these asides and what they reveal about Macbeth in terms of what he thinks and feels.

You might have noted that the asides reveal that the thought of being king, as the witches have predicted, begins to occupy his mind. The idea of murder comes into his mind but then he thinks that chance might make him king without him having to do anything to actively bring it about. The asides show that he has ambition to become king but also has misgivings about what he will need to do to bring it about.

> **KEY POINT**
>
> Some asides are much briefer than the example given here, sometimes consisting of just an odd word or two. Short or long, though, Shakespeare uses them for a reason and they will add something to the dialogue and drama.

Make sure that you are familiar with all the soliloquies given by the characters in the play you are studying. Be clear in your mind what information is given in these soliloquies and what they reveal about the characters.

Soliloquies

Some asides are much briefer than the one Macbeth uses here, but soliloquies tend to be longer and usually occur when no other characters are on stage.

For example, in this soliloquy from *Macbeth* Act 1 scene 7 (lines 1–28), Macbeth, spurred on by his wife, Lady Macbeth, is preparing to kill Duncan, the King.

MACBETH

If it were done when 'tis done, then 'twere well
It were done quickly. If the assassination
Could trammel up the consequence, and catch
With his surcease success; that but this blow
Might be the be-all and the end-all - here,
But here, upon this bank and shoal of time,
We'd jump the life to come. But in these cases
We still have judgment here, that we but teach
Bloody instructions, which being taught return
To plague th' inventor. This even-handed justice
Commends th' ingredience of our poisoned chalice
To our own lips. He's here in double trust:
First, as I am his kinsman and his subject,
Strong both against the deed; then, as his host,
Who should against his murderer shut the door,
Not bear the knife myself. Besides, this Duncan
Hath borne his faculties so meek, hath been
So clear in his great office, that his virtues
Will plead like angels, trumpet-tongued, against
The deep damnation of his taking-off;
And pity, like a naked new-born babe,
Striding the blast, or heaven's cherubim, horsed
Upon the sightless couriers of the air,
Shall blow the horrid deed in every eye,
That tears shall drown the wind. I have no spur
To prick the sides of my intent, but only
Vaulting ambition, which o'erleaps itself

Enter Lady Macbeth.   How now? What news?

Think about what is revealed about Macbeth's thoughts and feelings at this point in the play. Why do you think that Shakespeare uses a soliloquy at this point in the play?

Here are some points you might have noticed:

- Macbeth thinks over his decision to kill Duncan and feels that if he is going to do it, it would be better to get it over with quickly.
- He then begins to consider his decision to kill the king and, although it would have a good result in that he would gain the throne he also thinks about the risks if things go wrong.
- He also thinks about how, if he kills the king, the consequences could rebound on him.
- He begins to waver in his decision as he thinks about the king's qualities and how he trusts Macbeth. Note the use of the simile 'his virtues / will plead like angels'.
- By the end of the soliloquy he seems to have changed his mind about the killing, e.g. 'I have no spur' – and then Lady Macbeth arrives.
- The soliloquy at this point gives us an insight into how Macbeth is wrestling with his conscience over the planned murder and how he is having second thoughts about it. This serves to heighten the dramatic tension as we wait to see what he is going to do. This tension is heightened further by the arrival of Lady Macbeth who wants her husband to kill Duncan.

7.5 Shakespeare's language

LEARNING SUMMARY	After studying this section, you should be able to understand: • how Shakespeare uses poetry and prose • what the use of imagery adds to the play

Poetry and prose

AQA	E Lang	E Lit
	✓	✓

Shakespeare's plays are written mainly in verse (poetry), but he does use some prose too (i.e. ordinary writing that is not organised by rhymes or fixed line lengths).

Poetry

The kind of verse form that Shakespeare uses is called **blank verse**. This kind of verse form is ideal for writing dialogue because its rhythms are very close to the rhythm patterns of everyday speech.

Blank verse does not rhyme and is composed of lines that contain ten syllables. It is called **iambic pentameter**. An iamb is an unstressed syllable (⌣) followed by a stressed syllable (╱). Five iambs in a row make a line of iambic pentameter ('pent' means five in Greek, as in 'pentagon' or 'pentathlon'). This means that each line has ten syllables, as in this line from *Romeo and Juliet*:

But soft, what light through yonder window breaks?

However, where necessary for creating effects, or to make sense of the line, Shakespeare sometimes shortens or lengthens a line in order to express his meaning, or uses **enjambment**, where one line runs on to the next.

In this opening speech from *Twelfth Night*, Act 1 scene 1 (lines 1–15), Orsino, reveals that he is desperately in love. Read the speech carefully.

ORSINO	If music be the food of love, play on; Give me excess of it, that, surfeiting, The appetite may sicken, and so die. That strain again! it had a dying fall: O, it came o'er my ear like the sweet sound, That breathes upon a bank of violets, Stealing and giving odour! Enough; no more: 'Tis not so sweet now as it was before. O spirit of love! how quick and fresh art thou, That, notwithstanding thy capacity Receiveth as the sea, nought enters there, Of what validity and pitch soe'er, But falls into abatement and low price, Even in a minute: so full of shapes is fancy That it alone is high fantastical.

What do you notice about the ways in which Shakespeare uses blank verse here?

You might have noticed some of these points:
- Although most of the lines are written in iambic pentameter, sometimes Shakespeare inserts an extra syllable or two in order to express his meaning (as in lines 5 and 7, for example).
- The rhythm patterns closely follow those of normal speech.
- Some lines are divided into two by a pause (or **caesura**) and many of the lines run on (enjambment).

Prose

As well as using blank verse, Shakespeare also uses **prose** in his plays. It is often said that, in his plays, blank verse is used by important characters of high standing and that 'low' or comic characters use prose. This is often true but it is not always the case. Shakespeare uses prose in his plays for a variety of purposes and in a variety of **contexts** depending on what is happening in the text at that point and what effect he wants to achieve.

Prose is used in the following contexts:
- When characters read aloud letters, proclamations, challenges, etc.
- In circumstances where a character loses emotional control or descends into madness, e.g. Lady Macbeth's sleepwalking scene.
- Comic scenes, e.g. Sir Toby Belch and his friends in *Twelfth Night* (over half of *Twelfth Night* is written in prose).
- Situations where characters of low status, such as clowns, servants and drunkards are speaking.

> In order to decide why Shakespeare uses prose or verse you need to look closely at the text and at who is speaking, what they have to say and in what context they are saying it.

You should note, though, that these are not hard and fast rules and that Shakespeare was prepared to change the way in which he used language according to circumstances. For example, the Nurse in *Romeo and Juliet* speaks in both prose and verse depending on the context. In *Macbeth*, the porter is both a low and comic character. Appropriately, he speaks in prose when he is describing the effects of drink. Read the following extract:

PORTER	Marry, sir, nose-painting, sleep, and urine. Lechery, sir, it provokes, and unprovokes; it provokes the desire, but it takes away the performance. Therefore, much drink may be said to be an equivocator with lechery; it makes him, and it mars him; it sets him on, and it takes him off; it persuades him, and disheartens him; makes him stand to, and not stand to; in conclusion, equivocates him in a sleep, and, giving him the lie, leaves him.

Even here, the prose has a pattern to it because the contrasts in the effects brought on by drink are balanced against each other.

However, on occasion, a central and noble character will sometimes speak in prose, such as Brutus in *Julius Caesar*. In the following extract from Act 3 scene 2, for example, after the death of Caesar, Brutus speaks to the gathered crowd.

BRUTUS	Romans, countrymen, and lovers! hear me for my cause, and be silent, that you may hear: believe me for mine honour, and have respect to mine honour, that you may believe: censure me in your wisdom, and awake your senses, that you may the better judge. If there be any in this assembly, any dear friend of Caesar's, to him I say, that Brutus' love to Caesar was no less than his. If then that friend demand why Brutus rose against Caesar, this is my answer: --Not that I loved Caesar less, but that I loved Rome more. Had you rather Caesar were living and die all slaves, than that Caesar were dead, to live all free men? As Caesar loved me, I weep for him; as he was fortunate, I rejoice at it; as he was valiant, I honour him: but, as he was ambitious, I slew him. There is tears for his love; joy for his fortune; honour for his valour; and death for his ambition.

Here Brutus speaks to the people in prose rather than in verse to make his speech seem plain and simple and to put himself on the level of the ordinary citizens in the crowd. He claims to have loved Caesar as much as anyone in the crowd, but wants to convince them that Caesar had to die to prevent him making slaves of them all. He wants to put this message across in the language of the ordinary citizen to make it appear that he is one of them and has done what he has done for their sake. He uses prose to achieve this.

In *Much Ado About Nothing*, the comic character, Dogberry, always speaks in prose but in other parts of the play, Shakespeare switches between verse and prose for other characters, depending on the situation. In the following extract, Leonato is busy making arrangements for the banquet and masked ball, which is to take place that evening. He is interrupted when his brother, Antonio, arrives.

LEONATO	How now, brother, where is my cousin, your son? Hath he provided this music?
ANTONIO	He is very busy about it. But, brother, I can tell you strange news that you yet dreamt not of.
LEONATO	Are they good?
ANTONIO	As the events stamps them, but they have a good cover; they show well outward. The Prince and Count Claudio, walking in a thick-pleached alley in mine orchard, were thus much overheard by a man of mine: the Prince discovered to Claudio that he loved my niece your daughter and meant to acknowledge it this night in a dance, and if he found her accordant, he meant to take the present time by the top and instantly break with you of it.

Here, Antonio tells his brother that one of his servants has overheard Don Pedro confess to Claudio that he is in love with Hero. The informality of this context, as Leonato goes about the business of arranging matters and talks privately with his brother, is reflected in Shakespeare's choice of prose rather than verse to deliver the dialogue.

Shakespeare's use of imagery

AQA	E Lang	E Lit
	✓	✓

Imagery involves the use of words or phrases which create vivid pictures or create a sense of particular emotions in the minds of the reader or listener. Shakespeare's imagery uses **metaphors** and **similes**. A simile compares one thing with another using 'like' or 'as'. For example, Juliet's words to Romeo:
'My bounty is as boundless as the sea,
My love as deep.'

Another example is Beatrice's description of Benedick's friendship with Claudio:
'...he will hang upon him like a disease'.

A metaphor is also a form of **comparison** but, instead of using 'like' or 'as', it suggests that the thing being described and the thing being compared to it are the same. For example, Donalbain's warning to his brother Malcolm in *Macbeth*:
'There's daggers in men's smiles'

Sometimes a metaphor can be more developed. For example, in *Much Ado About Nothing*, Leonato expresses his feelings of anger and disappointment at what he believes to be his daughter's immoral behaviour:
'O, she is fallen
Into a pit of ink, that the wide sea
Hath drops too few to wash her clean again
And salt too little which may season give
To her foul-tainted flesh!'

Shakespeare often uses imagery to explore and add emphasis to a particular idea. In a play, there are sometimes groups of images that are repeated throughout the play, which build up a sense of the **themes**. For example, in *Romeo and Juliet*, Shakespeare sometimes uses images to do with the contrast between light and dark or night and day.

Here are a few examples:

- Romeo finds comfort in the darkness – 'I have night's cloak to hide me from their eyes.' (Act 2 scene 2)
- Juliet's beauty is associated with both night and light – 'O she doth teach the torches to burn bright. / It seems she hangs upon the cheek of night / Like a rich jewel in an Ethiop's ear.' (Act 1 scene 5)
- In the early morning after their only night spent together they do not want the light of dawn to break and Juliet tries to convince Romeo it is still night. But he realises that the light of dawn means they must part –
  '...Look love, what envious streaks
  Do lace the severing clouds in yonder east.
  Night's candles are burnt out...' (Act 3 scene 5)

> Look for the imagery in the play(s) you are studying and see if you can spot any repeated patterns.

Shakespeare also frequently uses **antithesis** to create effects. Antithesis is where one word or image is set against an opposite one to create a sense of contrast.

For example, in *Romeo and Juliet*, when Juliet is told by the Nurse that Romeo has killed Tybalt, her conflicting emotions are expressed through a series of antitheses, e.g. 'Beautiful tyrant, fiend angelical / Dove-feather'd raven, wolvish ravening lamb'.

> **KEY POINT**
>
> Apart from using imagery to enrich the descriptive qualities of the language, Shakespeare also uses it to highlight and develop key ideas and themes.

7.6 Endings

After studying this section, you should be able to understand:
- why the ending of a play is important
- techniques that Shakespeare uses to end his plays

Why the ending of a play is important

AQA — E Lang ✓ E Lit ✓

The ending of any play is very important as it leaves the audience with the final impression of the drama they have just spent two or three hours watching. In order for the play to have maximum impact, it is important that the ending is effective.

The ending of the play is important because it:
- develops from the action of the play and forms a natural conclusion
- draws together all the threads of the plot
- resolves and sorts out problems, confusions and conflicts that have developed through the course of the action
- creates a dramatic climax
- often has a sense of future happiness or reconciliation, or a sense that a new start is being made.

> You are sometimes asked to write about the effectiveness of the ending of a play. Make sure you have ideas in your mind about your response to the ending of the play(s) you are studying.

Think about the ending of the play you are studying. Which of the following key features apply to how the play ends?
- A sense of happiness
- Feelings of sadness
- Tragic consequences
- Confusions sorted out
- A sense of a new start
- Reconciliation and peace
- Conflicts resolved
- Friends reunited

Techniques used for ending plays

AQA — E Lang ✓ E Lit ✓

Put simply, Shakespeare's tragedies always end in the death of the central character and usually a number of other characters too – whereas, in the comedies, there are no deaths and things end happily. In *Romeo and Juliet*, for example, this is what happens:

> Romeo (thinking Juliet is dead) goes to the Capulet vault.

> He encounters Paris and kills him.

> He finds the body of Juliet and drinks his poison to die with her.

> Juliet wakes up from her drugged sleep to find Romeo dead. Grief stricken, she stabs herself to death.

This tragedy ends with the deaths of three characters, including the central characters of Romeo and Juliet.

However, Shakespeare does not leave the tragedy there. Tragic though the ending is, there is also a note of hope for the future in that the deaths of Romeo and Juliet have brought together the feuding Montagues and Capulets:

> PRINCE   A glooming peace this morning with it brings;
> The sun for sorrow will not show his head.
> Go hence to have more talk of these sad things;
> Some shall be pardoned, and some punished.
> For never was a story of more woe
> Than this of Juliet and her Romeo.

Romeo and Juliet Act 5, scene 3 (lines 304–309)

In a comedy, such as *Twelfth Night*, there are no such tragic deaths. Here is what happens in the final scene of *Twelfth Night*:

Viola is reunited with her twin brother, Sebastian, whom she thought had drowned at sea.

The confusion over Viola's disguise is sorted out and she and Orsino plan to marry.

Sebastian and Olivia love each other and they plan to marry.

Everyone is happy at the end, with the exception of Malvolio, who is angry at having been tricked.

PROGRESS CHECK

1 Look carefully at the play you are studying and make a brief plan of the way in which Shakespeare brings it to an end.

Sample GCSE question

This is part of a longer response to this element of the set task.

Explore Malvolio's dramatic function in *Twelfth Night*.

Malvolio contributes to several of the play's themes, though often not through choice. Malvolio's role in the subplot of the play – his behaviour during, and subsequent reaction to, Sir Toby, Maria and Feste's trick – is paramount because it contributes greatly to the comedic elements of the play. Sir Toby, Maria and Feste play on Malvolio's self-regard and ambition when they trick him into believing that Olivia is in love with him. The scenes that follow, where Malvolio capers around in yellow cross gartered stockings and smiles continuously, really show how reckless ambition can override good sense and offers the audience an important moral. The subplot involving Malvolio adds to the confusion and misguided love that surrounds the play, whilst providing a distraction from the main plot and making the play feel more complete.

Everything not being as it seems and the element of disguise are also key to `Twelfth Night´, what with its primary protagonist, Viola, disguising herself as a man, Cesario, and continuing this facade throughout the majority of the play. At first, Malvolio contributes indirectly to the `everything is not as it seems' aspect when he believes that Olivia is in love with him. He also contributes to the element of disguise in the play as, firstly, Maria's handwriting must be disguised as Olivia's in order for him to believe that the letter is from her and secondly, and more directly, when he must `disguise´ himself as a flamboyant courtier to impress Olivia. His most significant contribution to this aspect of the play is towards the end, when the majority of the play's characters believe him to be mad, though, of course, he isn't and this is merely a result of the trick that has been played on him. In Elizabethan times it was thought that to cure a mad person you should shut them in a darkened room until their sanity returned, and this is exactly the treatment that Malvolio's adversaries inflict upon him. This treatment is, however, far too harsh for modern audiences to find amusing. Malvolio also makes a rather surprising contribution to the theme of love through his attraction to Olivia, although this is less surprising when it becomes apparent that he sees love merely as a way of attaining `... greatness´. Malvolio's love for Olivia actually appears to reflect Orsino's to a degree: they are both misguided – Malvolio has been tricked and Orsino, it seems, is tricking himself: he barely knows Olivia and yet he believes himself to be in love with her – ; they are both relentless, as Malvolio proves by continuing to adhere to the letter, much to Olivia's bewilderment; and their respective loves are unrequited. Furthermore, Malvolio shows a high level of self-love, to the extent where Olivia says he is `... sick of self-love´. This self-love is also paralleled in Orsino, who is thoroughly convinced that Olivia will fall in love with him and is unfazed by her continued rejection.

Student begins by addressing the task directly and relevantly.

Opening paragraph gives a clear overview of the role of Malvolio.

Shows awareness of Malvolio's importance in contributing to developing ideas within the play.

Aware of contextual factors – the difference of perception between an Elizabethan audience and a modern-day one.

Interesting comparison between characters developed here.

Practice question

Macbeth

1 Answer both parts (a) and (b).

Part (a) How does Shakespeare show Macbeth's state of mind in the extract below?

Part (b) Explain how Shakespeare shows a different state of Macbeth's mind in another scene in the play.

(External exam question: English Literature, Unit 4)

MACBETH   Is this a dagger which I see before me,
The handle toward my hand? Come, let me clutch thee.
I have thee not, and yet I see thee still.
Art thou not, fatal vision, sensible
To feeling as to sight? or art thou but
A dagger of the mind, a false creation,
Proceeding from the heat-oppressed brain?
I see thee yet, in form as palpable
As this which now I draw.
Thou marshall'st me the way that I was going;
And such an instrument I was to use.
Mine eyes are made the fools o' the other senses,
Or else worth all the rest; I see thee still,
And on thy blade and dudgeon gouts of blood,
Which was not so before. There's no such thing:
It is the bloody business which informs
Thus to mine eyes.

8 Studying drama

The following topics are covered in this chapter:

- Approaching the text
- Opening scenes
- Presenting characters
- Settings, stage directions and themes

8.1 Approaching the text

LEARNING SUMMARY

After studying this section, you should be able to understand:

- the nature of drama texts
- how to begin to study your text

The nature of drama texts

AQA	E Lang	E Lit
	✓	✓

Before you begin this section it is worth noting that much of what was discussed in Chapter 7, in relation to Shakespeare, also applies to the study of other drama texts. Drama texts were written to be seen, rather than read, and the full meaning and impact of many of them can only be fully appreciated when they are seen in **performance**. When studying your text, keep this in mind and recognise that you are dealing with a work that is very different from a novel or short story.

> **KEY POINT**
>
> Drama texts are written to be **seen** rather than **read**.

Approaching a drama text

AQA	E Lang	E Lit
	✓	✓

Here are some suggestions of things you can do to familiarise yourself with a play before you look at it in detail:

Stage 1

1. **Read** the play all the way through. If you can read it with others, with people reading the parts aloud, this will help a great deal. Remember, drama is really a group activity.
2. See a live **performance** of the play if you can. If you can't, try to see a film or video version of it. If this is not possible, try to listen to it on audio tape or CD. (Your school, college or public library might be able to help in obtaining video or audio recordings.)
3. Make notes on any performance you see or hear. Keep a log book to record your initial impressions of characters, action, etc.

Stage 2

You are now ready to start looking at the play in more detail. Here are some things you can do to help develop your understanding further:

1 Have ideas about the characters – look at the **key speeches**.

2 Look for various meanings or 'patterns' in the play – this will help you to identify **themes**.

3 Think about the **structure** of the play and the **dramatic effects** that are created.

4 Look carefully at the language of the play, focusing on key speeches, soliloquies, dialogue between characters, etc.

Stage 3

If you are studying the text for an exam, you will need to make sure you have some detailed notes to revise from. It will help you a great deal if you adopt an organised and systematic approach to your note-making. Here are some suggestions:

> It is a good idea to select specific references from the text to support the points you make.

1 Make a brief **summary** of what happens in each scene / act. It's a good idea to note any key speeches or events here – you can use the summary as a quick reference to locate particular things in the text.

2 Keep a separate **character log**. Make notes on:
- Each occasion where a character appears in the play.
- What they say and do and the significance of this.
- Any important things they say or key speeches.
- What other characters say about them.

> Be aware of how all these elements link together in the play.

3 Keep notes on the **key ideas** (themes / issues raised in the play). Make notes on:
- **Themes** and how these are presented.
- How **language**, **images**, **symbols**, etc. develop these ideas.

PROGRESS CHECK

1 What key features should you look for in the play you are studying?

1. Characters, meanings / patterns in the play, themes, structure of the play, dramatic effects, language – key speeches, soliloquies, dialogue between characters.

8.2 Opening scenes

After studying this section, you should be able to understand:
- the dramatic function of an opening scene
- how some dramatists open their plays

The dramatic function of opening scenes

AQA   E Lang ✓   E Lit ✓

The way in which a play opens is very important because the opening is where the dramatist needs to capture the audience's interest and attention. There are many ways to do this, depending on the intended purpose of the scene and the effect that the dramatist wants it to have on the audience.

An opening scene can have a number of purposes, in any combination. For example, it can:
- Provide an **explanation** of what has happened before the play actually starts, giving background **information** that the audience needs to know in order to understand what is going on.
- Create a background **setting** against which the action of the play takes place.
- Create a particular **mood** or **atmosphere** that immediately captures the audience's attention.
- Introduce characters, perhaps revealing something about situations and relationships.
- Create a sense of intrigue or mystery that captures the audience's **attention** and makes them want to know more.

> **KEY POINT**
>
> The opening of a play can have a variety of purposes and can achieve its effects in various ways.

How plays can open

AQA   E Lang ✓   E Lit ✓

The following text is the opening of *An Inspector Calls* by J.B. Priestley. The text begins with very detailed stage directions describing both the setting and the characters. When watching a performance of the play, of course, all these details will be seen visually.

The play begins with the wealthy factory owner Mr Birling, his wife Mrs Birling, their daughter Sheila, son Eric and a young man, Gerald, seated at the table having a celebratory dinner. The maid, Edna, is serving them.

Read this opening through carefully.

BIRLING	Giving us the port, Edna? That's right. (*He pushes it towards Eric.*) You ought to like this port Gerald. As a matter of fact Finchley told me it's exactly the same port your father gets from him.
GERALD	Then it'll be good all right. The governor prides himself on being a good judge of port. I don't pretend to know much about it.
SHEILA	(*gaily, possessively*) I should jolly well think not, Gerald. I'd hate you to know all about port – like one of these purple-faced old men.
BIRLING	Here. I'm not a purple-faced old man.
SHEILA	No, not yet. But then you don't know all about port – do you?
BIRLING	(*noticing his wife has not taken any*). Now then, Sybil, you must take a little tonight. Special occasion, y'know, eh?
SHEILA	Yes, go on Mummy. You must drink our health.
MRS BIRLING	(*smiling*) Very well then, Just a little, thank you. (*To Edna, who is about to go, with tray.*) All right, Edna. I'll ring from the drawing-room when we want coffee. Probably in about half an hour.
EDNA	(*going*) Yes ma'am.

Edna goes out. They now have all the glasses filled. Birling beams at them and clearly relaxes.

From *An Inspector Calls* by J.B. Priestley

What impression do you get of the characters and situation from this opening of the play?

Here are some points you might have noted:
- All the characters seem very pleased with themselves. Birling appears to be in charge as the father, although Mrs Birling's instructions to the maid, Edna, are precise and suggest that she also has some authority.
- The reference to a 'special occasion' suggests that they are having a special celebration for something.
- Although Birling seems to be in charge here, he also seems to respect Gerald's father and makes a point of saying how good the port is and that it is the same kind that Gerald's father buys.
- They are obviously a very privileged and wealthy family who can afford to be waited on by servants.

You will see from this example that Priestley, as well as setting the scene for the play, conveys a good deal of important information to his audience in these opening lines. He does this whilst maintaining the interest of the audience through the dialogue, and also arouses interest in what exactly the special celebration might be about.

> **KEY POINT**
>
> Make sure that you are aware of the techniques that the dramatist uses to open the play you are studying.

8.3 Presenting characters

LEARNING SUMMARY	**After studying this section, you should be able to understand:** • the importance of characterisation • how dramatists present characters

The importance of characterisation

AQA	E Lang	E Lit
	✓	✓

Characters are at the centre of all drama and the effectiveness and success of a play often depends on how successfully the dramatist creates and presents characters. When watching or studying a play, you can learn about characters in three main ways:

• Through what they do, their actions on the stage.
• Through what they say.
• Through what other characters say about them.

It is important to look at all these aspects in the context of what is happening in the drama. For example, a character's words may not match what they actually do, or what one character says may not be the same as what another character says. Where this happens, the dramatist has created the effect deliberately for a particular purpose. You need to look carefully at all the evidence in order to reach your assessment of characters.

A useful way to gather information on characters is to keep a **character log** for each of the main characters in the play. Here is a brief example based on the character of Hobson from *Hobson's Choice* by Harold Brighouse.

Act / Scene	Character point	Evidence e.g. what they say / do – what others say about them	Supporting quotation	Lines / page
Act 1	Domineering	Tells his daughter what to do.	"I've a mind to take measures with the lot of you."	p5

PROGRESS CHECK

1. Choose a character from the play that you are studying and draw up a more detailed table based on the example above. What could you look at to help you form an idea of the character?

1. • What they do and how they act in the play.
   • What they say (and how they say it).
   • What other characters say about them.

KEY POINT

Each character has a role to play in the drama and the dramatist presents them in such a way as to fulfil that role.

How dramatists present characters

AQA	E Lang	E Lit
	✓	✓

In examining the characters in a play, you should make sure you consider all the possible ways you can **interpret** them and the **role** they **perform** in the play, and support your ideas with evidence from the text.

Look at this extract from *An Inspector Calls* by J.B. Priestley, where Arthur Birling, a wealthy, self-made man gives his son and prospective son-in-law the benefit of his experience.

> Birling   (*solemnly*) But this is the point. I don't want to lecture you two young fellows again. But what so many of you don't seem to understand now, when things are so much easier, is that a man has to make his own way – has to look after himself – and his family too, of course, when he has one – and so long as he does that he won't come to much harm. But the way some of these cranks talk and write now, you'd think everybody has to look after everybody else, as if we were all mixed up together like bees in a hive – community and all that nonsense. But take my word for it, you youngsters – and I've learnt in the good hard school of experience – that a man has to mind his own business and look after himself and his own – and –
>
> From *An Inspector Calls* by J.B. Priestley

We can learn a lot about Birling from what he has to say:

Character point	Evidence
Takes himself seriously.	Stage direction 'solemnly'
Aware that he lectures people – speaks down to them – patronising.	*'I don't want to lecture you two young fellows…* *But what so many of you don't seem to understand.'* *'youngsters'*
Believes that everyone has to look after himself and his own.	*'…a man has to make his own way… to look after himself'*
Doesn't agree with people who believe in 'community'.	Calls them *'cranks'* and calls it *'nonsense'*
He knows best.	*'I've learnt in the good hard school of experience'*

KEY POINT

Even a short extract can reveal a good deal about the character and the ways in which the dramatist presents them.

8.4 Settings, stage directions and themes

LEARNING SUMMARY	After studying this section, you should be able to understand:
	• the importance of setting
	• the importance of stage directions
	• how setting and stage directions can link to theme

The importance of setting and stage directions

	E Lang	E Lit
AQA	✓	✓

As mentioned earlier, a play is meant to be seen rather than read and, therefore, the dramatist is able to control the audience's responses by vision and sound as well as language. This means that the stage set and other external factors, such as **lighting**, **sound effects** and **props**, can be exploited for dramatic effect. Sometimes, stage directions suggest or reinforce ideas about the characters in a play, as well as giving information about the setting, actions or thematic ideas.

Different plays create a sense of setting and use stage directions in different ways. *Under Milk Wood* by Dylan Thomas was originally written as a radio play or 'play for voices' as Thomas put it. As it was written to be heard rather than seen it does not use stage directions in the normal way but instead the dialogue is interspersed by 'voices', which provide a commentary describing the setting, atmosphere and actions throughout the play.

Here is an extract from the opening of the play, in which the 'first voice' sets the scene, which is closely linked to the characters and ideas that the play will go on to develop.

[Silence]

FIRST VOICE (_Very softly_)

To begin at the beginning:

It is spring, moonless night in the small town, starless and bible-black, the cobblestreets silent and the hunched, courters'-and-rabbits' wood limping invisible down to the sloeblack, slow, black, crowblack, fishingboat-bobbing sea.

The houses are blind as moles (though moles see fine to-night in the snouting, velvet dingles) or blind as Captain Cat there in the muffled middle by the pump and the town clock, the shops in mourning, the Welfare Hall in widows' weeds. And all the people of the lulled and dumbfound town are sleeping now.

Hush, the babies are sleeping, the farmers, the fishers, the tradesmen and pensioners, cobbler, schoolteacher, postman and publican, the undertaker and the fancy woman, drunkard, dressmaker, preacher, policeman, the webfoot cocklewomen and the tidy wives. Young girls lie bedded soft or glide in their dreams, with rings and trousseaux, bridesmaided by glowworms down the aisles of the organplaying wood. The boys are dreaming wicked or of the bucking ranches of the night and the jollyrodgered sea. And the anthracite statues of the horses sleep in the fields, and the cows in the byres, and the dogs in the wetnosed yards; and the cats nap in the slant corners or lope sly, streaking and needling, on the one cloud of the roofs.

You can hear the dew falling, and the hushed town breathing.

Only your eyes are unclosed to see the black and folded town fast, and slow, asleep. And you alone can hear the invisible starfall, the darkest-beforedawn minutely dewgrazed stir of the black, dab-filled sea where the Arethusa, the Curlew and the Skylark, Zanzibar, Rhiannon, the Rover, the Cormorant, and the Star of Wales tilt and ride.

From Under Milk Wood by Dylan Thomas

Notice the vividness of the description here to create a strong sense of the setting and atmosphere.

1 How does Thomas use language in the opening of *Under Milk Wood* to create effects?

1. • He creates a vivid impression of the scene by using language that appeals to the listener's imagination and creates a series of visual images.
   • He lists the different inhabitants of the town and suggests what they are doing – dreaming.
   • He combines words together to create a descriptive effect, e.g. 'wetnosed yards', 'dewgrazed'.

Thematic ideas

AQA A | E Lang ✓ | E Lit ✓

Look at the following extract from the opening of the play. One of the themes that is explored in the play *An Inspector Calls* is the differences in the ways in which people are treated depending on their social class.

The stage directions in this extract describe the setting and the characters, which gives the audience a clear impression of the social context of the play.

At the rise of the curtain, the four Birlings and Gerald are seated at the table, with Arthur Birling at one end, his wife at the other, Eric downstage and Sheila and Gerald seated upstage. Edna, the parlourmaid, is just clearing the table, which has no cloth, of dessert plates and champagne glasses etc., and then replacing them with decanter of port, cigar box and cigarettes. Port glasses are already on the table. All five are in evening dress of the period, the men in tails, white ties, not dinner-jackets. Arthur Birling is a heavy looking, rather portentous man in his middle fifties with fairly easy manners but rather provincial in his speech. His wife is about fifty, a rather cold woman and her husband's social superior. Sheila is a pretty girl in her early twenties, very pleased with life and rather excited. Gerald Croft is an attractive chap about thirty, rather too manly to be a dandy but very much the easy well-bred young man-about-town. Eric is in his early twenties, not quite at ease, half shy, half assertive. At the moment they have all had a good dinner, are celebrating a special occasion, and are pleased with themselves.

From *An Inspector Calls* by J.B. Priestley

1 Write down the impression you form of the scene in the opening of *An Inspector Calls*, and the context from the stage directions given here. Give reasons for your ideas.

1. • The Birlings are a wealthy family – the setting is grand with port and champagne. They also have a maid to serve them.
   • They are dressed in evening dress and bow ties – further evidence of their social standing.
   • Mr Birling speaks with a provincial accent suggesting he has risen from a lower class. Mrs Birling seems to come from a socially higher background.
   • They are having a special celebration for some reason and are all very pleased with themselves.

Stage directions can give important information about a play.

The play *An Inspector Calls* examines a number of themes which are interlinked. For example:

Social responsibility, reputation and personal integrity ➤ Moral judgements ➤ Personal conflicts ➤ Truth and lies

These themes are explored in various ways throughout the play.

At the end of the play, just before the Inspector leaves, he sums up his thoughts on the suicide of Eva Smith and the part that the Birling family and Gerald Croft played in it.

Inspector	*(taking charge, masterfully)* Stop!
	(They are suddenly quiet, staring at him.)
	And be quiet for a moment and listen to me. I don't need to know any more. Neither do you. This girl killed herself – and died a horrible death. But each of you helped to kill her. Remember that. Never forget it. *(He looks from one to the other of them carefully.)* But then I don't think you ever will. Remember what you did, Mrs Birling. You turned her away when she most needed help. You refused her even the pitiable little bit of organised charity you had in your power to grant her. Remember what you did –
Eric	*(unhappily)* My God – I'm not likely to forget.
Inspector	Just used her for the end of a stupid drunken evening, as if she was an animal, a thing, not a person. No, you won't forget. *(He looks at Sheila)*
Sheila	*(bitterly)* I know. I had her turned out of a job. I started it.
Inspector	You helped – but didn't start it. *(Rather savagely, to Birling)* You started it. She wanted twenty-five shillings a week instead of twenty-two and sixpence. You made her pay a heavy price for that. And now she'll make you pay a heavier price still.
Birling	*(unhappily)* Look, Inspector – I'd give thousands – yes, thousands –
Inspector	You're offering the money at the wrong time, Mr Birling. *(He makes a move as if concluding the session, possibly shutting up notebook etc. then surveys them sardonically.)* No, I don't think any of you will forget. Nor that young man, Croft, though he at least had some affection for her and made her happy for a time. Well, Eva Smith's gone. You can't do her any more harm. And you can't do her any good now, either. You can't even say 'I'm sorry, Eva Smith.'
Sheila	*(who is crying quietly)* That's the worst of it.
Inspector	But just remember this. One Eva Smith has gone – but there are millions and millions and millions of Eva Smiths and John Smiths still left with us, with their lives, their hopes and fears, their suffering and chance of happiness, all intertwined with our lives, and what we think and say and do. We don't live alone. We are members of one body. We are responsible for each other. And I tell you that the time will soon come when, if men will not learn that lesson, then they will be taught it in fire and blood and anguish. Good night.

From *An Inspector Calls* by J.B. Priestley

PROGRESS CHECK

❶ Make a list of the thematic ideas you can see in this extract and explain what the stage directions reveal.

1. Thematic ideas:
- Social responsibility – we all live in the world together and should help each other. We have a responsibility to look after those less fortunate than ourselves in society.
- Birling is concerned about his public reputation and is willing to pay 'millions' if it would put things right. Note how he thinks of everything in terms of money.
- Sheila shows awareness of how she has acted and takes responsibility, showing remorse.
- Mrs Birling did not help Eva Smith even though she could have done and so exemplifies exactly the selfish lack of concern for others that Priestley condemns throughout the play.

Stage directions:
- The stage directions emphasise that the Inspector is in charge of the situation and has had enough of the bickering.
- They reveal the feelings of the characters and the Inspector's attitude towards the Birlings.

Sample GCSE question

This is part of a longer response to the set task.

Eric says of his mother 'You don't understand anything. You never did. You never even tried.'

How does Priestley present the character of Mrs Birling and her relationship with her family in *An Inspector Calls*?

You would be advised to spend about 45 minutes on this question.

It is clear from the start of the play that Mrs Birling is not a character that we will warm to. She is portrayed as being cold and snobbish and we are told that she is "...about fifty, a rather cold woman and her husband's social superior". She is obviously from a higher class background than her husband and she knows it.

Clear focus right from the start with appropriate quotation to support comments.

Like Mr Birling, she exhibits a smug self-satisfaction and it is clear that she is very pleased with herself and her own importance. However, it soon becomes apparent that she has little understanding either of her offspring or the world around her. For example, she is completely surprised by the discovery that her son is a heavy drinker and has been for two years. She is also surprised by the revelation that Alderman Meggarty is a "...notorious womaniser as well as being one of the worst sots and rogues in Brumley".

Sound evaluation of characters.

Appropriate textual reference.

She shows a similar complete lack of understanding of her children. It seems that she has never really listened to or understood them. Her son, Eric, says of her "You don't understand anything. You never did. You never... even tried." It is obvious that her daughter, Sheila, is on a completely different wavelength from her mother too as she responds angrily when Mrs Birling tells her not to be childish. She accuses her mother of being childish herself and refusing to face the facts. She obviously feels that both her mother and her father are more interested in justifying their actions than accepting their guilt. In fact, Sheila's statement that her mother "hardened her heart" to Eva Smith and that this finally pushed Eva over the edge and finished her off suggests that Sheila feels that Mrs Birling has a huge responsibility for what has happened.

Provides clear evidence to support comments.

She likes to think that she knows what is going on, and the fact that she is "a prominent member of the Brumley Women's Charity Organisation" shows how she likes to feel important and feed her own ego. Ultimately it is she who seals the fate of Eva Smith when she rejects her pleas for help. Her treatment of Eva Smith shows that even though Eva was pregnant, Mrs Birling still had no qualms about turning her away — she really is the "cold" woman that Priestley describes at the beginning of the play.

Sound knowledge of the text on which to base assessment of character.

Supports view of Mrs Birling being a 'cold' woman.

Practice questions

Under Milk Wood by Dylan Thomas

1 Choose three characters from *Under Milk Wood* and examine how Thomas presents them in the play.

(Controlled Assessment task: English Literature, Unit 1)

The Crucible by Arthur Miller

2 Elizabeth Proctor is described as 'cold' by both John Proctor and Abigail.

How does Miller present Elizabeth Proctor? Is she a cold character in your view?

(Controlled Assessment task: English Literature, Unit 1)

Kindertransport by Diane Samuels

3 How does Samuels present the idea of separation and loss in the play?

(Controlled Assessment task: English Literature, Unit 1)

An Inspector Calls by J.B. Priestley

4 The Inspector tells the Birlings, 'We don't live alone. We are members of one body. We are responsible for each other.'

What does the Inspector mean here and how are his words significant to the message Priestley presents in the play?

(Controlled Assessment task: English Literature, Unit 1)

9 Exploring prose texts (contemporary prose and Literary Heritage prose)

The following topics are covered in this chapter:

- Novels and short stories
- Developing characters
- Exploring themes
- Openings
- Setting and context

9.1 Novels and short stories

LEARNING SUMMARY	After studying this section, you should be able to understand:
	- some of the features of novels and short stories
	- how to approach the study of novels and short stories

Features of novels and short stories

AQA	E Lang	E Lit
	✓	✓

Novels and short stories are in many ways very similar, both in their basic purpose and in the ways they set out to achieve it. Here are some of the things they often have in common:

- They tell stories.
- They seek to interest and entertain the reader.
- They usually contain characters.
- They usually use dialogue.
- They often explore ideas or themes.

There are ways in which short stories differ from novels, though. Here are some ideas:

- Short stories are obviously shorter than novels. This fact can make a significant difference to the ways in which they are written.
- The story may be much narrower in style than a novel and perhaps deal with a single idea rather than a range of ideas, or perhaps cover a much shorter time span than a novel. For example, many short stories focus on a single incident, moment in time or experience.

- Because the writer does not have the space to develop many characters, short stories often contain fewer characters than novels.
- The action usually focuses on the main plot in a short story and the story does not deal with secondary or sub-plots.

Approaching the text

AQA	E Lang	E Lit
	✓	✓

As part of your course you will study a variety of texts of different kinds. These fall into the following broad categories:

- Novels or stories from the **Literary Heritage**. These are texts which have stood the test of time and have become part of our literary heritage.

  Texts of this kind on the AQA specification are:
  1. *Pride and Prejudice* by Jane Austen
  2. *Wuthering Heights* by Emily Brontë
  3. *Great Expectations* by Charles Dickens
  4. *The Withered Arm and Other Wessex Tales* by Thomas Hardy
  5. *Animal Farm* by George Orwell

- Novels or stories from different cultures. These texts present different cultures and ways of life, and are often set in different parts of the world (and sometimes different times).

  Texts of this kind on the AQA specification are:
  1. Short stories from the AQA Anthology *Sunlight on the Grass:*
     - *On Seeing the 100% Perfect Girl One Beautiful April Morning* (Japan) by Haruki Murakami
     - *Something Old, Something New* (Scotland/Sudan) by Leila Aboulela
     - *Anil* (Malaysia) by Ridjal Noor
  2. *Of Mice and Men* (America) by John Steinbeck
  3. *Mister Pip* (New Zealand) by Lloyd Jones
  4. *Purple Hibiscus* (Nigeria) by Chimamanda Ngozi Adichie
  5. *To Kill a Mockingbird* (America) by Harper Lee
  6. *Rabbit-proof Fence* by Doris Pilkington

- **Contemporary prose, novels or stories**. These are more recently written texts, which present a wide variety of themes and contexts.

  Texts of this kind on the AQA specification are:
  1. Short stories from the AQA Anthology *Sunlight on the Grass:*
     - *Compass and Torch* by Elizabeth Baines
     - *When the Wasps Drowned* by Clare Wigfall
     - *My Polish Teacher's Tie* by Helen Dunmore
     - *The Darkness Out There* by Penelope Lively
     - *On Seeing the 100% Perfect Girl One Beautiful April Morning* by Haruki Murakami
  2. *Lord of the Flies* by William Golding
  3. *Martyn Pig* by Kevin Brooks
  4. *Touching the Void* by Joe Simpson
  5. *The Woman in Black* by Susan Hill

Keep a notebook or a 'log' for your work on the text. Jot down your ideas on plot, setting, characters, style, etc. as you go along.

Here are some ways in which you can approach your text and help to develop your understanding of it quickly:

> Read the text through from beginning to end to get an overall picture of the story.

> Write a brief **summary** outlining the key points of the plot and the key characters.

> Now go back and look over the story again.

> Gain an **overview** – you will need to have a clear understanding of the plot and key ideas, the structure of the story, how events relate to each other, etc.

> Think about the **narrative viewpoint** – who tells the story – is it told in the first person ('I') or the third person ('He', 'She')?

> Know the characters – who they are, what they do, how they relate to other characters, their function in the story, etc.

> Be aware of the **setting** and **context** of the story, e.g. **where** it is set, **when** it is set.

> Have ideas on the ways in which the writer uses **language** and **style** and of the **effects** that are created.

PROGRESS CHECK

1. What does the term 'setting' mean?
2. How do short stories differ from novels?

1. Where the action of the story takes place.
2. They are short, contain fewer characters, and cover a narrower range of ideas or narrower plot.

9.2 Openings

LEARNING SUMMARY

After studying this section, you should be able to understand:

- why openings are important
- narrative viewpoint

Why openings are important

AQA	E Lang	E Lit
	✓	✓

The opening of a novel or short story is very important because it is here that the writer must **capture the interest** of the reader and make them want to read on. A writer often begins the story by presenting important situations, characters or themes right from the start.

Here are the openings from two novels. Read them through carefully and think about what you learn from each and what **effect** is created.

You might like to think about:

- Who the narrator is.
- Which characters are introduced and what you learn about them.
- What setting or context is created.
- What you notice about the writer's style.
- Whether it makes you want to read on, and why.

It is a truth universally acknowledged, that a single man in possession of a good fortune, must be in want of a wife.

However little known the feelings or views of such a man may be on his first entering a neighbourhood, this truth is so well fixed in the minds of the surrounding families, that he is considered as the rightful property of some one or other of their daughters.

'My dear Mr Bennet,' said his lady to him one day, 'have you heard that Netherfield Park is let at last?'

Mr Bennet replied that he had not.

'But it is,' returned she; 'for Mrs Long has just been here, and she told me all about it.'

Mr Bennet made no answer.

'Do not you want to know who has taken it?' cried his wife impatiently.

'You want to tell me, and I have no objection to hearing it.'

This was invitation enough.

'Why, my dear, you must know, Mrs Long says that Netherfield is taken by a young man of large fortune from the north of England; that he came down on Monday in a chaise and four to see the place, and was so much delighted with it that he agreed with Mr Morris immediately; that he is to take possession before Michaelmas, and some of his servants are to be in the house by the end of next week.'

'What is his name?'

'Bingley.'

'Is he married or single?'

'Oh! single, my dear, to be sure! A single man of large fortune; four or five thousand a year. What a fine thing for our girls!'

'How so? How can it affect them?'

'My dear Mr Bennet,' replied his wife, 'how can you be so tiresome! You must know that I am thinking of his marrying one of them.'

From *Pride and Prejudice* by Jane Austen

1801. - I have just returned from a visit to my landlord - the solitary neighbour that I shall be troubled with. This is certainly a beautiful country! In all England, I do not believe that I could have fixed on a situation so completely removed from the stir of society. A perfect misanthropist's heaven: and Mr. Heathcliff and I are such a suitable pair to divide the desolation between us. A capital fellow! He little imagined how my heart warmed towards him when I beheld his black eyes withdraw so suspiciously under their brows, as I rode up, and when his fingers sheltered themselves, with a jealous resolution, still further in his waistcoat, as I announced my name. 'Mr. Heathcliff?' I said.

A nod was the answer.

'Mr. Lockwood, your new tenant, sir. I do myself the honour of calling as soon as possible after my arrival, to express the hope that I have not inconvenienced you by my perseverance in soliciting the occupation of Thrushcross Grange: I heard yesterday you had had some thoughts - '

'Thrushcross Grange is my own, sir,' he interrupted, wincing. 'I should not allow any one to inconvenience me, if I could hinder it - walk in!'

The 'walk in' was uttered with closed teeth, and expressed the sentiment, 'Go to the Deuce:' even the gate over which he leant manifested no sympathising movement to the words; and I think that circumstance determined me to accept the invitation: I felt interested in a man who seemed more exaggeratedly reserved than myself.

When he saw my horse's breast fairly pushing the barrier, he did put out his hand to unchain it, and then sullenly preceded me up the causeway, calling, as we entered the court, - 'Joseph, take Mr. Lockwood's horse; and bring up some wine.'

From *Wuthering Heights* by Emily Brontë

These are two very different openings but in both, the writers want to capture the readers' attention. In order to do this, various techniques are used.

> **KEY POINT**
>
> Writers use various techniques, which combine to make the openings of their stories effective.

Let's compare these techniques and the effects they create.

Pride and Prejudice	Wuthering Heights
• Austen writes in the third person and combines description, dialogue and comments from the narrator to achieve her effects. • Austen introduces key themes – the ideas of marriage and money. • Dialogue is used, which brings the scene to life and tells us something about the characters. • The reader is given background information and the beginnings of the plot through the dialogue. • The opening creates interest and makes the reader want to find out if Mrs Bennet will be successful in marrying off one of her daughters to Mr Bingley.	• The story is written in the first person and the narrator begins by setting the scene and giving details about his first encounter with Mr Heathcliff. • The date, 1801 at the opening of the chapter gives a historical context to what follows. • The narrator, Mr Lockwood, gives his initial response to Heathcliff, which is clearly of a surly, suspicious and unwelcoming character, e.g. 'I beheld his black eyes withdraw so suspiciously under their brows'. • Dialogue is used to re-create the exchange of words between Lockwood and Heathcliff and give a sense of the characters' voices and manner of speech. • The narrator gives a sense of Heathcliff's attitude through the use of adjectives, e.g. '**black** eyes', '**jealous** resolution', and adverbs, e.g. '**sullenly** preceded me'. • He gives the reader an insight into what he imagines Heathcliff to be thinking, e.g. 'The "walk in" was uttered with closed teeth, and expressed the sentiment, "Go to the Deuce:"'.

PROGRESS CHECK

1. Look at this opening. What techniques does Hardy use to create a sense of characters?

It was an eighty-cow dairy, and the troop of milkers, regular and supernumerary, were all at work; for, though the time of year was as yet but early April, the feed lay entirely in water-meadows, and the cows were 'in full pail.' The hour was about six in the evening, and three-fourths of the large, red, rectangular animals having been finished off, there was opportunity for a little conversation.

'He do bring home his bride to-morrow, I hear. They've come as far as Anglebury to-day.'

The voice seemed to proceed from the belly of the cow called Cherry, but the speaker was a milking-woman, whose face was buried in the flank of that motionless beast.

'Hav' anybody seen her?' said another.

There was a negative response from the first. 'Though they say she's a rosy-cheeked, tisty-tosty little body enough,' she added; and as the milkmaid spoke she turned her face so that she could glance past her cow's tail to the other side of the barton, where a thin, fading woman of thirty milked somewhat apart from the rest.

From *The Withered Arm* by Thomas Hardy

1. Description of the scene; Direct speech to give the reader information through the characters themselves; The use of non-standard English to create a sense of the characters' voices; A brief, initial impression of the bride as seen through the eyes of the characters.

Narrative viewpoint

AQA	E Lang	E Lit
	✓	✓

When examining your novel or short story, it is important that you establish at the start what kind of **narration** the writer has chosen. Here are two extracts from different stories.

In a few days Mr. Bingley returned Mr. Bennet's visit, and sat about ten minutes with him in his library. He had entertained hopes of being admitted to a sight of the young ladies, of whose beauty he had heard much; but he saw only the father. The ladies were somewhat more fortunate, for they had the advantage of ascertaining, from an upper window, that he wore a blue coat and rode a black horse.

An invitation to dinner was soon afterwards dispatched; and already had Mrs. Bennet planned the courses that were to do credit to her housekeeping, when an answer arrived which deferred it all. Mr. Bingley was obliged to be in town the following day, and consequently unable to accept the honour of their invitation, &c. Mrs. Bennet was quite disconcerted. She could not imagine what business he could have in town so soon after his arrival in Hertfordshire; and she began to fear that he might be always flying about from one place to another, and never settled at Netherfield as he ought to be. Lady Lucas quieted her fears a little by starting the idea of his being gone to London only to get a large party for the ball; and a report soon followed that Mr. Bingley was to bring twelve ladies and seven gentlemen with him to the assembly.

From *Pride and Prejudice* by Jane Austen

While leading the way upstairs, she recommended that I should hide the candle, and not make a noise; for her master had an odd notion about the chamber she would put me in, and never let anybody lodge there willingly. I asked the reason. She did not know, she answered: she had only lived there a year or two; and they had so many queer goings on, she could not begin to be curious.

Too stupefied to be curious myself, I fastened my door and glanced round for the bed. The whole furniture consisted of a chair, a clothes-press, and a large oak case, with squares cut out near the top resembling coach windows. Having approached this structure, I looked inside, and perceived it to be a singular sort of old-fashioned couch, very conveniently designed to obviate the necessity for every member of the family having a room to himself. In fact, it formed a little closet, and the ledge of a window, which it enclosed, served as a table. I slid back the panelled sides, got in with my light, pulled them together again, and felt secure against the vigilance of Heathcliff, and every one else.

Wuthering Heights by Emily Brontë

In the first extract, the narration is told in the third person. Jane Austen tells her story as if she is able to observe everything that is going on and how the characters behave and even feel or what they think. The narrator is all seeing and all knowing. This kind of narration is called **third person** or **omniscient narration**.

In the second extract, the narration is told in the first person. Emily Brontë tells this part of her story from the point of view of the character, Mr Lockwood, the new tenant at Thrushcross Grange. The narrator is also a character in the story and so the reader sees everything through the eyes of the character telling the story. This kind of narration is called **first person narration**.

> **KEY POINT**
>
> Different kinds of narration achieve different effects. First-person narration is more personal and the character is able to direct the reader's attention and invite them into the experience. Third-person narration can give the reader an insight into what characters are thinking and why they act as they do, but is more distanced from them.

9.3 Developing characters

LEARNING SUMMARY

After studying this section, you should be able to understand:
- how writers reveal characters
- how characters and relationships are developed

How writers reveal characters

AQA	E Lang	E Lit
	✓	✓

A good deal of the interest in a novel or short story comes from the characters that the writer creates, the things they do and the things that happen to them. We often respond to these characters as if they were people with whom we can **empathise** or who we disapprove of. However, we must remember that these characters are just that. They are the **creations** of the writers and they do not have lives outside the pages of the novel or short story. If we find the characters **convincing**, then it is the writer's skill that has made us feel like this. In studying a novel or short story, it is important to be aware of the ways in which writers **present** the characters and the methods they use to reveal them to us.

Writers can use a number of methods to present their characters:
- **Description** – writers can describe their characters, telling us what they look like, their physical appearance, how they dress, etc.
- **Dialogue** – what the characters say can give important information about a character. It is also important to take into account what other characters say about a character in building up your picture.
- **Actions** – how the characters behave and react in particular situations will contribute to your view of them.
- **Thoughts and feelings** – the writer can reveal, either through a character's own words or thoughts, or through those of the narrator, the character's innermost thoughts and feelings.
- **Imagery and symbols** – writers sometimes describe characters using metaphors or similes, or link them with something symbolically. For example, in *Wuthering Heights*, Emily Brontë often links Heathcliff with fire or the colour black, which is symbolic of his temperament.

Keep a 'log' to record key passages and quotations for each important character and build this up as you work through the text.

KEY POINT

When examining characters, look at:
- Their actions.
- What they say.
- What others say about them.
- Their relationships with other characters.
- The ways in which the writer uses language to describe and present them.

Development of characters and relationships

AQA	E Lang	E Lit
	✓	✓

One of the things you might be asked to do when studying a novel is to **explore** the way in which a character is **presented** and how they **change** and **develop** during the course of the story. In order to do this, it can help if you:
- Choose a few passages or episodes from different parts of the novel in which the character you are examining plays a key part.
- Make sure these passages show different things about the character or the way they develop.
- Look at descriptive passages, dramatic moments or episodes, for example, where the character is faced with a decision, is in conflict with others or is experiencing emotional turmoil.

> In your notes or reading log it can help if you build up a record of key moments or episodes from the novel where each of your main characters appears.

In *Lord of the Flies* by William Golding, a plane carrying schoolboys has crashed on a tropical island. No adults have survived and the boys have to survive by fending for themselves. One of the characters, Jack Merridew, quickly shows his desire to be 'chief' of the boys.

The character of Jack changes a great deal during the course of the novel, moving from a rather surly schoolboy to a savage, prepared to kill others. Here are some of the key moments illustrating this change.

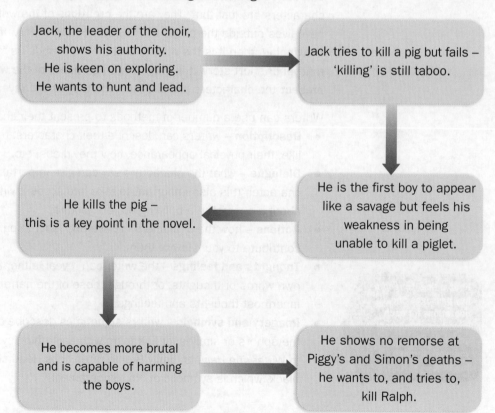

Jack, the leader of the choir, shows his authority.
He is keen on exploring.
He wants to hunt and lead.

Jack tries to kill a pig but fails – 'killing' is still taboo.

He is the first boy to appear like a savage but feels his weakness in being unable to kill a piglet.

He kills the pig – this is a key point in the novel.

He becomes more brutal and is capable of harming the boys.

He shows no remorse at Piggy's and Simon's deaths – he wants to, and tries to, kill Ralph.

Now let's look at how Golding presents this character at various points in the novel. Here is the point where we first meet Jack.

> Their bodies, from throat to ankle, were hidden by black cloaks which bore a long silver cross on the left breast and each neck was finished off with a hambone frill. The heat of the tropics, the descent, the search for food, and now this sweaty march along the blazing beach had given them the complexions of newly washed plums. The boy who controlled them was dressed in the same way though his cap badge was golden. When his party was about ten yards from the platform he shouted an order and they halted, gasping, sweating, swaying in the fierce light. The boy himself came forward, vaulted on to the platform with his cloak flying, and peered into what to him was almost complete darkness.
>
> "Where's the man with the trumpet?"
>
> Ralph, sensing his sun-blindness, answered him.
>
> "There's no man with a trumpet. Only me."
>
> The boy came close and peered down at Ralph, screwing up his face as he did so. What he saw of the fair-haired boy with the creamy shell on his knees did not seem to satisfy him. He turned quickly, his black cloak circling.
>
> "Isn't there a ship, then?"
>
> Inside the floating cloak he was tall, thin, and bony: and his hair was red beneath the black cap. His face was crumpled and freckled, and ugly without silliness. Out of this face stared two light blue eyes, frustrated now, and turning, or ready to turn, to anger.
>
> "Isn't there a man here?"
> Ralph spoke to his back.
> "No we're having a meeting. Come and join in."
> The group of cloaked boys began to scatter from close line. The tall boy shouted at them.
> "Choir! Stand still!"
>
> From *Lord of the Flies* by William Golding

Golding marks Jack out as being different from the others by making him stand out. They are all dressed in black (which gives a menacing feel) but Jack stands out from the others with his golden cap badge which indicates his authority.

Golding also tells us that Jack is the one who controls them, although he is only referred to as 'the boy' here, which adds mystery to his character.

The dialogue reveals Jack's authority. When Jack speaks, we can see his commanding attitude through the sharp questions he fires at Ralph and his shouted order 'Choir! Stand still!'.

Other features are mentioned which also indicate Jack's power and violent potential, e.g. 'ready to turn, to anger'.

Now look at this next passage, from later in the novel, where Jack kills a pig.

> Jack was on top of the sow, stabbing downward with his knife. Roger found a lodgement for his point and began to push till he was leaning with his whole weight. The spear moved forward inch by inch and the terrified squealing became a high-pitched scream. Then Jack found the throat and the hot blood spouted over his hands. The sow collapsed under them and they were heavy and fulfilled upon her. The butterflies still danced, preoccupied in the centre of the clearing.
>
> At last the immediacy of the kill subsided. The boys drew back, and Jack stood up, holding out his hands.
>
> "Look."
>
> He giggled and flinked them while the boys laughed at his reeking palms. Then Jack grabbed Maurice and rubbed the stuff over his cheeks. Roger began to withdraw his spear and the boys noticed it for the first time. Robert stabilized the thing in a phrase which was received uproariously.
>
> "Right up her ass!"
>
> "Did you hear?"
>
> "Did you hear what he said?"
>
> "Right up her ass!"
>
> This time Robert and Maurice acted the two parts; and Maurice's acting of the pig's efforts to avoid the advancing spear was so funny that the boys cried with laughter.
>
> At length even this palled. Jack began to clean his bloody hands on the rock. Then he started work on the sow and paunched her, lugging out the hot bags of coloured guts, pushing them into a pile on the rock while the others watched him. He talked as he worked.
>
> From *Lord of the Flies* by William Golding

By now, Jack's character has developed.

Jack takes the lead role in killing the sow – 'Jack was on top of the sow'. The vivid description of him 'stabbing downward with his knife' gives an impression of the violence he is capable of. This is further emphasised by the fact that it is Jack who cuts the pig's throat and 'the hot blood spouted over his hands'.

Afterwards, the description of Jack holding out his blood-covered hands as he 'giggled and flinked them' suggests that he is excited and is revelling in the killing and the blood, perhaps even showing off. He then wipes the blood on Maurice's cheeks, suggesting that he is performing a kind of ritual.

The relaxed way in which he pulls out the guts of the pig indicates that he is not squeamish in any way about killing. The simple sentence at the end of this extract also stresses his nonchalant attitude towards killing.

In this final extract from near the end of the novel, Jack's descent into savagery is complete as he tries to kill Ralph.

> The rock struck Piggy a glancing blow from chin to knee; the conch exploded into a thousand white fragments and ceased to exist. Piggy, saying nothing, with no time for even a grunt, travelled through the air sideways from the rock, turning sideways as he went. The rock bounded twice and was lost in the forest. Piggy fell forty feet and landed on his back across that square, red rock in the sea. His head opened and stuff came out and turned red. Piggy's arms and legs twitched a bit, like a pig's after it has been killed. Then the sea breathed again in a long slow sigh, the water boiled white and pink over the rock; and when it went, sucking back again, the body of Piggy was gone.
>
> This time the silence was complete. Ralph's lips formed a word but no sound came.
>
> Suddenly Jack bounded out from the tribe and began screaming wildly.
>
> "See? See? That's what you'll get! I meant that! There isn't a tribe for you any more! The conch is gone –"
>
> He ran forward, stooping.
>
> "I'm Chief!"
>
> Viciously, with full intention, he hurled his spear at Ralph. The point tore the skin and flesh over Ralph's ribs, then sheared off and fell in the water. Ralph stumbled, feeling not pain but panic and the tribe, screaming now like the Chief, began to advance. Another spear, a bent one that would not fly straight, went past his face and one fell from on high where Roger was. The twins lay hidden behind the tribe and the anonymous devils' faces swarmed across the neck. Ralph turned and ran. A great noise as of sea-gulls rose behind him. He obeyed an instinct that he did not know he possessed and swerved over the open space so that the spear went wide. He saw the headless body of the sow and jumped in time. Then he was crashing through foliage and small boughs and was hidden by the forest.
>
> From *Lord of the Flies* by William Golding

Golding creates a striking presentation of Jack here. The death of Piggy is a symbol that all the restraining influences of 'civilised' behaviour have gone. Immediately, Jack 'bounded out' and 'began screaming wildly', which gives the impression that he is excited by Piggy's death and is out of control. The use of the adverbs 'wildly' and 'viciously' and the verb 'stooping' imply Jack's animalistic behaviour. His threats confirm that he has lost all restraint and is now dangerous, e.g. 'See? See? That's what you'll get!'. The sense of threat is confirmed as he 'viciously' throws the spear at Ralph and injures him.

The emphasis on the word 'Chief' and the fact that from now on Golding refers to Jack as 'the Chief' shows that his dominance is now complete.

> **KEY POINT**
>
> When writing about a character, focus on specific details from the text that show important aspects of that character and the ways in which he / she develops.

9.4 Setting and context

> **LEARNING SUMMARY**
>
> **After studying this section, you should be able to understand:**
> - the importance of setting and context
> - how writers create atmosphere

Setting and context

AQA | E Lang ✓ | E Lit ✓

The imaginary 'world' within which a novel or short story is set can be an important element for several reasons:

- It forms the backdrop against which the action of the story takes place.
- It can be closely linked to the characters and experiences, and can reflect these.
- It can perform a symbolic function to develop ideas the writer wants to put across to the reader.
- It can present a world in which a character is a misfit, or a world with which he or she is in conflict.

For example, *To Kill a Mockingbird* by Harper Lee is set in Maycomb, a small town in the deep south of the USA during the great Depression of the 1930s. Here is how Harper Lee describes the setting seen through the eyes of the novel's narrator and central character, the young girl, Scout.

> Maycomb was an old town, but it was a tired old town when I first knew it. In rainy weather the streets turned to red slop; grass grew on the sidewalks, the court-house sagged in the square. Somehow, it was hotter then; a black dog suffered on a summer's day; bony mules hitched to Hoover carts flicked flies in the sweltering shade of the live oaks on the square. Men's stiff collars wilted by nine in the morning. Ladies bathed before noon, after their three o'clock naps, and by nightfall were like soft teacakes with frostings of sweat and sweet talcum.
>
> From *To Kill a Mockingbird* by Harper Lee

Think about the aspects of the setting that are shown in this short extract. Here are some points you might have noticed:

- The town is described as 'a tired old town', giving the impression that it is, perhaps, shabby and has seen better days.
- This impression is developed further with a vivid description of the streets turning to mud after rain, the grass growing on the sidewalks and the court-house that 'sagged' in the square.
- Alliteration is used to emphasise the descriptions of the setting, e.g. 'grass grew', 'sagged in the square'.
- It is set in a time when people still used mules to pull carts.
- The weather is very hot, and this is emphasised by adjectives such as 'sweltering', the comparative 'hotter', and the simile describing the ladies as being 'like soft teacakes with frostings of sweat and sweet talcum'.

In Emily Brontë's *Wuthering Heights* the **social and historical context** within which the novel is set is an important element in the setting. In this extract, Mr Earnshaw returns home with an orphan he has found on the streets of Liverpool.

It seemed a long while to us all - the three days of his absence - and often did little Cathy ask when he would be home. Mrs. Earnshaw expected him by supper-time on the third evening, and she put the meal off hour after hour; there were no signs of his coming, however, and at last the children got tired of running down to the gate to look. Then it grew dark; she would have had them to bed, but they begged sadly to be allowed to stay up; and, just about eleven o'clock, the door-latch was raised quietly, and in stepped the master. He threw himself into a chair, laughing and groaning, and bid them all stand off, for he was nearly killed - he would not have such another walk for the three kingdoms. 'And at the end of it to be flighted to death!' he said, opening his great-coat, which he held bundled up in his arms. 'See here, wife! I was never so beaten with anything in my life: but you must e'en take it as a gift of God; though it's as dark almost as if it came from the devil.'

We crowded round, and over Miss Cathy's head I had a peep at a dirty, ragged, black-haired child; big enough both to walk and talk: indeed, its face looked older than Catherine's; yet when it was set on its feet, it only stared round, and repeated over and over again some gibberish that nobody could understand. I was frightened, and Mrs. Earnshaw was ready to fling it out of doors: she did fly up, asking how he could fashion to bring that gypsy brat into the house, when they had their own bairns to feed and fend for? What he meant to do with it, and whether he were mad? The master tried to explain the matter; but he was really half dead with fatigue, and all that I could make out, amongst her scolding, was a tale of his seeing it starving, and houseless, and as good as dumb, in the streets of Liverpool, where he picked it up and inquired for its owner. Not a soul knew to whom it belonged, he said; and his money and time being both limited, he thought it better to take it home with him at once, than run into vain expenses there: because he was determined he would not leave it as he found it. Well, the conclusion was, that my mistress grumbled herself calm; and Mr. Earnshaw told me to wash it, and give it clean things, and let it sleep with the children.

From *Wuthering Heights* by Emily Brontë

PROGRESS CHECK

1 What do you learn from this extract about the social and historical context in which the novel was written?

1. • Orphan children lived on the streets in the cities.
    • No one knew or cared where the child had come from or where his parents were.
    • When Mr Earnshaw found the child he was 'half dead with fatigue' and starving.
    • The society of the time had no formal structure in place to care for such homeless children.
    • Mrs Earnshaw's apparently hard-hearted response to her husband bringing the child home was, perhaps, typical of the attitude that many people at that time would have had in that situation.

KEY POINT

The setting of a novel or short story is important and often links with a story's themes and ideas.

Creating atmosphere

AQA   E Lang ✓   E Lit ✓

Closely associated with the setting of a novel or short story is the **atmosphere** that a writer creates. In order to create a sense of atmosphere, writers often use **description**. In studying your own novel or story, you need to be aware of how writers use language to create a particular atmosphere.

Look carefully at the following extract from *Great Expectations* by Charles Dickens.

> Ours was the marsh country, down by the river, within, as the river wound, twenty miles of the sea. My first most vivid and broad impression of the identity of things, seems to me to have been gained on a memorable raw afternoon towards evening. At such a time I found out for certain, that this bleak place overgrown with the nettles was the churchyard; and that Philip Pirrip, late of this parish, and also Georgina wife of the above, were dead and buried; and that Alexander, Batholomew, Abraham, Tobias and Roger, infant children of the aforesaid, were also dead and buried; and that the dark flat wilderness beyond the churchyard, intersected with dykes and mounds and gates, with scattered cattle feeding on it, was the marshes; and that the low leaden line beyond, was the river; and that the distant savage lair from which the wind was rushing, was the sea; and that the small bundle of shivers growing afraid of it all and beginning to cry was Pip.
>
> "Hold your noise'" cried a terrible voice, as a man started up horn among the graves at the side of the church porch. "Keep still, you little devil, or I'll cut your throat"
>
> A fearful man, all in coarse grey, with a great iron on his leg. A man with no hat, and with broken shoes, and with an old rag tied round his head. A man who had been soaked in water and smothered in mud, and lamed by stones, and cut by flints, and stung by nettles and torn by briars: who limped, and shivered and glared and growled: and whose teeth chattered in his head as he seized me by the chin.
>
> "O! Don't cut my throat, sir," I pleaded in terror. "Pray don't do it, sir."
>
> From *Great Expectations* by Charles Dickens

Here Dickens creates a sense of the bleakness and isolation of the marshes coupled with a feeling of danger and Pip's fear.

Dickens creates this atmosphere through his use of language. For example:

- The vastness of the marsh country as the river 'wound, twenty miles of the sea'.
- Pip's personal memory of 'raw afternoons' giving a sense of cold bleakness.
- The description of the churchyard as a 'bleak place overgrown with nettles'.
- The references to the dead buried in the graveyard.
- The description of the sea as 'the distant savage lair from which the wind was rushing'.
- The description of Pip as a 'small bundle of shivers growing afraid of it all'.
- The use of direct speech and the threatening language of the man.
- The detailed description of the appearance of the man.
- The use of repeated sentence structures helps to build up tension, e.g. 'A fearful man…', 'A man with no hat…', 'A man who had been soaked in water…'.
- The long sentence in the first paragraph of the extract, consisting of a number of descriptions separated by semi-colons, also helps to create a tense atmosphere.

All these **descriptions** and **images** work together to create an atmosphere of fear, threat and danger.

> **KEY POINT**
>
> When writing about your text, make sure that you use specific examples with comments on their effects to illustrate how a writer uses language to create a sense of atmosphere.

9.5 Exploring themes

LEARNING SUMMARY

After studying this section, you should be able to understand:
- why themes are important
- how to approach the study of themes in a text

Why themes are important

AQA
| E Lang | E Lit |
| ✓ | ✓ |

Novels and short stories often do more than simply 'tell a story'. Writers use their 'stories' to **explore** particular **themes** and **ideas** and to present ideas on them.

When we talk about a **theme** we are really talking about the idea that lies behind the story as a whole and which the writer is interested in developing through the story. Often, novels contain several themes and the writer uses the story to make the reader think about these ideas or to put particular **messages** across to the reader.

For example, *Pride and Prejudice* explores a number of themes, which include:
- Attitudes to money.
- Society and class.
- Marriage.
- Social conventions.

Through her novel, Jane Austen explores all of these things, presenting the reader with characters and situations that show different views and ideas towards them.

> **KEY POINT**
>
> Be aware of the themes and ideas that are explored in the text you are studying. What message is the writer trying to put across?

Approaching the study of themes

AQA
| E Lang | E Lit |
| ✓ | ✓ |

When studying your novel or story it is a good idea to make a list of the main ideas or themes in the book. It can help you sort out your ideas in your mind if you draw a **diagram** or a **pattern note** (sometimes called mapping or a spidergram) that summarises each theme.

Here is one student's summary of the themes in *To Kill a Mockingbird* by Harper Lee.

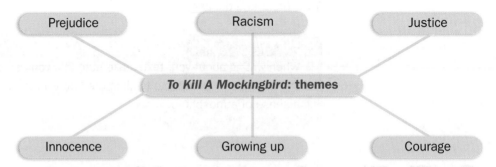

Having decided on the key themes in the text, you now need to think about each of them in turn, how each relates to the main storyline and what ideas the writer is exploring. Again, it can be useful to **summarise** your ideas in a pattern note.

Here are the student's notes on the theme of prejudice.

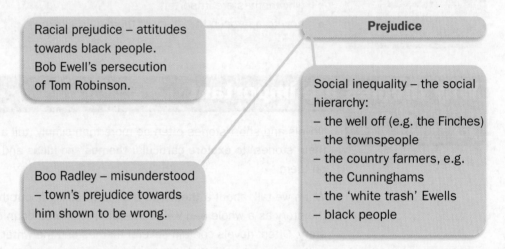

It can help if you include page references with your notes so that you can find particular sections easily.

Using your summary, you can now make more detailed notes on each theme. Make sure you include specific examples to support your points and make sure that you comment on them. Just quoting without commenting on what the quote shows is not helpful. Make sure that you do not use lots of long quotations though – they should be **short** and **to the point**.

Sample GCSE question

This is part of a longer response to this element of the set task.

How does Harper Lee present adults through Scout's eyes in *To Kill a Mockingbird*? You should write about TWO adults in your answer.

Harper Lee's presentation of adults through Scout's eyes shows that adults are a hugely varied people, who, in many cases, should be respected despite the fact that they can be flawed; Scout, of course, has a simplified child's view of the world.

Atticus is by far the most important character in the book as he is the adult by which Scout measures all others. Atticus is Scout and Jem's father, and in the very first chapter Scout describes him as a 'satisfactory' parent as, 'He played with us, read to us and treated us with courteous detachment'. His attitude to his children is, for the period, very liberal - a trait that the other adults of Maycomb find unusual. Atticus is, however, considered by most of his neighbours to be the 'gentleman' of Maycomb, going out of his way to aid those in trouble, a virtue that he tries to teach Scout, along with diplomacy, as it is a better way than fighting to resolve problems.

Atticus is also a humble character, a virtue that is dramatically shown when a rabid dog lurches into town and even though Atticus is the best marksman and doesn't own a gun, the townspeople of Maycomb go to him with their guns and request that he shoot the dog. Atticus's humility over his talent is so great that even his children didn't know of his ability with a gun. In the end it's one of the neighbours who tells them, '...didn't you know his nickname was 'Ol One Shot' when he was a boy? Why, down at the Landing when he was coming up, if he shot fifteen times and hit fourteen doves he'd complain about wasting ammunition.'

Maycomb's admiration for Atticus is as strong as the townspeople's suspicion and fear of the novel's other significant character, Boo Radley.

To Scout and her brother Jem, Boo Radley is a source of both fear and fascination. The mystery often overruns their imaginations to create images and exaggerations like, 'Inside the house lived a malevolent phantom.'

The fascination comes from his uniqueness in Maycomb's society, as he is a recluse and has strange and sometimes abusive relatives. Scout and Jem's fear stems from the example of the adults of Maycomb's misplaced fear, as they attribute anything that goes wrong to be of his doing even when the facts are to the contrary. For example, they believed he mutilated cats and chickens even after another man was caught and admitted to the crime. They even go so far as to believe that when the azaleas freeze in bad weather it is because he has breathed on them and that when his pecan trees shake their fruit into the school yard the nuts should lay untouched by the children as Radley pecans will kill you. All of this fear stems from their fear of the unknown and their inability to understand why he would live his life the way he does.

Good introductory paragraph focused on the question and indicating Scout's view of things.

Identification of the importance of Atticus and his influence on Scout.

Illustrates some of Atticus's qualities although has drifted from focus on how he is seen through Scout's eyes.

Quotation to support previous point.

Comments on admiration for Atticus and then moves on to another character, Boo Radley.

Comments on Scout and Jem's view of Boo Radley.

Expands and develops ideas about why Scout and Jem fear Boo Radley.

Highlights how Scout is influenced by the stories about Boo in the town and how she cannot understand, from her viewpoint as a child, why he lives as he does.

Practice questions

Jane Austen: *Pride and Prejudice*

1 Compare the relationship between Elizabeth and Darcy, and Jane and Bingley. How well matched do you think the couples are?

(External exam question: English Literature, Unit 1)

Emily Brontë: *Wuthering Heights*

2 Heathcliff and Edgar are very different characters.
Compare Brontë's presentation of these two characters.

(External exam question: English Literature, Unit 1)

William Golding: *Lord of the Flies*

3 Explore Golding's presentation of Jack in *Lord of the Flies*. What is the importance of his role in the novel?

You should look carefully at language and actions in your answer.

(External exam question: English Literature, Unit 1)

10 Studying poetry

The following topics are covered in this chapter:

- **Reading poetry**
- **Features of poetry**
- **Poetry in context**
- **Comparing poems**

10.1 Reading poetry

LEARNING SUMMARY

After studying this section, you should be able to understand:

- how to get the most out of reading poetry
- how to approach studying a poem

Reading poetry

AQA E Lang ✓ E Lit ✓

You will need to study a range of poetry, both from the English Literary Heritage, and contemporary poetry.

> Your study will focus mainly on the poems in the AQA Anthology *Moon on The Tides*. But remember that in the exam you will also have to answer a question on an unseen poem.

The first thing to recognise about poetry is that it comes in many **different forms** and it can be about any topic you can think of. Your work for GCSE will involve studying specific poems in some detail, but you can do a number of things to help you prepare for your poetry study. Here are some ideas:

- **Read** as many poems as you can to get a feel of the different forms that poetry can take and the ways in which poets use language in different ways to explore their ideas.
- Keep a **reading 'log'** and make a **note** of any interesting ideas, images, etc. that strike you as particularly effective.
- Read poems **aloud** (in the privacy of your own room if you prefer). Reading a poem aloud can often help you to understand it better and can also help you to get a feel of the **rhythm** and/or **rhyme** pattern.
- Ask yourself **questions** about the poems you read. These three questions are very important ones:
  - **What** is the poem about?
  - **How** does the poet use language in the poem?
  - **Why** does the poet use language in this way – why do they structure the poem in a particular way and what effect does he or she want to create?

This means that you will consider:

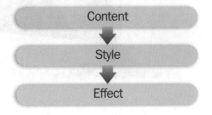

Content

↓

Style

↓

Effect

10 Studying poetry

PROGRESS CHECK

1 What three questions should you ask yourself when studying a poem?

1. • What is the poem about?
   • How does the poet use language in the poem?
   • Why does the poet use language in this way?

Studying poems

AQA — E Lang ✓ E Lit ✓

When studying specific poems as part of your course, it is important that you are clear in your mind what you are doing and what you want to achieve.

Having a **planned** approach to studying your poems can help you.

Here is a way of doing this:

Read the poem through carefully several times (aloud if possible).

↓

Write down your initial responses to it, making a note of any ideas that come into your head.

↓

Write down your thoughts about the subject or theme of the poem.

↓

Make a note of the ways in which the poet uses language, e.g. the vocabulary, metaphors, similes and images of the poem.

↓

Describe what kind of tone or atmosphere the poem has and how this is created.

↓

Make a note of other effects created in the poem, e.g. rhyme, rhythm, alliteration, onomatopoeia.

↓

Sum up your ideas about the poem and how the poem 'works' as a whole.

148

10.2 Features of poetry

LEARNING SUMMARY	**After studying this section, you should be able to understand:**
	• how poets create tone, mood and atmosphere
	• what imagery is and how poets use it
	• how rhyme and rhythm can affect a poem

Tone, mood and atmosphere

AQA	E Lang	E Lit
	✓	✓

The ideas of **tone** and **mood** are closely linked to the '**voice**' of the poem, in that it is the speaker's tone – whether it be happy, melancholy, bitter, regretful, angry, meditative, etc. – that creates a sense of the mood or atmosphere a poem establishes.

The tone, mood and atmosphere of a poem are the products of many factors, such as:

- The poet's choice of words.
- The imagery used.
- The rhyme and rhythm patterns established.
- The sound effects created through features such as alliteration and onomatopoeia.
- The context or situation the poem describes.

Now look at the following two poems. Both are concerned with the idea of death but the mood, tone and atmosphere created in each are very different.

In *On My First Sonne* Jonson confronts the idea of his son's death. Read the poem carefully.

On My First Sonne

Farewell, thou child of my right hand, and joy;
My sinne was too much hope of thee, lov'd boy,
Seven yeeres tho'wert lent to me, and I thee pay,
Exacted by thy fate, on the just day.
O, could I loose all father, now. For why
Will man lament the state he should envie?
To have so soone scap'd worlds, and fleshes rage,
And, if no other miserie, yet age?
Rest in soft peace, and ask'd say here doth lye
Ben Jonson his best piece of poetrie.
For whose sake, hence-forth, all his vowes be such,
As what he loves may never like too much.

Ben Jonson

In *Mid-Term Break*, Seamus Heaney writes about the death of his younger brother, who died at a young age as the result of a road accident. Read this poem (on the following page).

Mid-Term Break

I sat all morning in the college sick bay
Counting bells knelling classes to a close.
At two o'clock our neighbours drove me home.

In the porch I met my father crying –
He had always taken funerals in his stride –
And Big Jim Evans saying it was a hard blow.

The baby cooed and laughed and rocked the pram
When I came in, and I was embarrassed
By old men standing up to shake my hand

And tell me they were "sorry for my trouble".
Whispers informed strangers I was the eldest,
Away at school, as my mother held my hand

In hers and coughed out angry tearless sighs.
At ten o'clock the ambulance arrived
With the corpse, stanched and bandaged by the nurses.

Next morning I went up into the room. Snowdrops
And candles soothed the bedside; I saw him
For the first time in six weeks. Paler now,

Wearing a poppy bruise on his left temple,
He lay in the four foot box as in his cot.
No gaudy scars, the bumper knocked him clear.

A four foot box, a foot for every year.

Seamus Heaney

Think about how these two poems differ in terms of the tone, mood and atmosphere created.

Here are some examples of **how** the poets have created tone, mood and atmosphere in these poems. (There are many other techniques used in the poems too.)

Both *On My First Sonne* and *Mid-Term Break* have a tone of sadness, but *On My First Sonne* has a more 'accepting' tone than *Mid-Term Break*, which has an undercurrent of anger and frustration. Both poems are very personal, and both express the poets' feelings and their attempts to come to terms with the tragic deaths. Heaney uses the first person in *Mid-Term Break* to recount his brother's death, whilst Jonson uses the second person to speak directly to his son.

On My First Sonne:
- The poem is written in the form of an **elegy** (i.e. a song or poem of mourning), which immediately produces a mood of sadness.
- **Religious imagery** is used, e.g. 'child of my right hand', which might emphasise the boy's innocence.
- The diction is sometimes religious and accepting, e.g. 'sinne', 'just', but it is sometimes quite angry, e.g. 'rage', 'miserie'. This results in changes to the tone throughout the poem and reflects the poet's changing mood as he tries to come to terms with his son's death.
- The poem is written in **rhyming couplets**, imposing a pattern on the poem that contains the poet's grief.

- The **rhetorical questions** in the middle of the poem seem to represent the poet's grief and give a tone of confusion about why his son died.

Mid-Term Break:
- The sad mood of the poem is immediately signalled by the reference to *'bells knelling'*, which has **connotations** of death and funerals.
- The image of the father crying emphasises the intensity of the grief.
- **Enjambment** is used (the lines run on), which highlights that the grief and suffering are continuous.
- The poem has eight stanzas, all of which follow a pattern of three lines, except for the last stanza, which is just one line. This helps to stress the information in the poem and ensures that the poem ends with a tone of sadness.
- The poem is written simply, almost in a conversational manner, perhaps to convey the simplicity of life and death.
- The tone of the poem is not evoked through emotive words; it is evoked through the direct description of events.
- The ending of the poem and the revelation that his brother was only four years old comes as a shock, and the **alliteration** and **assonance** used here help to give a final emphasis of this tragic death.

> **KEY POINT**
>
> When writing about how poets create particular moods or atmospheres, always use specific details from the poems and analyse the effects they have on the reader.

Imagery

AQA   E Lang ✓   E Lit ✓

Poets often use **imagery** in their poems. Imagery is where language is used in such a way as to help us form a kind of 'mental picture' of the thing that is being described or the idea that is being explored.

Images can work in a number of ways. For example, a poet can literally describe something, as Mary Ann Evans does at the beginning of her poem, *In a London Drawing-room*:

'The sky is cloudy, yellowed by the smoke.
For view there are the houses opposite
Cutting the sky with one long line of wall'

In this example, Evans describes what she can see literally and so this is called a **'literal image'**. However, sometimes the thing that is being described is compared to something else in order to make the description more vivid. This kind of imagery is called **'figurative'**. Figurative imagery includes similes, metaphors and personification.

Similes

You can spot **similes** easily because they usually make the **comparison** quite clear, often by using the words 'like' or 'as'. For example, in *In a London Drawing-room*, Evans continues her description using a simile:

'Cutting the sky with one long line of wall
Like a solid fog.'

Here she uses the simile of the fog to emphasise how the wall cuts out the light of the sky – like a *'solid fog'* would do.

Metaphors

Metaphors are very similar to similes in that they also create a comparison, but instead of saying something is 'like' or 'as' something, it actually says it *is* that thing.

For example, in his **sonnet**, *Upon Westminster Bridge*, William Wordsworth describes London, which can be seen as the 'heart' of the country, early in a morning saying, *'And all that mighty heart is lying still'*. Obviously, the city isn't literally a 'heart' but Wordsworth is using a metaphor to describe it.

Personification

Another form of imagery is personification. This is created through the technique of attributing human qualities or feelings to something that is not human.

In his poem, *Futility*, Wilfred Owen uses metaphors and personification to create his effects. Read the poem through carefully.

Futility

Move him into the sun –
Gently its touch awoke him once,
At home, whispering of fields unsown.
Always it woke him, even in France,
Until this morning and this snow.
If anything might rouse him now
The kind old sun will know.
Think how it wakes the seeds, –
Woke, once, the clays of a cold star.
Are limbs, so dear-achieved, are sides,
Full-nerved – still warm – too hard to stir?
Was it for this the clay grew tall?
– O what made fatuous sunbeams toil
To break earth's sleep at all?

Wilfred Owen

In this poem, the sun is personified as if it is a living being that the poet feels might still have the power to restore life to the dead soldier.

The poet remembers how the sun has always woken the young man both at home in England and even in France where he has been fighting – until this morning. If anything can rouse the soldier 'The kind old sun will know'. Even the power of the sun, of course, cannot restore life to the dead soldier and the poem ends with another example of personification, in which the sunbeams are described as living things that have given life but to no purpose – just to see it wasted in this way.

Aural imagery

Apart from images created through words, poets often make use of images that are created through **sound**.

Alliteration involves the **repetition** of the same consonant **sound**, usually at the beginning of each word. For example, in Gerard Manley Hopkins's poem *The Windhover* he describes a kestrel hovering:

'I caught this morning morning's minion, kingdom of daylight's dauphin, dapple-down-drawn Falcon,'

Here, he uses alliteration of the 'm' and 'd' sounds.

Sometimes the alliteration can come at the end of words too, as in the line from another of Hopkins's poems *Spring*:

'When weeds, in wheels, shoot long and lovely and 'lush','

Here the 'w', 'l' and 'sh' sounds are alliterated, which adds a softness – a peacefulness – to the poem, and allows the line to flow smoothly.

Students generally find alliteration easy to spot in a poem but the main thing is to be able to describe its effects, and this can be more difficult. There are certain things to look out for:
- The way that alliteration can help to affect and create the **tone** within a poem.
- The way that its regularity or irregularity can affect rhythm.

Assonance is another kind of **aural** device involving **repetitions**. This time the repetition is of a **vowel sound** and again it is used to create a particular effect in a poem. For example, D.H. Lawrence uses it in his poem *Storm in the Black Forest*:

*'Now it is almost night, from the bronzey soft sky
Jugfull after jugfull of pure white liquid fire, bright white.'*

The poem moves from the heavy 'o' sounds of 'bronzey soft sky' to the short sharp sound of the 'i' in 'liquid fire, bright white'. So, from the still, heavy sky the lightning strikes and the atmosphere changes with the change in sound.

Onomatopoeia is another kind of aural device in which the actual sounds of words reflect their meanings. Simple examples would be words like 'bang' or 'crash'. However, poets often use this device in more complex ways. Here, Wilfred Owen uses onomatopoeia to create a sense of the sound of gunfire in *Anthem for Doomed Youth*:

*'Only the monstrous anger of the guns.
Only the stuttering rifles' rapid rattle
Can patter out their hasty orisons'*

You might have noticed some alliteration here too.

> **KEY POINT**
>
> The important thing is not to simply 'spot' features but to be able to explain and comment on the effects they create in a poem and what they contribute towards its overall effectiveness.

Rhyme and rhythm

	E Lang	E Lit
AQA	✓	✓

Rhyme

Rhyme can make an important contribution to the overall **impact** of a poem. Rhyme is such a strong feature of poetry that often people expect poems to rhyme, even though many do not. Like several of the other features that we have

In writing about the use of rhyme in a poem, you must comment on the effects it creates.

looked at, rhyme is quite easy to spot but it is rather more difficult to explain its effect on a poem. In order to establish this, each poem needs to be looked at individually.

Here are some possible effects to look for:
- The sound effects created, for example, a 'musical' quality; a jarring, discordant effect.
- The emphasis that it places on certain words, giving them a prominence.
- It draws lines and stanzas together, linking ideas and images.
- It creates a pattern.
- It can give a sense of ending or finality – for example, the rhyming couplet is often used to give a sense of ending as in Shakespeare's *Sonnet XVIII*:
  'So long as men can breathe or eyes can see,
  So long lives this, and this gives life to thee.'

A.E. Housman, in his poem *With Rue my Heart is Laden,* uses a straightforward rhyme scheme:

With rue my heart is laden	A
For golden friends I had,	B
For many a rose-lipt maiden	A
And man a lightfood lad.	B
By brooks too broad for leaping	C
The lightfoot boys are laid;	D
The rose-lipt girls are sleeping	C
In fields where roses fade.	D

Here, Housman uses an ABAB, CDCD rhyme scheme, in that alternate lines rhyme.

PROGRESS CHECK

1 What effect do you think the ABAB, CDCD rhyme scheme has on Housman's poem?

1. It is simple and straightforward, suited to the simple message of the poem. It also creates a cyclical pattern that reflects the events of the poem.

Rhythm

Another kind of pattern in poetry can be created through the **rhythm**, which consists of **patterns** of recurring **stresses** and **pauses**. The rhythm in a poem is, perhaps, more difficult to identify than some of the other features we have looked at. Often, it helps to read the poem aloud in order to get a feel for the rhythm pattern.

Look back at pages 149–150 and re-read *On My First Sonne* and *Mid-Term Break* and note how the very different rhythm patterns affect the poems.

KEY POINT

The rhythm pattern of a poem has an important influence on the overall effect the poem creates.

10.3 Poetry in context

After studying this section, you should be able to understand:

- social, cultural and historical contexts
- how to approach poems from the Literary Heritage
- how to approach contemporary poems
- how to approach poetry from different cultures and traditions

Social, cultural and historical contexts

AQA — E Lang ✓ E Lit ✓

In studying AQA English Literature, one of the things you must do is relate texts to their social, cultural and historical contexts and literary traditions. To understand this, it is important to recognise that texts, such as poems, are not created in a vacuum but are the product of many influences that affect the ways in which writers write and the ways in which we read and interpret their work. Becoming aware of this background information can help you to understand and appreciate the poetry texts you read, and help you form your responses more effectively.

> Although any or all of these features can be important when writing about a poem, the poem itself should be at the centre of your discussion. Students often go wrong by writing more about the historical background or the life of the poet than about the poem itself.

The social, historical and cultural contexts can consist of a variety of factors. Here are some things you could consider in placing a text in 'context':

- The life or biography of the poet.
- Other works that the poet has written.
- The historical period in which the poem was written.
- The place or event that gave rise to the poem.
- The ways in which the language used in the poem reflects the period in which it was written.
- The particular culture within which the poem was written.
- The social background of the poet, or the theme or setting of the poem.

Poems from the Literary Heritage

AQA — E Lang ✓ E Lit ✓

Generally speaking, poems considered to be representative of the 'literary heritage' of England, Wales or Ireland were written some time ago and are considered to have been influential and significant over time. Obviously, such poems can cover a very wide range of poetic styles, encompassing the work of Chaucer written in the 13th Century, and poems written in the 20th Century, such as those of Wilfred Owen, Dylan Thomas or Ted Hughes.

There is a huge variety of poetry covered by the period and so it is very difficult to generalise about the features you might encounter. However, in studying some poetry written in an earlier period than our own you might find some of the following:

- Some of the **language** used might be **archaic** (old-fashioned words and phrases that we don't use anymore) so you might have to look up the meanings of particular words. The language of Chaucer is an obvious example of this.
- The poem might be to do with **ideas** or **themes** that we no longer relate to in our own time.

- The poem might contain **references** that meant something to the reader at the time the poem was written, but which you now need to look up to fully understand.
- The **style** in which the poet writes might be unfamiliar to you today.

Some of these factors could apply to modern poetry too, but you are more likely to encounter them in poetry that was written some time in the past.

> **KEY POINT**
>
> You sometimes need to work at a poem in order to begin to develop an understanding of it.

Read the following two verses from the poem, *The Affliction of Margaret* by William Wordsworth, written in 1807.

From **The Affliction of Margaret**

Where art thou, my beloved Son,
Where art thou, worse to me than dead?
Oh find me, prosperous or undone!
Or, if the grave be now thy bed,
Why am I ignorant of the same
That I may rest; and neither blame
Nor sorrow may attend thy name?

Seven years, alas! to have received
No tidings of an only child;
To have despaired, have hoped, believed,
And been for evermore beguiled, -
Sometimes with thoughts of very bliss!
I catch at them, and then I miss;
Was ever darkness like to this?

William Wordsworth

What is immediately striking about Wordsworth's language is that some of the words used are quite different to our modern language. For example, words such as 'art' and 'thou' are used where we would now use 'are' and 'you'. However, most of the words are the same as those we would use today, for example, 'son', 'dead', 'ignorant'.

The context of this poem is a woman who hasn't heard from her son in seven years and does not know whether he is alive or dead. This is a situation that we can still relate to today, although the experience was far more common then than now.

To His Coy Mistress by Andrew Marvell is another poem in which the historical context of the poem influences the ways in which language is used and the ideas are explored. Read the poem through carefully.

To His Coy Mistress

Had we but world enough, and time,
This coyness, Lady, were no crime,
We would sit down and think which way
To walk and pass our long love's day.
Thou by the Indian Ganges' side
Shouldst rubies find; I by the tide
Of Humber would complain. I would
Love you ten years before the Flood,
And you should, if you please, refuse
Till the conversion of the Jews.
My vegetable love should grow
Vaster than empires, and more slow;
An hundred years should go to praise
Thine eyes, and on thy forehead gaze,
Two hundred to adore each breast,
But thirty thousand to the rest;
An age at least to every part,
And the last age should show your heart.
For, Lady, you deserve this state,
Nor would I love at lower rate.
But at my back I always hear
Time's wingèd chariot hurrying near;
And yonder all before us lie
Deserts of vast eternity.
Thy beauty shall no more be found,
Nor, in thy marble vault, shall sound
My echoing song; then worms shall try
That long preserved virginity,
And your quaint honour turn to dust,
And into ashes all my lust:
The grave's a fine and private place,
But none, I think, do there embrace.
Now therefore, while the youthful hue
Sits on thy skin like morning dew,
And while thy willing soul transpires
At every pore with instant fires,
Now let us sport us while we may,
And now, like amorous birds of prey,
Rather at once our time devour
Than languish in his slow-chapt power.
Let us roll all our strength and all
Our sweetness up into one ball,
And tear our pleasures with rough strife
Through the iron gates of life.
Thus, though we cannot make our sun
Stand still, yet we will make him run.

Andrew Marvell

The poem presents a satire on conventional Elizabethan love poetry. It also plays on the idea of the transience of human life, a major preoccupation of the Elizabethans. It is basically a seduction poem. The poet is trying to persuade his lady to allow him to make love to her. In order to do this he puts to her a series of apparently logical reasons why she should give in to his wishes.

Marvell uses rich and elaborate imagery and hyperbole to add weight to his persuasion. For example he tells her how, in an ideal world, his love would never be diminished by time and that he would love her 'ten years before the Flood'. His use of biblical imagery is also designed to add gravity to his words. He also stresses how they do not have the luxury of unlimited time for:

> '…at my back I always hear
> Time's wingèd chariot hurrying near;
> And yonder all before us lie
> Deserts of vast eternity.'

Contemporary poetry

AQA	E Lang	E Lit
	✓	✓

Contemporary poems also cover a very broad range, but they will have been written much closer to our own time. They often deal with themes and issues relating to modern life and are written in the kind of language we are familiar with.

Read the following poem, *My Grandmother*, by Elizabeth Jennings.

My Grandmother

She kept an antique shop – or it kept her.
Among Apostle spoons and Bristol glass,
The faded silks, the heavy furniture,
She watched her own reflection in the brass
Salvers and silver bowls, as if to prove
Polish was all, there was no need of love.

And I remember how I once refused
To go out with her, since I was afraid.
It was perhaps a wish not to be used
Like antique objects. Though she never said
That she was hurt, I still could feel the guilt
Of that refusal, guessing how she felt.

Later, too frail to keep a shop, she put
All her best things in one long, narrow room.
The place smelt old, of things too long kept shut,
The smell of absences where shadows come
That can't be polished. There was nothing then
To give her own reflection back again.

And when she died I felt no grief at all,
Only the guilt of what I once refused.
I walked into her room among the tall
Sideboards and cupboards – things she never used
But needed: and no finger-marks were there,
Only the new dust falling through the air.

Elizabeth Jennings

Many of Jennings's poems explore themes of family, relationships, suffering and loneliness. In this poem she explores a very personal memory of the guilt she still feels about the way she behaved towards her grandmother on a particular occasion.

Structure:

- The poem is divided into four stanzas, each of which develops the idea further:
  - Stanza 1 describes her grandmother.
  - Stanza 2 describes the incident that causes her guilt.
  - Stanza 3 shows her grandmother in retirement.
  - Stanza 4 tells us how, after her grandmother has died, the poet reflects on her grandmother's life and her own memories.

Themes:

- The poet explores her own feelings of inadequacy in dealing with her memories of her relationship with her grandmother.
- In a broader sense, the poet seems to explore the difficulties in relationships and with people's feelings as opposed to the inanimate objects her grandmother collected around herself.

Language:

- The language used appears simple and straightforward, using ordinary words and phrases. This conceals the complexity of the feelings it explores.
- The image of dust is used in the final stanza and carries connotations of death (as in 'ashes').
- The language is descriptive – note the use of adjectives, e.g. 'faded silks', 'brass salvers', 'silver bowls'.
- The poem is written in the first person and sounds like a story being told.

> **KEY POINT**
>
> Think about the ways in which the different elements of the poem work together to create the overall effect.

Poetry from different cultures and traditions

AQA	E Lang	E Lit
	✓	✓

The idea of 'different cultures' is a very broad one, covering the tremendously diverse range of cultures in the world.

Poems that are rooted in different cultures can have particular features that you should look out for and comment on.

Non-standard English and dialect forms

Some poetry from different cultures, rather than using Standard English, uses the **non-standard English** and/or **dialect** forms of the particular **cultural background** from which it comes.

Sometimes a poet might use a mixture of **Standard English** and a **dialect form** in order to **emphasise** a particular idea. For example, in his poem *Half-Caste*, a poem about the poet's objection to the term 'half-caste' to mean 'of mixed race', John Agard mixes West Indian patois with Standard English. Look at the following extract from the poem.

From **Half-Caste**

Excuse me
standing on one leg
I'm half-caste

Explain yuself
wha yu mean
when yu say half-caste

John Agard

PROGRESS CHECK

1. Why do you think Agard mixes dialect form with Standard English in this poem?

1. By using this technique he emphasises the theme of his poem – that of being 'Half-Caste' – the half dialect, half Standard English emphasises this. The poet considers this an offensive term – the theme of the poem is the anger he feels about prejudiced views of his mixed race. It also gives a sense of the dual 'voice' that the poet possesses.

10.4 Comparing poems

LEARNING SUMMARY

After studying this section, you should be able to understand:

● what features to look for in each poem
● how to plan and write your response

Features to look for

AQA	E Lang	E Lit
	✓	✓

As part of the AQA GCSE English Literature course, one of the things you will need to do is explore relationships and comparisons between texts, selecting and evaluating relevant material. One of the ways in which you might be asked to do this is to compare two poems.

When comparing poems you need to look for all the features that you look for when studying a single poem. You need to look at the:

● **Content** of the poem.
● **Tone** and **mood** of the poem.
● **Form** in which it is written and **structured.**
● Ways in which **language** is used.

However, you also need to compare these features in both poems.

You will need to look at each poem individually to plan your response, but when writing your response you need to integrate your ideas on both poems.

> When writing your response, avoid writing an analysis of one poem and then the other and comparing them in a final paragraph. Integrate your comments on the poems throughout.

Planning and writing your response

AQA   E Lang ✓   E Lit ✓

Here's one way in which you could approach the task of comparing poems.

Planning your response

1. Read both poems through carefully and get an overall **sense** of what each poem is about and how the poets **handle** their topics.

2. Re-read the first poem and make **brief notes** either around the poem, if you are able, or on a separate sheet, noting key words, phrases, images, etc. and your **response** to it. Do the same with the second poem.

3. Note down some **brief** quotations from each poem that you will use to illustrate your ideas. You could underline or circle these if you are allowed to write on the copy of the poem.

4. Make two lists – one headed **similarities** and one headed **differences** – and list the main points under each heading.

Writing the response

It is important that you avoid writing an essay on each poem and then try to join them together. The best responses are those that **integrate** the ideas in **parallel** throughout the essay. Here's one way you could approach this:

Introduction

Introductory paragraph commenting on what each poem is about and capturing the 'flavour' of each.

Main body

Several paragraphs based on your detailed reading of the poems. It is a good idea to make a point about the first poem and then a point about the second poem, and so on.

It can help you to structure your ideas in a logical way, e.g. one paragraph could compare the way each uses imagery, while another paragraph could focus on structure.

Conclusion

A concluding paragraph, summing up the main similarities and differences, saying which poem you find more effective and why, if you are asked this.

KEY POINT

Keep both poems at the centre of your focus and don't be tempted to write all about one and then the other.

1 Read the following two poems. How might you compare them if you were writing a response to a comparison question on them?

The Little Lamb

Little Lamb, who made thee?
Dost thou know who made thee?
Gave thee life, and bid thee feed
By the stream and o'er the mead;
Gave thee clothing of delight,
Softest clothing, woolly, bright;
Gave thee such a tender voice,
Making all the vales rejoice?
Little Lamb, who made thee?
Dost thou know who made thee?

Little Lamb, I'll tell thee,
Little Lamb, I'll tell thee,
He is called by thy name,
For he calls himself a Lamb.

He is meek, and he is mild;
He became a little child.
I a child, and thou a lamb,
We are called by his name.
Little Lamb, God bless thee!
Little Lamb, God bless thee!

William Blake

The Eagle

HE clasps the crag with crooked hands;
Close to the sun in lonely lands,
Ringed with the azure world, he stands.

The wrinkled sea beneath him crawls;
He watches from his mountain walls,
And like a thunderbolt he falls.

Alfred, Lord Tennyson

1. Here are some ideas of features you might compare:
- The content – the way in which the eagle is portrayed, compared to the view of the lamb in Blake's poem. The eagle represents the beauty, power and violence of nature; the lamb is portrayed as small and gentle, and is even compared to Jesus Christ – 'meek' and 'mild', and a 'little child'.
- Specific details of how language is used in each poem with examples and comments on effects created, e.g. alliteration is used in both poems – soft 'l' and 'm' sounds in *The Little Lamb* to portray the lamb as harmless, and hard 'c' sounds in *The Eagle*, to give an impression of violence.
- The tone of each poem, e.g. *The Eagle* has a tone of power and violence, whilst *The Little Lamb* has a tone that is softer and almost child-like, although a joyous and celebratory tone is created at the end.
- The structure of each poem, e.g. use of rhyme and the effect created. In *The Eagle*, all three lines of each stanza rhyme, forming rhyming triplets. In *The Little Lamb*, a simple rhyme scheme is used, with a lot of repetition, which gives a more simple, child-like tone.

Sample GCSE question

Read the poem below and answer the question that follows.

War Photographer

In his darkroom he is finally alone
with spools of suffering set out in ordered rows.
The only light is red and softly glows,
as though this were a church and he
a priest preparing to intone a Mass.
Belfast. Beirut. Phnom Penh. All flesh is grass.

He has a job to do. Solutions slop in trays
beneath his hands which did not tremble then
though seem to now. Rural England. Home again
to ordinary pain which simple weather can dispel,
to fields which don't explode beneath the feet
of running children in a nightmare heat.

Something is happening. A stranger's features
faintly start to twist before his eyes,
a half-formed ghost. He remembers the cries
of this man's wife, how he sought approval
without words to do what someone must
and how the blood stained into foreign dust.

A hundred agonies in black-and-white
from which his editor will pick out five or six
for Sunday's supplement. The reader's eyeballs prick
with tears between bath and pre-lunch beers.
From aeroplane he stares impassively at where
he earns a living and they do not care.

Carol Ann Duffy

Explain how Duffy uses language, structure and form to explore her ideas about the work of the war photographer.

Support your answer with examples from the poem.

Sample GCSE question

The initial tone of the poem, `War Photographer´ conveys the tragedy and turmoil of the war zone, with `... finally alone´ conveying the photographer´s relief at finally being away from the terrible sights that his job had forced him to witness. This is then contrasted with the impassive way in which the editor of the newspaper will `pick out´ five or six of the photographer´s pictures. The phrase `pick out´ is casual and suggests that the editor is not affected by the `hundred agonies´ that lay before him. Although the readers of the newspaper´s eyes will initially `prick with tears´, they too are ultimately unaffected by the pictures.

The war photographer is not named in Duffy´s poem, and is instead referred to as `he´. This is perhaps to create a sense of detachment, which reflects the emotional detachment conveyed by the editor and the readers towards the end of the poem.

There is also an element of innocence in `War Photographer´, where Duffy describes the children in the war zones — `running children in a nightmare heat´ — and the innocent man who has been killed. This emphasises injustice, and enables the reader to make comparisons between this and their own lives.

The first stanza of `War Photographer´ has religious overtones, which sets the scene for the rest of the poem. The description of the man sitting in a darkened room with red glowing light, and the hushed atmosphere is reminiscent of a church. The idea that Duffy presents, of the photographer being like a priest preparing a mass, gives the poem and the process a sense of solemnity. Instead of the words of the service, the names of war zones are given, which enables the reader to contrast between the peaceful solemnity of church and the horrors of the war zones.

There are many metaphors and contrasts in the poem. `War Photographer´ contrasts the horrors of the war zones with everyday English life. The metaphors in `War Photographer´ are expressive and help to convey the suffering of the people at wartime: `nightmare heat´, `a half-formed ghost´, `a hundred agonies´.

The poem´s ending is powerful and makes a lasting impression on the reader. The revelation that the war photographer too is impassive towards those he photographs is shocking, even though we know it is probably essential to have some degree of emotional detachment in his line of work, to ensure his own emotional survival. His admittance that the people who will see his pictures in the Sunday supplements `... do not care´ about the people in the war zone makes the reader consider the way that they receive and react to similar pictures themselves.

Effective introduction establishes the tone of the poem supported by reference.

Aware of contrasts in poem.

Perceptive point suggesting the emotional detachment the war photographer must have in order to do his job, but also the emotional detachment of others viewing the photographs.

Relevant idea about the suffering of the innocents and the injustice of war.

Explores interesting idea of religious connotations.

Sound ideas on the use of metaphors in the poem.

Good concluding paragraph summing up the key ideas and implications of the poem. Awareness of how the poem makes us question our own attitudes and reactions too.

Practice questions

1 Relationships

Compare how feelings towards a parent or relative are expressed in *Praise Song for My Mother* and one other poem from 'Relationships'.

(External exam question: English Literature, Unit 2)

2 Character and Voice

Compare how the poet creates a sense of an individual voice in *Checking Out Me History* and one other poem from 'Character and Voice'.

(External exam question: English Literature, Unit 2)

3 Theme

Explore the ways in which love is presented in a range of contemporary and Literary Heritage poems.

(Controlled Assessment task: English Literature, Unit 5)

4 Characterisation and voice

Explore the ways in which relationships are presented in a range of contemporary and Literary Heritage poems.

(Controlled Assessment task: English Literature, Unit 5)

11 Speaking and listening

The following topics are covered in this chapter:

- **What speaking and listening involves**
- **Presenting**
- **Discussing and listening**
- **Role playing**

11.1 What speaking and listening involves

LEARNING SUMMARY	After studying this section, you should be able to understand:
	• the importance of speaking and listening to your course
	• the range of activities that your speaking and listening assessment will consist of

The importance of speaking and listening

	E Lang	E Lit
AQA	✓	✗

The speaking and listening element of your AQA GCSE English Language course carries 20% of the overall marks and so it is an important aspect of the work that you will do.

You must be able to do the following:
- Communicate clearly and purposefully through speech; structure and sustain talk, adapting it to different situations and audiences; use Standard English and a variety of techniques as appropriate.
- Listen and respond to speakers' ideas and perspectives, and how they construct and express meanings.
- Interact with others, shaping meanings through suggestions, comments and questions and drawing ideas together.
- Create and sustain different roles.

Speaking and listening activities

	E Lang	E Lit
AQA	✓	✗

You will be assessed in **three** different activities. Broadly, these will cover:
- An individual activity involving presenting and listening to information and ideas.
- Discussing, listening, interacting and responding in a group situation.
- Role playing.

11.2 Presenting

LEARNING SUMMARY	After studying this section, you should be able to understand:
	• the kind of skills you will need to give an individual presentation
	• the kinds of tasks you might be asked to do
	• how to do well in this task

Skills for giving an individual presentation

AQA	E Lang	E Lit
	✓	✗

Here are the key speaking and listening skills you will need when giving an individual presentation. You will need to:

- **Communicate your ideas clearly and effectively** – you need to make sure that you express yourself clearly so that your audience can follow and understand what you are saying.
- **Present information and ideas** – you need to make sure that you are familiar with the information and ideas you are talking about so you can be clear in presenting them.
- **Use Standard English** as appropriate – you should make sure that you speak in Standard English and avoid slang or colloquial expressions (unless you have incorporated them into your talk to achieve a particular effect).
- **Speak in a structured and sustained way** – you should make sure that your presentation is well-structured, that your ideas link together effectively, and that you speak fluently. In general, your talk should last about five minutes.
- Choose and adapt the language you use to be **appropriate to your audience** – you should always take into account the kind of audience you are talking to when thinking about the language that you use in your presentation.
- **Respond appropriately to the questions and views of others** – listen carefully to the questions asked at the end of your presentation and answer them as fully as you can. If you do not know the answer to a question, do not be afraid to say so. Be tolerant of the views expressed by your audience and recognise that not everyone will take the same view as you.

See pages 26–28 for techniques used in planning and making a speech.

In some cases, you might be able to use visual aids to illustrate your presentation or make use of PowerPoint to help make your presentation more effective.

Remember though, that you will be assessed on your speaking and listening skills and not on the quality of your visual aids.

Careful **planning** is of key importance in delivering an effective presentation.

Here is one way of planning a talk on a particular topic:

1. Think carefully about the topic of your talk and write down all your ideas on it. Remember, if you have a choice, choose to talk about something that you know about.
2. Decide on the key focus of your talk and write down a structure for your ideas. Do not write out your talk as if it were an essay; instead, think through your key ideas in your mind.

3 If you are going to use visual aids or PowerPoint, decide how they will fit in with your talk and make sure that they are used for a purpose. For example, there is no point in using PowerPoint if you simply put slides up on the screen and read out what they say to your audience.

4 When you are happy with your structure it can be useful to write down key words on a piece of card as memory prompts. Do not write more than a word or two on the cards. It is really important that your talk is presented in a natural way. Reading out from pre-prepared notes is not fulfilling the requirements for speaking and listening – all it shows is that you can read aloud.

> **KEY POINT**
>
> Careful planning is important in delivering an effective presentation.

Possible presenting tasks

AQA	E Lang	E Lit
	✓	✗

Here are some examples of the kinds of task that you might be asked to do as part of your assessment:

1 Prepare an individual talk to the class about a topic that you are interested in. After your talk is finished you then hold a question and answer session in which you answer questions put to you by members of your class.

2 Take on the role of a character in a text that you have studied and deliver a monologue to your class. Speaking in the role of that character, explain why you behave in the way that you do in the text.

3 Present an argument for a subject that you feel strongly about.

4 Prepare a presentation in which you explain, with the use of examples, what you found through a detailed examination of a particular speech made by a well-known person.

How to do well when presenting

AQA	E Lang	E Lit
	✓	✗

In order to achieve a good mark in this part of the AQA GCSE English Language course, you need to do the following:

- Put your information, ideas and feelings across confidently, making sure that you emphasise the key points and issues.
- Shape your talk to suit the demands of the particular task and audience.
- Use non-verbal features to suit the situation and purpose.
- Use language to suit the context of the task.
- Make appropriate use of Standard English, vocabulary and grammar.

If you do all these things, you should achieve a good mark for your presentation.

11.3 Discussing and listening

LEARNING SUMMARY	**After studying this section, you should be able to understand:**
	• the kind of skills you will need to take part in group discussions
	• the kinds of tasks you might be asked to do
	• how to do well in this task

Skills for taking part in group discussions

AQA	E Lang	E Lit
	✓	✗

Here are the key speaking and listening skills you will need when taking part in group discussions. You will need to:

- **Interact with and respond to others** – listen carefully to what others have to say and respond in a thoughtful way to them.
- **Make a range of effective contributions** – make well-thought out and relevant comments and contributions to the discussion.
- **Express ideas clearly, accurately and appropriately** – make sure that your responses are relevant and sensible and that you express yourself using appropriate language.
- **Listen and respond to others' ideas and perspectives** – be aware that others may hold different views to you and listen to what they have to say.
- **Challenge what you hear where appropriate** – challenge people's statements and opinions, but do this in a polite and appropriate way.
- **Shape meaning through asking questions and making comments and suggestions** – ask well-thought-out questions and make comments which present a real contribution to, and help to shape, the discussion.

> **KEY POINT**
>
> Remember that good listening skills, as well as good speaking skills, are important in taking an effective part in group discussion.

Possible discussing and listening tasks

AQA	E Lang	E Lit
	✓	✗

Here are some examples of the kinds of task that you might be asked to take part in as part of your assessment:

1. In a group of three or four, discuss a topic that has recently been in the news and has caused a good deal of controversy.
2. In a group of three or four, discuss interpretations and ideas on a set text you have all studied.
3. In a small group, take part in a problem-solving exercise of some kind.
4. In a group of three or four, discuss a speech that you have studied as part of your study of spoken language.

How to do well in discussing and listening

AQA	E Lang	E Lit
	✓	X

In order to achieve a good mark in this part of the AQA GCSE English Language course, you need to do the following:

- Challenge, develop and respond to what you hear in a thoughtful and considerate way.
- Ask appropriate and apt questions.
- Analyse and reflect on the ideas put forward by other members of the group and use your ideas to develop the discussion.
- Help to sustain the discussion by encouraging quieter members of the group to contribute.

> **KEY POINT**
>
> Remember that you will be assessed not only on what you have to say yourself, but also on how you listen to, respond to and interact with others. Avoid trying to dominate the discussion yourself, but listen, respond and encourage others to contribute too.

11.4 Role playing

LEARNING SUMMARY

After studying this section, you should be able to understand:

- the kind of skills you will need in carrying out role play
- the kinds of tasks you might be asked to do
- how to do well in this task

Skills for role playing

AQA	E Lang	E Lit
	✓	X

Here are the key speaking and listening skills you will need in taking part in a role play. You will need to:

- Create and sustain different roles.
- Take part in a range of real-life contexts.
- Experiment with language to engage the audience.

Possible role play tasks

AQA	E Lang	E Lit
	✓	X

Here are some examples of the kinds of task that you might be asked to take part in as part of your assessment:

1. Create a role from a situation that you are familiar with, such as within a school or college context, and develop your character around that basis.

2. Work with a partner to simulate an interview situation for a particular job.

3. Work with a partner to create an interview of a character from a text that you have studied.

4. Give an individual improvisation based on a particular situation that you have been given.

Speaking and listening 11

Although some role play situations can be planned, you are not allowed to use written scripts, or even scripts that have been learned, in your role play.

How to do well in role play

AQA	E Lang	E Lit
	✓	✗

In order to achieve a good mark in this part of the AQA GCSE English Language course, you need to do the following:

- Create convincing characters and roles.
- Use carefully selected verbal and non-verbal techniques to make your role play effective.
- Respond sensitively and skilfully in different situations and scenarios.
- Explore ideas and issues, and relationships in a variety of formal and informal scenarios.
- Choose appropriate dramatic approaches.

1. What are the three main areas that you will be assessed on for speaking and listening?
2. Describe the two key skills that you need in order to do well in speaking and listening.

1. Individual presentation; Discussing and listening; Role play.
2. You need to be able to use spoken language effectively and appropriately to suit a variety of audiences and purposes; you need to have effective listening skills and be able to respond in a sensitive and appropriate way to what others have to say.

171

Controlled Assessment Speaking and Listening practice tasks

The following are some examples of the type of Controlled Assessment tasks you might have to do for English Language Unit 2: Speaking and Listening.

Presenting

1. Prepare a talk to the class in which you tell them about your favourite charity and try to persuade them to become involved with it.

2. Give a presentation to the class in which you describe an interesting place that you have visited recently.

3. Present to the school your views on a controversial issue.

4. Present a proposal to the class, in which you outline the improvements that you would like to see carried out in your town.

Discussing and listening

1. Work in a small group to discuss your favourite film.

2. In a group of three or four, prepare the front page for a local newspaper, creating appropriate headlines, stories, etc.

3. In a small group, listen to a recording of a TV news programme and discuss your views and ideas on it.

4. Work in a group of three or four and discuss your ideas on a current environmental issue.

Role playing

1. Perform in a pair an interview in which one of you takes the role of a character from a Shakespeare play you have studied and the other takes the role of interviewer.

2. Present two different characters' responses to seeing an argument in the street.

3. Perform in a pair a situation where a teacher is trying to persuade an uncooperative student to do his/her work.

4. Take the role of a councillor at a council meeting, speaking in opposition to the closure of a local school.

Practice questions answers

Chapter 1

1.
- You should be clear about the audience and purpose of your article.
- Express your views clearly on the contribution of the Internet (positive or negative) on education.
- Your writing should clearly be in article form, e.g. with an appropriate headline.
- It should be written in language to address the readership of a school magazine, and that will capture the readers' attention and keep them interested.
- Your writing must show a good level of technical accuracy in terms of spelling, punctuation and grammar.

2.
- You should be clear about the audience and purpose of your writing.
- The key focus is writing about your memorable experience.
- Your piece of writing should convey the experience vividly and you should use language effectively in order to achieve this.
- Keep in mind that this piece of writing is intended to be read by and interest the readers of a school or college magazine.
- Your writing must show a good level of technical accuracy in terms of spelling, punctuation and grammar.

3.
- You should provide an effective range of advice points.
- The writing should include clear, practical ideas closely focused on camping.
- You should show clear awareness of the advice leaflet form, e.g. using bullet points, blocks of text.
- It should show effective use of language closely linked to task, purpose and audience.
- It should make use of language techniques associated with giving advice, e.g. imperatives, modal verbs.
- Your writing must show a good level of technical accuracy in terms of spelling, punctuation and grammar.

4.
- Your response should be written in formal letter form using formal letter conventions.
- Explain your argument clearly either for or against the plans for a wind farm, using language techniques associated with writing to argue, e.g. connectives, rhetoric, personal experiences.
- Offer evidence or examples to support your ideas.
- Use language effectively to express your ideas.
- Your writing must show a good level of technical accuracy in terms of spelling, punctuation and grammar.

Chapter 2

1. You should comment on and analyse how the writer has:
- used style and tone to capture the reader's attention and make their writing personal and appropriate
- used fact and opinion
- used individual words and phrases, and the effects that they create
- used language devices such as imagery and alliteration for effect
- used sentence structure and paragraphs to organise ideas and sustain the reader's interest and attention.

2. Your research should focus clearly on:
- the techniques the speakers use and the effects they achieve
- the ways in which the speeches are structured
- how language is used to create specific effects, e.g. use of rhetoric, emotive / sensational language
- the overall impact and effectiveness of the speeches

3. You have some flexibility in how you approach this task but it is likely that you will examine some or all of the following:
- register – formal or informal

- humour, sarcasm
- slang and colloquial language, accent and dialect
- intonation and features of speech, e.g. fillers, pauses, repetition
- context
- vocabulary, e.g. technical, emotive.

Chapter 3

1.
- You should have a clear focus on your chosen pet.
- You should give an effective range of advice points.
- The writing must give clear, practical ideas closely focused on the care of your chosen pet.
- You must show clear awareness of the advice leaflet form, e.g. using bullet points, blocks of text.
- You should demonstrate effective use of language closely linked to task, purpose and audience.
- It should make use of language techniques associated with giving advice, e.g. imperatives, modal verbs.
- Your writing must show a good level of technical accuracy in terms of spelling, punctuation and grammar.

2.
- You should be clear about the audience and purpose of your article.
- You should express your views clearly on the greatest threat to continued human life.
- Your writing should clearly be in article form, e.g. with an appropriate headline.
- It should be written in language to capture the reader's attention and keep them interested.
- Your writing must show a good level of technical accuracy in terms of spelling, punctuation and grammar.

3.
- You should give an effective range of advice points linked to imaginative writing.
- It should offer clear, practical ideas that the intended age group can try for themselves.
- Your writing must show clear awareness of the advice leaflet form, e.g. using bullet points.
- It should make use of language techniques associated with giving advice, e.g. imperatives, modal verbs.
- You should demonstrate effective use of language closely linked to task, purpose and audience, e.g. fairly simple language that the age group will understand.
- Your writing must show a good level of technical accuracy in terms of spelling, punctuation and grammar.

4.
- You must show clear use of a review form focusing on your chosen film.
- You should express your ideas clearly.
- You should support your ideas with details of character, plot, camerawork, etc.
- You should conclude your review effectively.
- Your writing should show effective use of language closely linked to task, purpose and audience.
- Your writing must show a good level of technical accuracy in terms of spelling, punctuation and grammar.

5.
- The drama script form should be used, i.e. the people's names on the left, the speech on the right.
- You have flexibility in terms of the actor interviewed.
- You have flexibility in what they say, although the kinds of questions asked and their replies should be in keeping with the actor and the kind of work they do.
- You should show effective use of language closely linked to task, purpose and audience.
- Your writing must show a good level of technical accuracy in terms of spelling, punctuation and grammar.

Chapter 4

1.
- You should be clear about the audience and purpose of your article.

Practice questions answers

- Express your views clearly on how you would like to see computer / Internet facilities improved at your local library.
- Your writing should clearly be in article form, e.g. with an appropriate headline.
- It should be written in language to address the readership of a local newspaper, and that will capture the readers' attention and keep their interest.
- Your writing must show a good level of technical accuracy in terms of spelling, punctuation and grammar.
2. • You should be clear about the audience and purpose of your article.
- Express your views clearly on the amount of violence and bad language on television, and provide evidence / examples.
- Your writing should clearly be in the form of an editorial.
- It should be written in language to address the readership of a local newspaper.
- Your writing must show a good level of technical accuracy in terms of spelling, punctuation and grammar.
3. • Make sure that your talk is focused on the topic of the advantages and disadvantages of the Internet.
- Structure your talk effectively with an effective opening that captures the attention of your listeners, e.g. by using a rhetorical question.
- Develop your ideas, with evidence or illustrations as your talk develops.
- Conclude with an effective ending.
- It is important that your talk is interesting and keeps your listeners' attention throughout.

Chapter 5
1. • Your response should be written in formal letter form using formal letter conventions.
- Explain your arguments for saving the bus service clearly and effectively.
- You should offer evidence or examples to support your ideas.
- You should use language effectively to express your ideas.
- You should use persuasive language techniques, e.g. emotive language, rhetoric, exaggeration and repetition.
- Your writing must show a good level of technical accuracy in terms of spelling, punctuation and grammar.
2. • You should be clear about the audience and purpose of your article.
- Express your views clearly on the contribution of the Internet in various contexts (good or bad).
- Your writing should clearly be in article form, e.g. with an appropriate headline.
- It should be written in language to address the readership of a local newspaper and that will capture the readers' attention and keep them interested.
- Your writing must show a good level of technical accuracy in terms of spelling, punctuation and grammar.
3. • All the essential information relating to the visit should be given, e.g. place, time, costs, clothing required.
- The information should be clearly structured so that all points are easy to read and understand.
- You should show clear awareness of information leaflet form, e.g. using bullet points, blocks of text.
- You should show effective use of language closely linked to task, purpose and audience.
- Your writing must show a good level of technical accuracy in terms of spelling, punctuation and grammar.

Chapter 6
1. • Script form should be used, i.e. the people's names on the left, the speech on the right.
- You have flexibility in terms of the kind of story you are to be interviewed about and the specific questions you are being asked.
- You have flexibility in what you say in response, although it should be linked to the key task.
- You should show effective use of language closely linked to task, purpose and audience.
- Your writing must show a good level of technical accuracy in terms of spelling, punctuation and grammar.
2. • Your response should be in informal letter form using the normal conventions of letter writing.
- You have flexibility in the story and character you choose.
- What your character has to say in the letter should be in keeping with events, their behaviour, etc. in the story.
- You should capture the authentic 'voice' of the character, e.g. if the character is American, use American terms, such as 'Fall', for 'Autumn'.
- Your writing must show a good level of technical accuracy in terms of spelling, punctuation and grammar.
3. • You should show clear use of a review form focusing on your chosen book.
- Express your ideas clearly.
- Support your ideas with details of elements such as characters, plot, setting and structure.
- You should show effective use of language closely linked to task, purpose and audience – your purpose is given here – i.e. a book review but you can decide on the audience, so your language may be aimed at children, teenagers or adults – make sure it is appropriate to the book you are reviewing.
- Conclude your review effectively.
- Your writing must show a good level of technical accuracy in terms of spelling, punctuation and grammar.

Chapter 7
1 (a) • The fact that Macbeth sees an illusory dagger, and is seeing things, suggest a disturbed state of mind.
- Macbeth recognises that the image of the dagger is the product of his 'heat-oppressed brain'.
- He cannot get the image of the dagger out of his mind and he realises that it is guiding him to the place where he will murder Duncan.
- The language he uses (words associated with death and murder, alliteration, questions to himself) expresses his disturbed state of mind, e.g. 'gouts of blood', 'bloody business'.
- His language reveals that he is tormented by the idea of murder but he is going to go through with it.
(b) There are several scenes you could choose from, for example, the final scene where he is confronted by Macduff:
- Here all his fear has gone and he fights like a warrior.
- His language in this scene (he thinks he is invincible: 'I bear a charmed life' shows that he is prepared to face his fate).

Chapter 8
1. • You have a free choice of characters, but you should obviously choose ones that you can write something about.
- Examine how they are presented in the play.
- Look at the way Thomas uses language to create a picture of them – their appearances, their personalities, their behaviour.

- Write about their roles in the play.
2. You could discuss:
  - Elizabeth's response on discovering her husband's affair with Abigail, and Abigail's view of her.
  - Her virtuous nature – a good and kindly mother.
  - Religious – she tries to forgive John, but she has reached a point which she cannot go beyond.
  - She cannot bring herself to name her husband as a lecher.
  - Whatever view you take make sure that you support it with evidence from the text.
3. You could discuss:
  - Eva separated from family and evacuated to England, and the effects that this has on her.
  - Years later she wants to erase the memory of the separation from her parents.
  - When her mother comes looking for her, the loss suffered by mother and daughter is clearly more than physical separation.
  - Explore your ideas in detail and make sure that you support them with references from the play.
4. You could discuss:
  - The whole message that the Inspector brings is that we are all in the world together and need to look after each other.
  - He illustrates through the play how the actions of one individual or individuals can affect the life of another individual.
  - His view cuts across social barriers and class – everyone is of equal worth.
  - The different responses of the members of the Birling family and Gerald illustrate the differing views of his message.
  - Make sure you support your ideas with references from the text.

Chapter 9
1. You could discuss:
  - Elizabeth has many admirable qualities but she can be sharp tongued and inclined to make hasty judgments.
  - This leads her initially to reject Darcy.
  - Darcy too is proud, hasty and sometimes judges too harshly.
  - The reader can see, though, that these two characters are ideally matched and, in many ways, the novel is concerned with them overcoming all the obstacles that face them before Elizabeth realises her mistake in being prejudiced against Darcy and the two get together.
  - Jane and Bingley are immediately attracted to each other and Austen presents them as a potential couple throughout the novel.
  - Jane and Bingley are very similar in nature and behaviour – both are friendly and good-natured and always think the best of others.
  - Jane's mellow nature forms a contrast to her sister's more fiery spirit.
  - Bingley's friendliness contrasts with Darcy's aloofness and pride.
  - Give your view on how well-matched you think the couples are, and back it up with references from the text.
2. You could discuss:
  - Heathcliff is presented with many of the qualities of a 'hero' figure – handsome, powerful and charismatic.
  - He also has less attractive features – he is brutal, dishonest, vindictive and immoral.
  - These two opposing sets of features combine to create a mysterious, unconventional and intriguing character.

- Edgar represents morality and accepted values as contrasted against Heathcliff's immorality and rejection of conventional behaviour and values.
- Edgar lacks the physical strength of Heathcliff and sometimes appears feeble. But he does possess an inner moral strength and is humane and unselfish which, in the end, gives him a quiet dignity.
- You must support your ideas with references from the text.
3. You could discuss:
  - Jack is a leader – he already leads the choir at the beginning of the novel.
  - His methods are the complete opposite of Ralph's.
  - His natural aptitude for hunting degenerates into a lust for killing.
  - He reverts to the primitive and savage.
  - He is irresponsible and has no patience or constructive ideas, e.g. he soon grows tired of debates and hut-building.
  - He abuses his power as a leader and, free from social restraints, the latent evil within his character emerges.
  - Give details on how language is used to portray Jack's role, e.g. violent diction, authoritarian dialogue by Jack, references to animalistic behaviour.
  - You must support your ideas with references from the text.

Chapter 10
1. You could discuss:
  - Nichols' attitude towards her mother.
  - The significance of the metaphors, e.g. in lines 2, 5 and 8.
  - Her use of repetition and its effect.
  - The effect of the final line.
  - You must make comparative points with your chosen poem, supported by references to the poems.
2. You could discuss:
  - Agard's use of non-standard English and its effects.
  - His use of metaphors and the effects created.
  - The significance of the historical references.
  - His use of rhythm and rhyme.
  - You must make comparative points with your chosen poem, supported by references to the poems.
3. - Focus closely on the ways in which love is presented in your chosen texts.
  - Choose your texts carefully and make sure that you have plenty of ideas about them.
  - Analyse the ways in which language is used and the effects created.
  - Use specific examples of vocabulary, imagery, etc. to illustrate and support the points you make.
  - Look at other poetic techniques, such as the use of rhythm, rhyme, tone and structure.
  - Compare the texts effectively, using references to the poems to support your ideas.
4. - Focus closely on the ways in which relationships are presented in your chosen texts.
  - Choose your texts carefully and make sure that you have plenty of ideas on them.
  - Analyse the ways in which language is used and the effects created.
  - Use specific examples of vocabulary, imagery, etc. to illustrate and support the points you make.
  - Look at other poetic techniques, such as the use of rhythm, rhyme, tone and structure.
  - Compare the texts effectively, using references to the poems to support your ideas.

Unit 1 Understanding and producing non-fiction texts

Time allowed: 2 hours 15 minutes

Instructions
Use black ink or black ball-point pen.
Answer all questions.
You must not use a dictionary.

Information
The maximum mark for this paper is 80.
There are 40 marks for Section A and 40 marks for Section B.
You are reminded of the need for good English and clear presentation in your answers.
All questions should be answered in continuous prose.
You will be assessed on the quality of your reading in Section A.
You will be assessed on the quality of your writing in Section B.

Section A: READING

Answer **all** questions in this section.
This section is worth 40 marks.
(The reading materials for this section are at the end of the paper.)

1. Read **Item 1**, the item from the *Big Issue* called 'In his own words'. What do you learn from Brian Rowe's account about how he came to be a *Big Issue* vendor? *(8 marks)*

2. Now read **Item 2**, the fact sheet about child labour. How do the headline and layout add to the effectiveness of the text? *(8 marks)*

3. Now read **Item 3**, the article on the drought in Africa. What views of the drought are expressed by the various charity agencies? *(8 marks)*

4. Now refer to **Item 3**, 'More on Horn of Africa Drought' and either **Item 1** or **Item 2**. You are going to compare two texts, one of which you have chosen.

   Compare the ways in which language is used for effect in the two texts. Give some examples and explain what the effects are. *(16 marks)*

Section B: WRITING

Answer **both** questions in this section.
This section is worth 40 marks.

5. Write a letter to a friend describing to them the sights you saw and experiences that you had on a memorable visit to a place that had a special effect on you. *(16 marks)*

6. Some people believe that money raised by charities should be spent on helping to create an environment where people can provide for themselves, rather than keep providing aid.

   Write an article for a newspaper in which you put forward your views on the most effective ways charities can provide help to people who need it. *(24 marks)*

Materials for English Language Unit 1

The three items that follow are:

- **ITEM 1:** An article from the *Big Issue* in which a *Big Issue* vendor tells his story of how he came to be a vendor.
- **ITEM 2:** Part of a Fact Sheet from the Save the Children organisation giving information about the use of child labour.
- **ITEM 3:** An article from *The Mirror* Online about the effects of drought in Africa.

Item 1

IN HIS OWN WORDS...

MR BRIAN ROWE - BIG ISSUE VENDOR & SURVIVOR OF THE FALKLANDS WAR 1982

I was born in Witham Essex in 1959, I have five brothers and three sisters.

I left school at 16 and joined the Royal Navy as a Gunner on HMS Cardiff. After seven years service, I was sent to the Falklands to serve my country. I used to fire shells but never saw the impact of what I was doing or the people that I may have killed. That's what I was trained to do so I didn't think about it at the time.

For me, the Falklands experience was horrible and it preyed on my mind for months and years afterwards. I was more affected by the experience than I realised. I thought I would come home to a hero's welcome but when I didn't, that's when the shock set in. I found it hard to cope after coming home and eventually took voluntary redundancy in 1984. The Services never supported me after I left and I was never properly diagnosed. I still believe I had post traumatic stress disorder but nobody helped so I tried to cope on my own.

I had left the structure of family and school and then the Navy and without that structure it was hard to cope. Simple things like paying bills and managing finances were alien to me – we didn't have to do that at school or in the forces. After a year out of the Navy my wife left me and we got divorced, that's when I had a breakdown.

"I still believe I had post traumatic stress disorder but nobody helped so I tried to cope on my own."

She has since remarried and I haven't seen my son since he was 6 years old. A day doesn't go by that I don't think of them. My son would be 25 now and has done well and went to university. I am just disappointed in myself for not being there for him.

I drifted to London and saw people selling the Big Issue and I eventually decided to have a go. I have been selling for five years now and it has made a big difference to my life. In the last few months I have got off the streets and am now living in a hostel in Victoria.

I love meeting people – that's the best part of selling the Issue. It's great when people stop and say hello, it's nice to feel part of the community and feel that people actually care.

Some people still say "Get a job" or "Tramp". I have been attacked, punched, head butted and spat at. What can you do – you just have to laugh it off. I think many people see me and presume I have always been homeless, they don't know my personal history. They don't realise I'm just like them – could they one day be like me?

"It's great when people stop and say hello, it's nice to feel part of the community and feel that people actually care."

I have been homeless for 13 years and done lots of jobs including kitchen fitting, plumbing and electrics, I have even worked in a factory. I liked the kitchen fitting and plumbing – perhaps that is something I could do one day.

Somebody asked me what I would love to do in the future and I'd love to be a handy man on a desert island! More realistically, I'd love to see Spurs play – I'm a life long fan but I haven't been able to afford to go in over 16 years. Maybe one day, when we lift the premiership trophy - I'll be there!

 **Save the Children**

Child Labour

Globally, 1 in 6 children work. Around 60% of these children work in hazardous conditions, such as in mines or in agriculture using dangerous machinery, chemicals or pesticides. An estimated 8.4 million children are trapped in the unconditional worst forms of child labour including slavery, trafficking, debt bondage, prostitution, work in armed conflict, pornography and other illicit activities.

What is child labour?

Not all children's work is child labour. Child labour is work that is exploitative or likely to be hazardous; work that interferes with child's education or is harmful to their health or physical and emotional development. In its worst forms, child labour involves children being separated from their families, living in slavery-like conditions or being exposed to serious hazards and illnesses.

Safe, light, part-time, legal work that does not affect children's health and personal development or interfere with their schooling is not child labour and is generally regarded as a positive experience.

Why do children work?

"Had I not got a job, I could not secure even a single meal a day, let alone clothes, medicines and other necessities".
14 year old homeless girl, Dhaka, Bangladesh

Poverty is one of the major factors pushing children into work. In situations of extreme poverty, families depend upon children's income for survival. Children who suffer most from discrimination are more likely to be forced into the worst jobs.

Children can be pushed into work because they lack access to good quality education that is relevant to their lives. Their families may be unable to afford the costs of schooling or the poor quality of education on offer means that they decide that work offers them better opportunities for developing skills.

Facts and Figures
- **218 million** children aged 5 - 17 are involved in child labour world wide
- **126 million** children work in hazardous conditions
- **22,000** working children die each year in work related accidents
- **8.4 million** children are involved in the worst forms of child labour
- **300,000** children are involved in armed conflict
- **1.2 million** children are trafficked each year into exploitative work in mines, factories, armed conflict or sex work.
- The *highest numbers* of child labourers are in the Asia/Pacific region, where there are **122 million** working children
- The *highest proportion* of child labourers is in Sub Saharan Africa, where **26% of children** (49 million) are involved in work.
- **69%** of child labourers work in the agricultural sector.
- **22%** of child labour is in the services sector including working for traders, in restaurants and hotels and domestic work.
- **9%** of child labour is in industry, mining and construction
- The ILO estimates that, over a period of 20 years, the total costs of eliminating child labour and replacing it by universal education would be US $768 billion. Over the same period, the benefits would be $5,106billion.

Culture and tradition affect attitudes to work. In some communities, work is seen to be the best option for teaching children the skills they will need as adults.

Conflict, natural disaster, severe illness or economic transition can increase the risk of children becoming entangled in child labour. The death of family members, disruption to livelihoods and the risk of separation of children from their families place children at increased risk of exploitation. In regions badly affected by HIV/AIDS, for example, children may have to work to support the household when adults become sick or die.

Item 3

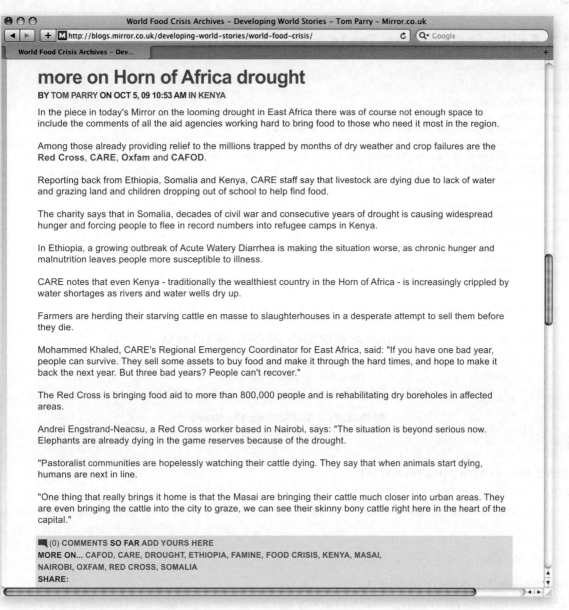

World Food Crisis Archives – Developing World Stories – Tom Parry – Mirror.co.uk

http://blogs.mirror.co.uk/developing-world-stories/world-food-crisis/

World Food Crisis Archives – Dev...

more on Horn of Africa drought

BY TOM PARRY ON OCT 5, 09 10:53 AM IN KENYA

In the piece in today's Mirror on the looming drought in East Africa there was of course not enough space to include the comments of all the aid agencies working hard to bring food to those who need it most in the region.

Among those already providing relief to the millions trapped by months of dry weather and crop failures are the **Red Cross**, **CARE**, **Oxfam** and **CAFOD**.

Reporting back from Ethiopia, Somalia and Kenya, CARE staff say that livestock are dying due to lack of water and grazing land and children dropping out of school to help find food.

The charity says that in Somalia, decades of civil war and consecutive years of drought is causing widespread hunger and forcing people to flee in record numbers into refugee camps in Kenya.

In Ethiopia, a growing outbreak of Acute Watery Diarrhea is making the situation worse, as chronic hunger and malnutrition leaves people more susceptible to illness.

CARE notes that even Kenya - traditionally the wealthiest country in the Horn of Africa - is increasingly crippled by water shortages as rivers and water wells dry up.

Farmers are herding their starving cattle en masse to slaughterhouses in a desperate attempt to sell them before they die.

Mohammed Khaled, CARE's Regional Emergency Coordinator for East Africa, said: "If you have one bad year, people can survive. They sell some assets to buy food and make it through the hard times, and hope to make it back the next year. But three bad years? People can't recover."

The Red Cross is bringing food aid to more than 800,000 people and is rehabilitating dry boreholes in affected areas.

Andrei Engstrand-Neacsu, a Red Cross worker based in Nairobi, says: "The situation is beyond serious now. Elephants are already dying in the game reserves because of the drought.

"Pastoralist communities are hopelessly watching their cattle dying. They say that when animals start dying, humans are next in line.

"One thing that really brings it home is that the Masai are bringing their cattle much closer into urban areas. They are even bringing the cattle into the city to graze, we can see their skinny bony cattle right here in the heart of the capital."

(0) COMMENTS SO FAR ADD YOURS HERE
MORE ON... CAFOD, CARE, DROUGHT, ETHIOPIA, FAMINE, FOOD CRISIS, KENYA, MASAI, NAIROBI, OXFAM, RED CROSS, SOMALIA
SHARE:

*CARE – CARE International – a charity that cares for vulnerable people in some of the world's poorest countries
*CAFOD – Catholic Agency for Overseas Development – a charity working to alleviate poverty and suffering in developing countries

English Literature

Unit 1 Exploring Modern Texts

Time allowed: 1 hour 30 minutes

Instructions
Use black ink or black ball-point pen.
Answer two questions.
Answer one question from Section A. Answer one question from Section B.
This is an open text examination. You must have a copy of the AQA Anthology, *Sunlight on the Grass* and / or the text you have studied in the examination room. The texts must not be annotated, and must not contain additional notes or materials.
You must not use a dictionary.

Information
The maximum mark for this paper is 60.
There are 30 marks for Section A and 30 marks for Section B.
You will be marked on your ability to:
- use good English
- organise information clearly
- use specialist vocabulary where appropriate.

Advice
You are advised to spend about 45 minutes on Section A and about 45 minutes on Section B.

Section A: MODERN PROSE OR DRAMA

Answer **one** question from this section on the text you have studied.
This section is worth 30 marks.
You are advised to spend about 45 minutes on this section.

Anthology – *Sunlight on the Grass*

EITHER

Question 1 Answer both parts (a) and (b).

(a) Write about the ways Dunmore presents her characters in *My Polish Teacher's Tie*.

(b) Go on to write about the ways in which characters are presented in one other story from the Anthology.

(30 marks)

OR

Question 2 Answer both parts (a) and (b).

(a) Write about how the relationship between the boy and his father is presented in *Compass and Torch*.

(b) Go on to write about the way in which a relationship between two people is presented in one other story from the Anthology.

(30 marks)

William Golding: *Lord of the Flies*

EITHER

Question 3

Explore Golding's presentation of Ralph in *Lord of the Flies*. What is the importance of his role in the novel?

(30 marks)

OR

Question 4

What is the importance of Piggy's role in *Lord of the Flies*?

(30 marks)

Kevin Brooks: *Martyn Pig*

EITHER

Question 5

How does Brooks present Martyn in the opening chapter of the novel?

(30 marks)

OR

Question 6

Which chapter did you find most effective? Explain how Brooks made this chapter particularly effective for you.

(30 marks)

Susan Hill: *The Woman in Black*

EITHER

Question 7

Choose a section from the novel that you find particularly effective. What methods does Hill use to make this part of the novel effective to you?

(30 marks)

OR

Question 8

What do you think about the ending of the novel? How effective do you find the methods that Hill uses to draw the novel to a conclusion?

(30 marks)

Joe Simpson: *Touching the Void*

EITHER

Question 9

Touching the Void has been described as 'brilliant, vivid, gripping'. Write about an episode from the book which you find particularly gripping. How does Simpson use language in your chosen episode to create his effects?

(30 marks)

OR

Question 10

How does Simpson present Simon's reaction when Joe arrives at the camp, and what does this reveal about the relationship between the two climbers?

(30 marks)

Dylan Thomas: *Under Milk Wood*

EITHER

Question 11

How does Thomas present Captain Cat and what does he add to the play?

(30 marks)

OR

Question 12

What methods does Thomas use to achieve comic effects in *Under Milk Wood*?

(30 marks)

Arthur Miller: *The Crucible*

EITHER

Question 13

Explore the function of Reverend Hale in the *The Crucible*. How does he change during the course of the play and what is your view of the character?

(30 marks)

OR

Question 14

How does Miller present Abigail and what is her importance in the play?

(30 marks)

Diane Samuels: *Kindertransport*

EITHER

Question 15

One of the questions posed by *Kindertransport* is, 'What future grows out of a traumatized past?' How does Eva's past shape her future?

(30 marks)

OR

Question 16

Write about your own responses to the play. You should focus on one or two episodes and explore the effects created here.

(30 marks)

J.B. Priestley: *An Inspector Calls*

EITHER

Question 17

How do you respond to the ending of *An Inspector Calls*? Explore the dramatic techniques Priestley uses to create dramatic effect in the final section of the play.

(30 marks)

OR

Question 18

How does Priestley present the character of Arthur Birling? Explore his role in the play.

(30 marks)

Dennis Kelly: *DNA*

EITHER

Question 19

How effective do you find the opening of the play? Explore the techniques that Kelly uses to create dramatic effect here.

(30 marks)

OR

Question 20

Write about your own responses to the play. You should explore the effects created by specific sections.

(30 marks)

Answer **one** question from this section on the text you have studied.
This section is worth 30 marks.
You are advised to spend about 45 minutes on this section.

EITHER

John Steinbeck: *Of Mice and Men*

Question 21

Read the passage and then answer the questions which follow.

> Evening of a hot day started the little wind to moving among the leaves. The shade climbed up the hills toward the top. On the sand-banks the rabbits sat as quietly as little grey, sculptured stones. And then from the direction of the state highway came the sound of footsteps on crisp sycamore leaves. The rabbits hurried noiselessly for cover. A stilted heron laboured up into the air and pounded down river. For a moment the place was lifeless, and then two men emerged from the path and came into the opening by the green pool. They had walked in single file down the path, and even in the open one stayed behind the other. Both were dressed in denim trousers and in denim coats with brass buttons. Both wore black, shapeless hats and both carried tight blanket rolls slung over their shoulders. The first man was small and quick, dark of face, with restless eyes and sharp, strong features. Every part of him was defined: small, strong hands, slender arms, a thin and bony nose. Behind him walked his opposite, a huge man, shapeless of face, with large, pale eyes, with wide, sloping shoulders; and he walked heavily, dragging his feet a little, the way a bear drags his paws. His arms did not swing at his sides, but hung loosely and only moved because the heavy hands were pendula.
>
> The first man stopped short in the clearing, and the follower nearly ran over him. He took off his hat and wiped the sweat-band with his forefinger and snapped the moisture off. His huge companion dropped his blankets and flung himself down and drank from the surface of the green pool; drank with long gulps, snorting into the water like a horse. The small man stepped nervously beside him.
>
> 'Lennie!' he said sharply. 'Lennie, for God's sakes don't drink so much.' Lennie continued to snort into the pool. The small man leaned over and shook him by the shoulder. 'Lennie. You gonna be sick like you was last night.'
>
> Lennie dipped his whole head under, hat and all, and then he sat up on the bank and his hat dripped down on his blue coat and ran down his back. 'Tha's good,' he said. 'You drink some, George. You take a good big drink.' He smiled happily.

(a) How do the details in this passage add to your understanding of the relationship between George and Lennie?

(b) How does Steinbeck use the characters of George and Lennie in the novel as a whole to comment on life in America in the 1930s? *(30 marks)*

OR

Chimamanda Ngozi Adichie: *Purple Hibiscus*

Question 22

Read the passage and then answer the questions that follow.

> Things started to fall apart at home when my brother, Jaja, did not go to communion and Papa flung his heavy missal across the room and broke the figurines on the etagere. We had just returned from church. Mama placed the fresh palm fronds, which were wet with holy water, on the dining table and then went upstairs to change.
>
> Later, she would knot the palm fronds into sagging cross shapes and hang them on the wall beside our gold-framed family photo. They would stay there until next Ash Wednesday, when we would take the fronds to church, to have them burned for ash. Papa, wearing a long, gray robe like the rest of the oblates, helped distribute ash every year. His line moved the slowest because he pressed hard on each forehead to make a perfect cross with his ash-covered thumb and slowly, meaningfully enunciate every word of "dust and unto dust yon shall return."
>
> Papa always sat in the front pew for Mass, at the end beside the middle aisle, with Mama, Jaja, and me sitting next to him. He was first to receive communion. Most people did not kneel to receive communion at the marble altar, with the blond life-size Virgin Mary mounted nearby, but Papa did. He would hold his eyes shut so tight that his face tightened into a grimace and then he would stick his tongue out as far as it could go. Afterward, he sat back on his seat and watched the rest of the congregation troop to the altar, palms pressed together and extended, like a saucer held sideways.

(a) How effective do you find this as an opening to the novel?

(b) How is Kambili's father presented in the novel? *(30 marks)*

OR

Lloyd Jones: *Mister Pip*

Question 23

Read the passage and then answer the questions that follow.

> Everyone called him Pop Eye. Even in those days when I was a skinny thirteen-year-old I thought he probably knew about his nickname but didn't care. His eyes were too interested in what lay up ahead to notice us barefoot kids.
>
> He looked like someone who had seen or known great suffering and hadn't been able to forget it. His large eyes in his large head stuck out further than anyone else's – like they wanted to leave the surface of his face. They made you think of someone who can't get out of the house quickly enough.
>
> Pop Eye wore the same white linen suit every day. His trousers snagged on his bony knees in the sloppy heat. Some days he wore a clown's nose. His nose was already big. He didn't need that red light bulb. But for reasons we couldn't think of he wore the red nose on certain days that may have meant something to him. We never saw him smile. And on those days he wore the clown's nose you found yourself looking away because you never saw such sadness.
>
> He pulled a piece of rope attached to a trolley on which Mrs Pop Eye stood. She looked like an ice queen. Nearly every woman on our island had crinkled hair, but Grace had straightened hers. She wore it piled up, and in the absence of a crown her hair did the trick. She looked so proud, as if she had no idea of her own bare feet. You saw her huge bum and worried about the toilet seat. You thought of her mother and birth and that stuff.
>
> At two-thirty in the afternoon the parrots sat in the shade of the trees and looked down at a human shadow one third longer than any seen before. There were only the two of them, Mr and Mrs Pop Eye, yet it felt like a procession.

(a) How does Jones create an impression of Mr and Mrs Pop Eye in this opening section of the novel?

(b) What is Mr Watts' significance in the novel as a whole? *(30 marks)*

OR

Harper Lee: *To Kill a Mockingbird*

Question 24

Read the passage and then answer the questions that follow.

'It's like bein'a caterpillar in a cocoon, that's what it is,' he said. 'Like somethin' asleep wrapped up in a warm place. I always thought Maycomb folks were the best folks in the world, least that's what they seemed like.

'We're the safest folks in the world,' said Miss Maudie.

'We're so rarely called on to be Christians, but when we are, we've got men like Atticus to go for us.'

Jem grinned ruefully. 'Wish the rest of the county thought that.'

'You'd be surprised how many of us do.'

'Who?' Jem's, voice rose. 'Who in this town did one thing to help Tom Robinson, just who?"

'His coloured friends for one thing, and people like us'.

People like Judge Taylor. People like Mr Heck Tate. Stop eating and start thinking, Jem. Did it ever strike you that Judge Taylor naming Atticus to defend that boy was no accident? That Judge Taylor might have had his reasons for naming him?'

This was a thought. Court-appointed defences were usually given to Maxwell Green, Maycomb's latest addition to the bar, who needed the experience. Maxwell Green should have had Tom Robinson's case.

'You think about that,' Miss Maudie was saying. 'It was no accident. I was sittin' there on the porch last night waiting, I waited and waited to see you all come down the sidewalk, and as I waited I thought, Atticus Finch won't win, he can't win, but he's the only man in these parts who can keep a Jury out so long in a case like that. And I thought to myself, well, we're making a step – it's just a baby-step, but it's a step.'

(a) How do the details in the passage add to the exploration of racism in the novel?

(b) How does Jem develop in the novel as a whole?

(30 marks)

Unit 2 Poetry Across Time

Time allowed: 1 hour 15 minutes

Instructions
Use black ink or black ball-point pen.
Answer two questions.
Answer one question from Section A. Answer one question from Section B.
For Section A, you must have a copy of the AQA Anthology, *Moon on the Tides* in the examination room.
The Anthology must not contain annotations.
You must not use a dictionary.

Information
The maximum mark for this paper is 54.
There are 36 marks for Section A and 18 marks for Section B.
You will be marked on your ability to:
- use good English
- organise information clearly
- use specialist vocabulary where appropriate.

Advice
You are advised to spend about 45 minutes on Section A and about 30 minutes on Section B.

Section A: POETRY CLUSTER FROM THE ANTHOLOGY
This section relates to the AQA Poetry Anthology that you have been using during the course.
Answer one question from this section on the poems you have studied in the *Anthology*. This section is worth 36 marks.
You are advised to spend about 45 minutes on this section.

EITHER

Character and Voice

Question 1

Compare the ways in which language is used to present a particular character in 'The Hunchback in the Park' and **one** other poem from 'Character and Voice'.   *(36 marks)*

OR

Question 2

Compare the ways in which a sense of voice is presented in 'My Last Duchess' and **one** other poem from 'Character and Voice'.   *(36 marks)*

OR

Place

Question 3

Compare the ways in which language is used to create a sense of place in 'Price We Pay for the Sun' and **one** other poem from 'Place'.   *(36 marks)*

OR

Question 4

Compare how poetic techniques are used to create effects in 'Storm in the Black Forest' and **one** other poem from 'Place'.   *(36 marks)*

OR

Conflict

Question 5

Compare how war is presented in 'The Charge of the Light Brigade' and **one** other poem from 'Conflict'.   *(36 marks)*

OR

Question 6

Compare how attitudes to war are explored in 'Futility' and **one** other poem from 'Conflict'.   *(36 marks)*

Relationships

Question 7

Compare how ideas about love are presented in Barrett Browning's 'Sonnet 43' and **one** other poem from 'Relationships'.

(36 marks)

OR

Question 8

Compare how language is used to achieve effects in 'Born Yesterday' and **one** other poem from 'Relationships'.

(36 marks)

Section B: RESPONDING TO AN UNSEEN POEM
Answer the question in this section.
This section is worth 18 marks.
You are advised to spend about 30 minutes on this section.

Question 1

Read the poem below and answer the question that follows.

Inversnaid

This darksome burn, horseback brown,
His rollrock highroad roaring down,
In coop and in comb the fleece of his foam
Flutes and low to the lake falls home.

A windpuff-bonnet of fawn-froth
Turns and twindles over the broth
Of a pool so pitchblack, fell-frowning,
It rounds and rounds Despair to drowning.

Degged with dew, dappled with dew
Are the groins of the braes that the brook treads through,
Wiry heathpacks, flitches of fern,
And the beadbonny ash that sits over the burn.

What would the world be, once bereft
Of wet and of wildness? Let them be left,
O let them be left, wildness and wet;
Long live the weeds and the wilderness yet.

Gerard Manley Hopkins

What do you think the poet is saying in this poem and how does he use language to achieve his effects?

(18 marks)

Unit 4 Approaching Shakespeare and the English Literary Heritage

Time allowed: 1 hour 30 minutes

Instructions
Use black ink or black ball-point pen.
Answer two questions.
Answer one question from Section A. Answer one question from Section B.
You must not use a dictionary.

Information
The maximum mark for this paper is 54.
There are 30 marks for Section A and 24 marks for Section B.
You will be marked on your ability to:
- use good English
- organise information clearly
- use specialist vocabulary where appropriate.

Advice
You are advised to spend about 50 minutes on Section A and about 40 minutes on Section B.

Section A: SHAKESPEARE
Answer **one** question from this section on the play you have studied.
This section is worth 30 marks.
You are advised to spend about 50 minutes on this section.

Macbeth

EITHER

Question 1 Answer both parts (a) and (b).

(a) How does Shakespeare show Lady Macbeth's thoughts and feelings in the extract below? *(15 marks)*

(b) Explain how Lady Macbeth persuades Macbeth to murder Duncan later in the play. *(15 marks)*

> Glamis thou art, and Cawdor, and shalt be
> What thou art promised: yet do I fear thy nature,
> It is too full o'th' milk of human kindness,
> To catch the nearest way. Thou wouldst be great,
> Art not without ambition, but without
> The illness should attend it. What thou wouldst highly,
> That wouldst thou holily: wouldst not play false,
> And yet wouldst wrongly win.
> Thou'dst have, great Glamis,
> That which cries, 'Thus thou must do, if thou have it;
> And that which rather thou dost fear to do
> Than wishest should be undone. Hie thee hither,
> That I may pour my spirits in thine ear,
> And chastise with the valour of my tongue
> All that impedes thee from the golden round,
> Which fate and metaphysical aid doth seem
> To have thee crowned withal.

OR

Question 2 Answer both parts (a) and (b).

(a) Read the following extract. How does Shakespeare use this opening scene of the play to capture the audience's attention and interest? *(15 marks)*

(b) Write about another part of the play which you found caught your attention and interest. Explain your reasons. *(15 marks)*

> ACT I SCENE I.
> An open place.
> *Thunder and lightning. Enter three Witches*
>
> | | |
> |---|---|
> | FIRST WITCH | When shall we three meet again |
> | | In thunder, lightning, or in rain? |
> | SECOND WITCH | When the hurlyburly's done, |
> | | When the battle's lost and won. |
> | THIRD WITCH | That will be ere the set of sun. |
> | FIRST WITCH | Where the place? |
> | SECOND WITCH | Upon the heath. |
> | THIRD WITCH | There to meet with Macbeth. |
> | FIRST WITCH | I come, Graymalkin! |
> | SECOND WITCH | Paddock calls. |
> | THIRD WITCH | Anon. |
> | ALL | Fair is foul, and foul is fair: |
> | | Hover through the fog and filthy air. |

Much Ado About Nothing

EITHER

Question 3 Answer both parts (a) and (b).

(a) How does Shakespeare convey Don John's thoughts and feelings in the passage below?   *(15 marks)*

(b) How does Shakespeare further show Don John's attitude through his words and actions elsewhere in the play?

(15 marks)

> DON JOHN   I had rather be a canker in a hedge than a rose in his grace, and it better fits my blood
> to be disdained of all than to fashion a carriage to rob love from any: in this, though I cannot
> be said to be a flattering honest man, it must not be denied but I am a plain-dealing
> villain. I am trusted with a muzzle and enfranchised with a clog; therefore I
> have decreed not to sing in my cage. If I had my mouth, I would bite; if I had
> my liberty, I would do my liking: in the meantime let me be that I am and seek
> not to alter me.

OR

Question 4 Answer both parts (a) and (b).

(a) How does Shakespeare convey Beatrice's attitude towards Benedick in the passage below?   *(15 marks)*

(b) Show how Shakespeare shows Beatrice exhibiting a different attitude towards Benedick in a passage from elsewhere in the play.

(15 marks)

> | | |
> |---|---|
> | BENEDICK | What, my dear Lady Disdain! are you yet living? |
> | BEATRICE | Is it possible disdain should die while she hath such meet food to feed it as Signior Benedick? Courtesy itself must convert to disdain, if you come in her presence. |
> | BENEDICK | Then is courtesy a turncoat. But it is certain I am loved of all ladies, only you excepted: and I would I could find in my heart that I had not a hard heart; for, truly, I love none. |
> | BEATRICE | A dear happiness to women: they would else have been troubled with a pernicious suitor. I thank God and my cold blood, I am of your humour for that: I had rather hear my dog bark at a crow than a man swear he loves me. |
> | BENEDICK | God keep your ladyship still in that mind! so some gentleman or other shall 'scape a predestinate scratched face. |
> | BEATRICE | Scratching could not make it worse, an 'twere such a face as yours were. |

EITHER

Question 5 Answer both parts (a) and (b).

(a) How does Shakespeare use imagery to express Romeo's feelings in the passage below?   *(15 marks)*

(b) How does Shakespeare use a different kind of imagery to express different feelings that Romeo experiences in a passage elsewhere in the play?   *(15 marks)*

> ROMEO
> He jests at scars that never felt a wound.
>
> [JULIET appears above at a window]
> But, soft! what light through yonder window breaks?
> It is the east, and Juliet is the sun.
> Arise, fair sun, and kill the envious moon,
> Who is already sick and pale with grief,
> That thou her maid art far more fair than she:
> Be not her maid, since she is envious;
> Her vestal livery is but sick and green
> And none but fools do wear it; cast it off.
> It is my lady, O, it is my love!
> O, that she knew she were!
> She speaks yet she says nothing: what of that?
> Her eye discourses; I will answer it.
> I am too bold, 'tis not to me she speaks:
> Two of the fairest stars in all the heaven,
> Having some business, do entreat her eyes
> To twinkle in their spheres till they return.
> What if her eyes were there, they in her head?
> The brightness of her cheek would shame those stars,
> As daylight doth a lamp; her eyes in heaven
> Would through the airy region stream so bright
> That birds would sing and think it were not night.
> See, how she leans her cheek upon her hand!
> O, that I were a glove upon that hand,
> That I might touch that cheek!

OR

Question 6 Answer both parts (a) and (b).

(a) How does Shakespeare use language to create a sense of tension in the passage below?   *(15 marks)*

(b) How does Shakespeare create tension in a different way in a passage from elsewhere in the play?   *(15 marks)*

| BENVOLIO | By my head, here come the Capulets. |
| MERCUTIO | By my heel, I care not. |

Enter TYBALT and others

TYBALT	Follow me close, for I will speak to them.
	Gentlemen, good den: a word with one of you.
MERCUTIO	And but one word with one of us? Couple it with something; make it a word and a blow.
TYBALT	You shall find me apt enough to that, sir, an you will give me occasion.
MERCUTIO	Could you not take some occasion without giving?
TYBALT	Mercutio, thou consortest with Romeo,--
MERCUTIO	Consort! what, dost thou make us minstrels? An thou make minstrels of us, look to hear nothing but discords: here's my fiddlestick; here's that shall make you dance. 'Zounds, consort!
BENVOLIO	We talk here in the public haunt of men:
	Either withdraw unto some private place,
	And reason coldly of your grievances,
	Or else depart; here all eyes gaze on us.
MERCUTIO	Men's eyes were made to look, and let them gaze;
	I will not budge for no man's pleasure, I.

EITHER

Question 7 Answer both parts (a) and (b).

(a) How does Shakespeare use language in this opening speech to set the mood for the play?   *(15 marks)*

(b) How is love talked of differently in a passage in another part of the play?   *(15 marks)*

Enter DUKE ORSINO, CURIO, and other Lords;
Musicians attending

DUKE ORSINO
If music be the food of love, play on;
Give me excess of it, that, surfeiting,
The appetite may sicken, and so die.
That strain again! it had a dying fall:
O, it came o'er my ear like the sweet sound,
That breathes upon a bank of violets,
Stealing and giving odour! Enough; no more:
'Tis not so sweet now as it was before.
O spirit of love! how quick and fresh art thou,
That, notwithstanding thy capacity
Receiveth as the sea, nought enters there,
Of what validity and pitch soe'er,
But falls into abatement and low price,
Even in a minute: so full of shapes is fancy
That it alone is high fantastical.

OR

Question 8 Answer both parts (a) and (b).

(a) How does Shakespeare use mistaken identity to amuse the audience and create interest in the development of the plot in the passage below from Act 4 scene 1?   *(15 marks)*

(b) Explain how Shakespeare uses mistaken identity elsewhere in the play to create dramatic impact.

(15 marks)

SIR ANDREW	Now, sir, have I met you again? There's for you. [Strikes Sebastian]
SEBASTIAN	[Striking Sir Andrew] Why, there's for thee, and there, and there. Are all the people mad?
SIR TOBY	Hold, sir, or I'll throw your dagger o'er the house.
FESTE	This will I tell my lady straight: I would not be in some of your coats for two pence. [Exit
SIR TOBY	Come on, sir; hold.
SIR ANDREW	Nay, let him alone: I'll go another way to work with him; I'll have an action of battery against him, if there be any law in Illyria: though I struck him first, yet it's no matter for that.
SEBASTIAN	Let go thy hand.
SIR TOBY	Come, sir, I will not let you go. Come, my young soldier, put up your iron: you are well fleshed; come on.
SEBASTIAN	I will be free from thee. What wouldst thou now? If thou darest tempt me further, draw thy sword.
SIR TOBY	What, what? Nay, then I must have an ounce or two of this malapert blood from you.

EITHER

Question 9 Answer both parts (a) and (b).

(a) How does Shakespeare reveal what is in Brutus's mind in the soliloquy (below)?   *(15 marks)*

(b) How does Brutus seek to persuade others that he has done the right thing in another speech
from the play?   *(15 marks)*

BRUTUS	It must be by his death: and for my part, I know no personal cause to spurn at him, But for the general. He would be crown'd: How that might change his nature, there's the question. It is the bright day that brings forth the adder; And that craves wary walking. Crown him?--that;-- And then, I grant, we put a sting in him, That at his will he may do danger with. The abuse of greatness is, when it disjoins Remorse from power: and, to speak truth of Caesar, I have not known when his affections sway'd More than his reason. But 'tis a common proof, That lowliness is young ambition's ladder, Whereto the climber-upward turns his face; But when he once attains the upmost round. He then unto the ladder turns his back, Looks in the clouds, scorning the base degrees By which he did ascend. So Caesar may. Then, lest he may, prevent. And, since the quarrel Will bear no colour for the thing he is, Fashion it thus; that what he is, augmented, Would run to these and these extremities: And therefore think him as a serpent's egg Which, hatched, would, as his kind, grow mischievous, And kill him in the shell.

OR

Question 10 Answer both parts (a) and (b).

(a) How does Shakespeare reveal Caesar's opinion of Cassius in the following passage?   *(15 marks)*

(b) Explain how Caesar's assessment of Cassius proves to be accurate through Cassius's own
words later in the play.   *(15 marks)*

CAESAR	Let me have men about me that are fat; Sleek-headed men and such as sleep o' nights: Yond Cassius has a lean and hungry look; He thinks too much: such men are dangerous.
ANTONY	Fear him not, Caesar; he's not dangerous; He is a noble Roman and well given.
CAESAR	Would he were fatter! But I fear him not: Yet if my name were liable to fear, I do not know the man I should avoid So soon as that spare Cassius. He reads much; He is a great observer and he looks Quite through the deeds of men: he loves no plays, As thou dost, Antony; he hears no music; Seldom he smiles, and smiles in such a sort As if he mock'd himself and scorn'd his spirit That could be moved to smile at any thing. Such men as he be never at heart's ease Whiles they behold a greater than themselves, And therefore are they very dangerous. I rather tell thee what is to be fear'd Than what I fear; for always I am Caesar. Come on my right hand, for this ear is deaf, And tell me truly what thou think'st of him.

Section B: PROSE FROM THE ENGLISH LITERARY HERITAGE

Answer **one** question on the novel or story collection you have studied.
This section is worth 24 marks.
You are advised to spend about 40 minutes on this section.

Jane Austen: *Pride and Prejudice*

EITHER

Question 11

How does Austen present Mr Bennet in *Pride and Prejudice*? Remember to write about the society he lives in.

(24 marks)

OR

Question 12

How does Austen present the role of women in society in *Pride and Prejudice*? Remember to write about the society they live in.

(24 marks)

Emily Brontë: *Wuthering Heights*

EITHER

Question 13

Referring in detail to two sections from the novel, show how Brontë presents different aspects of Catherine Earnshaw / Linton's character. Remember to write about the society she lives in.

(24 marks)

OR

Question 14

What do we learn about the values held by the characters in *Wuthering Heights*? Write about two or three characters from the novel in your answer. Remember to write about the society they live in.

(24 marks)

Charles Dickens: *Great Expectations*

EITHER

Question 15

How does Dickens explore issues to do with social class in *Great Expectations*? Remember to write about the society Dickens describes.

(24 marks)

OR

Question 16

Referring to two episodes from the novel, how does Dickens present Miss Havisham in different ways? Remember to write about the society she lives in.

(24 marks)

Thomas Hardy: *Hardy Short Stories*

EITHER

Question 17

How does Hardy present Rhoda Brook in *The Withered Arm* and one other character from a story of your choice? Remember to write about the society they live in.

(24 marks)

OR

Question 18

Referring to two of Hardy's stories, explore the ways in which he uses settings. Remember to write about the society he describes.

(24 marks)

George Orwell: *Animal Farm*

EITHER

Question 19

Referring to two episodes from the novel, explore how the animals are deceived and the methods the pigs use to control them.

(24 marks)

OR

Question 20

How does Orwell present the character of Boxer and what is his role in the novel?

(24 marks)

Answers

AQA English Language
Unit 1, Section A

1. You should mention:
- Fighting in the Falklands War had a mental impact on him.
- He was more affected by the experience than he realised.
- When he returned home after the war he found it hard to cope with life and he left the Navy.
- He believed he had post-traumatic stress but it was never properly diagnosed.
- He could not cope with normal life, his wife left him and they divorced.
- He then had a breakdown.
- He drifted to London and lived on the streets and later began selling the *Big Issue*.

2. You should mention:

Headline:
- The main heading 'Child Labour' makes it completely clear what the fact sheet is about – Child Labour.
- 'Save the Children' tells you which organisation has produced the fact sheet and the fact that it is a well-known organisation gives the information authority.

Layout:
- The introductory paragraph states the extent of the problem.
- Information is clearly laid out in blocks of text.
- Sub-headings pose questions that are answered in the text.
- The bullet point list gives extensive and comprehensive information.
- The list is boxed to separate it from the rest of the text.
- The direct quote from a girl stands out as it is in italic. The use of a real quote also adds to the effectiveness of the fact sheet.

3. You should discuss:
- Overall the agencies mentioned present a bleak picture of the situation.
- CARE draws attention to livestock dying and children dropping out of school to help find food. Civil war and drought year after year have forced people to flee their homes and become refugees creating widespread hunger.
- The Red Cross representative comments that the situation is worse than serious. Communities are losing the ability to feed themselves and their cattle are dying through lack of water.

4. Comparison is the key point here. Here are some points of comparison you might make between Item 3 and either Item 1 or Item 2.

Item 3
- Factual information based on reports from people who are there.
- Cause of the drought and famine highlighted.
- Direct speech used to give comments from people on the spot adds authority to the information.
- Descriptions of things they have seen.
- Use of negative vocabulary to create sense of seriousness of situation (e.g. 'widespread', 'malnutrition', 'crippled').

Item 1
- First-person style captures voice of speaker and makes the story personal.
- Background information given about life.
- Factual information about experiences.
- Details such as supporting Spurs.
- Layout with certain quotations from the text highlighted.
- A question is asked, which involves the readers and makes them think.

Item 2
- Factual and statistical information used.
- Questions asked and then answered.
- Use of quotations from a homeless girl.
- Vocabulary to express the nature of the jobs children do (e.g. 'trafficking', 'prostitution').
- Causes of the problem indicated.

Unit 1, Section B

5. and **6.** To achieve a good mark on these questions you need to:
- Write showing clear thinking and communicate in a convincing and compelling way.
- Capture the reader's attention with detailed and developed ideas and concepts and succinct argument.
- Make and sustain the purpose, intention and objective of writing the letter (Q.5) or article (Q.6), e.g. by affecting the reader, evoking a response.
- Write a letter (Q.5) to a friend or an article (Q.6), the tone of which is appropriate for the task.
- Sustain the purpose of writing the letter (Q.5) or article (Q.6).
- Use linguistic devices such as rhetorical questions, hyperbole, irony and description in an effective and appropriate way.
- Show use of appropriate discourse markers, e.g. 'Surely we cannot believe that....', 'Taking a positive view...', 'On the other hand...'.
- Write the whole text in continuous prose.
- Use paragraphs effectively to enhance meaning, e.g. the one-sentence paragraph for effect; longer paragraphs to develop ideas.
- Use a variety of structural features, e.g. different paragraph lengths, indented sections, dialogue, bullet points, to achieve particular effects.
- Present complex ideas in a coherent way.

AQA English Literature
Unit 1 Exploring Modern Texts
Section A: Modern Prose or Drama

1. (a) You should discuss:
- A description of narrator and her background.
- The impressions of teaching staff and the Head.
- Use of dialogue, e.g. the Head's attitude towards Mrs Carter.
- The impression of the 'Polish teacher' built up through the letters.
- The description of him when he comes to the school.
- The significance of his tie.

1. (b) Choose your own story to write about – make sure you focus on *how* the characters are *presented*, e.g. through descriptive language, dialogue and behaviour.

2. (a) You should discuss:
- The boy's eagerness to see his father.

- His desire to appear 'grown up'.
- His desire to please his father.
- The father's attitude towards his son and his fear that he has 'lost' him.
- The fact that the boy and the father are not named.

2. **(b)** Choose your own story and make sure you focus on how a *relationship* is presented, e.g. through descriptive language, dialogue and actions.

3. You should discuss:
   - Ralph is sensitive to the feelings of others, e.g. Piggy.
   - He is responsible and a natural leader, who has a natural air of authority and commands respect.
   - He shows both courage and compassion.
   - He believes in a democratic style of society as opposed to the kind run by Jack.
   - Ralph's failure to lead such a society symbolises a general failure to deal with the evil and anarchy.

4. You should discuss:
   - Piggy represents the voice of common-sense in a group where sense does not prevail.
   - His appearance marks him out as different, e.g. his size, glasses.
   - His intellectual point of view makes him the only 'adult-like' character on the island.
   - He applies his common-sense approach to dispelling the fears and illusions of the others.
   - Ultimately his death represents the rejection of rational thought by Jack and the others.

5. You should discuss:
   - Martyn's name and the effect it has had on him.
   - His relationship with his father.
   - His feelings about his father's drinking.
   - The kind of life he leads.
   - The effects created through the first-person narrative style.

6. • Select your chapter carefully.
   - Make sure that you have enough to say about it.
   - Look at the ways in which language is used in it to create effects.
   - Write about why you found the chapter effective.

7. • Select your section carefully and make sure you choose one you found effective.
   - Describe why you found this section particularly effective.
   - Analyse the ways in which Hill uses language to create her effects.
   - Make sure you comment on the effects of particular words, phrases, images, etc.

8. You should discuss:
   - Arthur Kipps' relief at leaving Crythin Gifford.
   - His hope that the curse has gone.
   - Hill apparently drawing the story to an end.
   - Arthur's marriage to Stella.
   - The 'shock' ending and the death of Stella and the child.
   - The language / structural techniques that Hill uses.

9. • Choose your episode carefully making sure that it is a part of the text that you found 'gripping'.
   - Focus on how Simpson uses language (e.g. imagery, description) and the effects that he creates.
   - Use specific examples of words and phrases and comment on them, e.g. how they create mood, atmosphere.
   - Make sure your comments are analytical.

10. You could discuss:
    - The strain Simon is under.
    - Simon's language to express his response to the fact Joe is alive.
    - His emotions – pity, horror, etc.
    - How he cares for Joe, e.g. laying him down gently and feeding him.
    - Simon's anxiety about Joe expressing their closeness.

11. You should discuss:
    - Captain Cat's role as an additional commentator in the play.
    - His detachment from the other characters.
    - As a member of the community he describes the other characters.
    - His attitude towards the children and his descriptions of them.
    - His private life and history.

12. You should discuss:
    - The description, e.g. the use of imagery.
    - The use of parody, e.g. through the Reverend Eli Jenkins.
    - The dialogue.
    - The presentation of the characters and their social background.
    - The contrast between serious and comic.

13. You should discuss:
    - The Reverend Hale's role as witch-hunter.
    - He is described as an 'intellectual'.
    - He takes pride in his job of exposing witches.
    - Through the course of the play he becomes convinced that Proctor and Mary Warren are telling the truth.
    - He becomes opposed to the witch trials and his failure to stop them breaks him.
    - You must also give your opinion of the character and support your view with references to the text.

14. You should discuss:
    - Abigail's role as the 'villain'.
    - Her lies and manipulations.
    - Throughout the play her motivations seem to consist purely of jealousy and a desire for revenge.
    - Her social position in Salem society.
    - The way the trial empowers her.
    - The language used to describe her, her dialogue and her actions.

15. You should discuss:
    - The trauma faced by Eva of being sent away by her mother.
    - The long-term consequences of her not being there for Eva.
    - How this impacts on her life as a grown up.
    - Eva's relationship with her own daughter.
    - The significance of the Ratcatcher.

16. • Explore your own responses and ideas about the play in detail, focusing on one or two specific episodes of the play.
    - Use references to the play to support your ideas.
    - Think about your ideas on the thematic ideas in the play.
    - Consider how effectively / powerfully Samuels presents the drama.
    - Pick out one or two parts that you found particularly moving / effective / interesting.

17. • Write about your own feelings at the end of the play (you do not need to 'explain' what you think has happened in terms of the strangeness of the events at the end). You should also discuss:
    - The way the characters have changed after the Inspector has left.
    - The effect of Gerald's information.
    - Mr and Mrs Birling's response to this.
    - The false sense of security shattered by the dramatic effect of the phone call.
    - You should also consider stage directions and dialogue.

18. You should discuss:
    - The 'self-made' man full of his own self-importance.
    - His relationship with his wife and son and daughter.
    - The importance he places on 'status'.
    - His attitude towards the Inspector.
    - His attitude towards his workers and Eva Smith.
    - His role as typifying the kind of 'I'm all right Jack' attitude that the Inspector condemns.

- The way he speaks and what he says.

19. Give a clear indication of how effective you find the opening of the play with specific remarks, e.g:
    - The use of questions.
    - The use of repetition.
    - The use of unfinished sentences.
    - How the audience is kept guessing.

20. Give clear views about your responses to the play, e.g:
    - Comment in detail about specific sections you have chosen, giving references to the text.
    - Comment on themes and ideas expressed.
    - Comment on dramatic techniques.

Unit 1 Exploring Modern Texts
Section B: Exploring Cultures

21. (a) You should discuss (with reference to the text):
    - Lennie is very child-like and relies on George to look after him and tell him what to do.
    - George has taken responsibility for Lennie. There are several possible reasons for this.
    - George likes Lennie and feels sorry for him.
    - Lennie is a companion to George.
    - George is the opposite of Lennie – he is quick-witted and intelligent, whereas Lennie is big and strong but he is like a small child.
    - George recognises that Lennie can be a liability as well as a companion.

    (b) You should discuss (with reference to the text):
    - America is going through a Depression and work and money are in short supply.
    - Lennie and George are typical of the thousands of itinerant labourers who roamed the country looking for work.
    - For those who had little, dreams were important.
    - Adversity created a kind of camaraderie amongst men like the men in the bunk house.
    - Men such as George and Lennie lived a rootless existence and they longed for somewhere to call their own where they could settle down.
    - Loneliness was common.

22. (a) • Give your own view on the effectiveness of the opening, supporting your view with references to the text.
    - Give reasons for your opinions with examples.
    - Consider language use and structure, e.g. description, narrative, sentence structure.

    (b) You should discuss (with reference to the text):
    - Kambili's father is generous and well-respected in the community.
    - He likes to show off his religious devotion.
    - At home, he is strict, narrow-minded and intolerant.
    - Although Kambili is afraid of him, she also loves him.
    - He sends Kambili and her brother away to live with their aunt when the military coup begins.

23. (a) You could discuss:
    - The physical description of him.
    - His white linen suit.
    - The use of language to describe Mrs Pop Eye.
    - Their actions and the descriptions of them.

    (b) You should discuss (with reference to the text):
    - Mr Watts as the storyteller to Matilda.
    - The only white man introduces *Great Expectations*, and introduces the children to the very different world created by Dickens.
    - Mr Watts mistakenly identified as 'Mr Dickens'.

24. (a) You should discuss:
    - Jem's question about who helped Tom Robinson.
    - Miss Maudie's response showing that some of the white people tried to help Tom Robinson.

    (b) You should discuss (with reference to the text):

- He begins as an innocent.
- The events of Tom Robinson's trial cause him great disillusionment.
- His realisation that justice does not always win leaves him confused.
- He later comes to realise the good in people too.
- In the end he loses his innocence without losing his hope.

Unit 2 Poetry Across Time
Section A: Poetry Cluster from the Anthology

1. You should mention:
   - The use of vocabulary to create a sense of isolation.
   - The use of imagery and other language devices.
   - The tone of the poem.
   - You must make comparative points with your chosen poem.

2. You should mention:
   - The poem is 'spoken' through the voice of a single speaker – dramatic monologue.
   - The 'flowery' speech which shrouds the true significance of what he has done.
   - The manipulation of the narrative by the speaker's voice.
   - You must make comparative points with your chosen poem.

3. You should mention:
   - Nichols' use of imagery and other language devices.
   - The use of vocabulary to create a sense of place.
   - The effect of the ending of the poem.
   - You must make comparative points with your chosen poem.

4. You should mention:
   - Lawrence's use of metaphor and other language techniques.
   - His use of vocabulary.
   - The effect of tone.
   - You must make comparative points with your chosen poem.

5. You should mention:
   - The use of repetition and rhythm and rhyme in 'The Charge of the Light Brigade'.
   - The idea that someone had 'blundered'.
   - Tennyson's attitude towards the charge and the men.
   - You must make comparative points with your chosen poem.

6. You should mention:
   - Owen's use of personification in 'Futility'.
   - His attitude towards the death of the young soldier.
   - His broader message and attitude towards war.
   - You must make comparative points with your chosen poem.

7. You should mention:
   - 'Sonnet 43' expresses the poet's intense love.
   - Her love is so great it is on a spiritual level.
   - The use of features including alliteration and repetition and the effects created.
   - You must make comparative points with your chosen poem.

8. You should mention:
   - The use of the opening metaphor in 'Born Yesterday'.
   - Larkin's use of vocabulary.
   - The key ideas of the poem.
   - You must make comparative points with your chosen poem.

Unit 2 Poetry Across Time
Section B: Responding to an Unseen Poem

1. You should discuss:
   - The poem as a celebration of the wildness of the scene, a celebration of nature, or of the purity of the unspoilt wilderness.

- The use of dialect words, e.g. 'burn', 'brae'.
- Unusual words, e.g. 'rollrock', 'windpuff'.
- The use of alliteration, e.g. 'degged with dew', 'wildness and wet'.
- The use of words created by combining words, e.g. 'fell-frowning', 'beadbonny'.
- The effect of the 'sprung rhythm' of the poem.

Unit 4 Approaching Shakespeare and the English Literary Heritage

Section A: Shakespeare

1. **(a)** You should discuss:
   - Lady Macbeth is pleased to hear of the honours bestowed on Macbeth (Glamis and Cawdor).
   - She feels he will be what the witches promised (i.e. king).
   - She feels he is too kind-hearted to actively seek to achieve this.
   - He is reluctant to 'play false' to achieve his ambitions.
   - She wants him to hurry home so she can persuade him to work to become king – 'that I can pour my spirits in thine ear'.
   - The use of metaphorical language by Lady Macbeth.

   (b) You should discuss:
   - Lady Macbeth plants the thought of killing Duncan in Macbeth's mind as soon as he returns.
   - She urges Macbeth to hide his feelings and let her take charge of everything.
   - When Macbeth changes his mind about the murder she is scornful and accuses him of cowardice.
   - She accuses him of lacking love for her.
   - She explains her plan to him and assures him they will not fail.

2. **(a)** You should discuss:
   - The storm creates a sense of violence and chaos and immediately captures the audience's attention.
   - The three witches establish the idea of the supernatural having an influence over events.
   - It creates a sense that forces of evil have been released.
   - The witches' words ('Fair is foul and foul is fair') turn normal values upside down – what is good is evil and what is evil is good.
   - The reference to fog and filthy air adds to the sense of unwholesome confusion.

   (b) Choose your passage carefully.
   - Make sure it is a passage that has caught your attention and interest.
   - Make sure you explain the effects created.
   - Give detailed references from the passage to illustrate how it creates impact.

3. **(a)** You should discuss:
   - Don John's words are a response to Conrade urging him to hide his ill-nature.
   - Don John expresses how he would rather be a 'canker' than something of 'grace'.
   - He appears to revel in his malicious nature.
   - He feels caged by his situation and likens himself to a muzzled dog.
   - If he had the opportunity he would 'bite'.

   (b) Choose your passage carefully, e.g:
   - Don John's conversation with Borachio in Act 2 scene 2.
   - His motives for his actions – several are mentioned but we do not know if they are true.
   - His dislike of the idea of marriage (Act 1 scene 3).
   - His grievance against Claudio (e.g. Act 1 scene 2).
   - The comparison of Don John and Don Pedro.

4. **(a)** You should discuss:
   - She picks up his comments and uses them to answer him back.
   - The tone of her banter – is it playful, affectionate, mocking, bitter?
   - Her words have more of an edge as the exchange continues (e.g. '...have been troubled by a pernicious suitor').
   - The reference to face scratching.

   (b) Select your passage carefully, e.g.
   - The final scene of the play (Act V, scene IV).
   - You could write about Beatrice revealing her feelings for Benedick publically for the first time.

5. **(a)** You should discuss:
   - The personification of Juliet as the sun.
   - The image of the 'envious moon'.
   - The image of 'envy / green'.
   - The comparison of Juliet's eyes with stars.
   - The idea of light linked with the 'brightness of her cheek'.
   - The idea of 'heaven' linked to Juliet.

   (b) Select your passage carefully.
   - There are several you could choose from – e.g. the final scene (Act 5 scene 3).
   - You could write about Romeo's extended personification of death.

6. **(a)** You should discuss:
   - Benvolio's opening remark – the appearance of the Capulets means trouble.
   - Mercutio's response and lack of concern.
   - Mercutio's provocative response to Tybalt's remark – '...make it a word and a blow'.
   - Mercutio's continued provocative talk and his response to Tybalt's language – e.g. Mercutio takes offence at his use of the word 'consort'.
   - Benvolio's attempted intervention and Mercutio's refusal to be moved.

   (b) Select your passage carefully, e.g.
   - Romeo's confrontation with Paris in the final scene.
   - You could write about Romeo's dangerous desperation and Paris's defying of him.

7. **(a)** You should discuss:
   - The opening reference to love, which is a major theme of the play.
   - The use of imagery of music as food.
   - The expression of the intensity of Orsino's love for Olivia.
   - The flowery nature of Orsino's language – perhaps indicating an excessive artificiality and exaggerated attitude.
   - The music imagery.

   (b) Select your passage carefully, e.g:
   - Orsino's attitude to love.
   - You could write about Olivia's expression of love for her dead brother.
   - You could write about the love she shows towards Cesario.
   - You could write about Viola's attitude towards love.

8. **(a)** You should discuss:
   - Sir Andrew's mistaken confidence in striking Sebastian based on his (mistaken) first meeting.
   - The mistaken identity proving unfortunate for Sir Andrew.
   - The amusement of the audience at seeing him beaten.
   - Sir Toby's intervention.
   - Sir Andrew's threat of legal action.

   (b) You could discuss:
   - Viola disguised as Cesario.
   - Sebastian mistaken for Cesario.

197

- Malvolio's inability to see through Feste's disguise.
- Malvolio's failure to see through the false letter written by Maria.
- How mistaken identity is essential for the plot.

9. **(a)** You should discuss:
   - Brutus decides that Caesar must die.
   - He has no personal reason to rebel against Caesar.
   - He fears Caesar's ambition and how being 'crown'd' might change his nature.
   - Use of the image 'bright day' bringing 'forth the adder' to emphasise this idea.
   - He fears greatness can be abused – 'when it disjoins / Remorse from power', i.e. power overrules feelings.

   (b) Select your passage carefully, e.g:
   - Act 3 scene 2 – Brutus speaks to the people after Caesar's death.
   - You could write about how he claims he did not kill Caesar because he did not love him but because he loved Rome more.
   - You could write about how he explains how Romans would have lived like slaves under Caesar.
   - You could write about how he speaks in prose here to address the plebeians on their level. Note the effect that his speech has.

10. **(a)** You should discuss:
    - His comments reveal that Cassius is not to be trusted.
    - He thinks too much and men who think 'are dangerous'.
    - Caesar says he does not know fear but if he did he would avoid Cassius.
    - His analysis of Cassius is perceptive – a man who has no personal life or interests – just a discomfort at the fact that others are more powerful than him.

    (b) You should discuss:
    - Later in the same scene, Cassius plots to turn Brutus against Caesar.
    - The plans to plant forged letters in Brutus's house.
    - He has recognised Brutus's weakest point and how to use it against Caesar.
    - Cassius has the ability to manipulate.

Unit 4 Approaching Shakespeare and the English Literary Heritage
Section B: Prose from the English Literary Heritage
11. You should discuss (with references to the text):
    - Mr Bennet's dialogue and the language used to describe him.
    - Mr Bennet adopts a rather detached attitude and distances himself from the rest of the family.
    - He can display a kind of sarcastic humour.
    - He is particularly close to Elizabeth and recognises her intelligence.
    - He has a dry wit which contrasts with his wife's hysteria, and this makes the reader see him as a sympathetic figure.
    - However, his detachment from the family can make him seem rather a weak father and he perhaps is too inclined to indulge Lydia's immature behaviour, which nearly leads to general disgrace when she elopes.
    - After this he proves largely ineffective and it is left to Darcy to rescue the situation.
    - His attitude towards society's conventional judgements.

12. You should discuss (with references to the text):
    - The novel presents a society in which a woman's reputation is of the utmost importance.
    - A woman was expected to behave in particular ways governed by social convention – ways not adhering to these social norms would invite ostracism from polite society.
    - When Lydia elopes with Wickham and the two live together unmarried, Austen shows the very serious implications this has. Through her actions, Lydia clearly broke one of the most important social rules.
    - Her disgrace not only threatens her but the entire Bennet family.
    - Darcy manages to save the situation but only by persuading Wickham to marry Lydia.

13. Choose your sections carefully. You could discuss (with references to the text):
    - Catherine's spirited nature is retained throughout the novel.
    - She has a dual nature which allows her to have feelings for both Heathcliff and Edgar.
    - She recognises that her feelings for Edgar are superficial whereas she describes her love for Heathcliff in spiritual terms.
    - She changes after her time at Thrushcross Grange.
    - Her attitude before her death.

14. Think about your character selection. You could discuss (with references to the text):
    - Considerations of class status often lie behind various characters' motivations.
    - For example, Catherine's decision to marry Edgar is based on her desire to improve her social status.
    - The Lintons have a much more solid status as members of the gentry than the Earnshaws, e.g. the Earnshaws do not possess a carriage, the Lintons have more land and a grander house.
    - Heathcliff rises from homeless orphan to 'gentleman'.
    - Nellie and Lockwood are aware of social distinctions.

15. You should discuss (with references to the text):
    - Magwitch at the bottom of the social class as a convict.
    - The lower class through Joe and Biddy.
    - The middle class through, e.g. Pumblechook.
    - The wealthy – Miss Havisham.
    - Central theme relates to social class – Pip learns that wealth and class are less important than love and affection, e.g. Drummle is upper class but a worthless individual, whereas Magwitch is a convict but has dignity and worth.

16. Choose your episodes carefully. You could discuss (with references to the text):
    - The daunting and bitter figure that Pip meets when he is a young boy.
    - Miss Havisham's growing realisation about what she has made Estella.
    - Miss Havisham's eventual sorrow at what she has done.

17. You should discuss (with references to the text):
    - The sympathetic portrayal of her – people look down on her and ignore her.
    - The idea of the illegitimate son to the farmer.
    - The idea that she possesses special powers and performs witchcraft.
    - Choice of other character, e.g. Gertrude Lodge.

18.
    - Select your stories carefully.
    - Focus on the use of settings.
    - Give specific examples, and explain their significance and effects.
    - Comment on the society he writes about.
    - Support your points with reference to the text.

19. You should discuss (with reference to the text):
    - Deception used to gain power: the pigs deceive the other animals by convincing them that certain events did or did not occur.
    - They pretend that the other animals are far better off than they are.
    - Their plans for the future are lies.
    - They assure the animals their dreams will come true.
    - They are deceived about the fate of Boxer.

20. You should discuss (with reference to the text):
- Boxer is a devoted citizen of the farm and its hardest worker.
- He fully supports the rebel cause.
- He is not the brightest of the animals and so falls easy prey to the scheming pigs.
- His fate serves to highlight Napoleon's ruthless tyranny.
- He represents the exploitation of ordinary workers.

ACKNOWLEDGEMENTS

p.15, 92, 183 *Of Mice and Men* by John Steinbeck. (Penguin 2000). Copyright © John Steinbeck 1937, 1965. Reproduced by permission of Penguin Books Ltd.

p.20 and p.34 Articles 'Fairtrade' and 'Is it Time to Kill Bambi?' from the RSPB magazine *Wingbeat*, the magazine for teenagers. Reproduced by kind permission of the RSPB.

p.27 Crown copyright material reproduced with the permission of the Controller of HMSO and the Queen's Printer for Scotland.

p.29 *The Perfect Storm* by Sebastian Junger. Reprinted by permission of HarperCollins Publishers Ltd. © 1997 Sebastian Junger.

p.37 *The Sound of Laughter* by Peter Kay, published by Century. Reprinted by permission of The Random House Group Ltd.

p.38–39 *Notes from a Small Island* by Bill Bryson. Reprinted by permission of The Random House Group Ltd.

p.42–43 *Fever Pitch* by Nick Hornby. (First published by Victor Gollancz 1992, Penguin Books 2000) Copyright © Nick Hornby, 1992. Reproduced by permission of Penguin Books Ltd.

p.43–44 *Pole to Pole* by Michael Palin. Reprinted by permission of The Orion Publishing Group Ltd.

p.50 Image of Loch Ness Monster © Everett Collection/Rex Features.

p.54 Chester Zoo leaflet, reprinted by permission of Chester Zoo.

p.55 Mars advert. Used with permission of Mars. MARS, TWIX, MILKY WAY and SNICKERS are registered trademarks. © Mars 2009

p.59 Harry Potter review by Edward Lawrenson, from *The Big Issue in the North* No.781 13-19 July 2009, used with kind permission.

p.72–73 Article 'Global: Destructive Fishing' from Greenpeace's *Connect* magazine, Summer 2009 Image: © Greenpeace/Hilton, article used with kind permission of Greenpeace.

p.79 Crown copyright material reproduced with the permission of the Controller of HMSO and the Queen's Printer for Scotland.

p.82 Leaflets for the Churchill Museum and Cabinet War Rooms, reproduced by kind permission of the Imperial War Museum.

p.90 Lemona's Tale by Ken Saro-Wiwa, first published 1996. Reprinted by permission of Ed Victor Ltd.

p.88, 140, 145, 185 *To Kill a Mockingbird* by Harper Lee, published by Vintage Classics, £7.99. First published in 1960.

p.88, 137, 138, 139 *Lord of the Flies* by William Golding. Reprinted by permission of the publishers, Faber and Faber Ltd., London.

p.120, 121, 122, 124, 126, 127 *An Inspector Calls* by J.B. Priestley. (An Inspector Calls and Other Plays first published by William Heineman 1948-50, first published by Penguin Books 1969, Penguin Classics 2000.) Copyright © J.B. Priestley 1947. Reproduced by permission of Penguin Books Ltd.

p.123 *Under Milk Wood* by Dylan Thomas, published by Orion. Reprinted by permission of David Higham Associates Ltd.

p.121 *Hobson's Choice* by Harold Brighouse. Reprinted by permission of Samuel French Ltd, representatives of the Estate.

p.150 *Mid-Term Break* by Seamus Heaney. Reprinted by permission of the publishers, Faber and Faber Ltd., London.

p.158 *My Grandmother* by Elizabeth Jennings, published by Carcanet Press. Reprinted by permission of David Higham Associates Ltd.

p.160 *Half-Caste* by John Agard. Reprinted by permission of the Caroline Sheldon Literary Agency.

p.163 *War Photographer* by Carol Ann Duffy. `War Photographer' is taken from "Standing Female Nude" by Carol Ann Duffy published by Anvil Press Poetry in 1985.

p.177 Brian's Story from *The Big Issue*, used with kind permission.

p.178 Excerpt taken from 'Child Labour: Fact sheet', Save the Children, 2005. Reproduced with permission of Save the Children.

p.179 Article 'More on Horn of Africa Drought' by Tom Parry, October 5th 2009 from the Daily Mirror Online. Reproduced with permission.

p.184 *Purple Hibiscus* by Chimamanda Ngozi Adichie. Reprinted by permission of HarperCollins Publishers Ltd. © 2003 Chimamanda Ngozi Adichie.

p.184 *Mister Pip* by Lloyd Jones. Reproduced by permission of John Murray (Publishers) Ltd..

p.185 *On the Train* from *Making the Beds for the Dead* by Gillian Clarke (2004). Reprinted by permission of Carcanet Press Limited.

p11   ©iStockphoto.com/Julien Grondin
p14   ©iStockphoto.com/Henk van Mierlo
p27   ©iStockphoto.com/Courtney Navey
p48   ©iStockphoto.com/Dainis Deric
p50   ©Everett Collection/Rex Features
      ©Jupiterimages / Photos.com / Thinkstock

All other images are ©2010 Jupiterimages Corporation and Lonsdale

Index

A Christmas Carol 90
A Walk in a Workhouse 40–41
Adjacency pairs 24
Advertising 52–56
    Analysing adverts 54
    Comparing adverts 55–56
Advice 77–80
    Layout 77–78
    Language 77–78
Alliteration 53, 95, 153
An Inspector Calls 120, 122, 124, 125
Analysing texts 18–19
Analysis 18
Anecdotes 70
Anthology 129
Antithesis 112
Arguments 65–70
    Beginning 65–66
    Developing 67–68
    Ending 69
    Planning 64–65
    Presenting 64–70
Asides 106–107
Assonance 53, 95, 153
Atmosphere 149–151
Audience 11–12, 18, 21, 78
Aural imagery 152–153
Autobiographies 36–38

Biographies 36–38

Characters 91–93
Colloquial language 24
Comparative devices 76
Connectives 69
Contemporary poetry 158–159
Contemporary prose 129
Context 12–13, 155
Contractions 24
Controlled Assessment 6
Creative writing 86–95

Description 135
Descriptive writing 93–95
Dialect 159–160
Dialogue 135
Discourse markers 69
Discussing and listening 169–170, 172
Documentary writing 40–41
Drama texts 117–125
    Characters 121–122
    Opening scenes 119–120

Elizabethan theatre 98
Emotive language 26
End-clipping 24
Exaggeration 53, 70, 76
Exclamations 26

Fact 35, 49, 66
False starts 24
Far from the Madding Crowd 11
Fever Pitch 42–43
Fillers 24
Film 57–61
First person narration 87–89
Functional skills 6
Futility 152

Great Expectations 142
Group discussions 169–170, 172

Hard Times 92, 95
Headings 35
Humour 53, 76
Hyperbole 70

Illustrations 35
Imagery 53, 95, 112, 135, 151–153
Imaginative writing 86–95
Imperatives 53, 78
Information 80–83
    Presenting 80–83
Interviews 60–61

Julius Caesar 111

Language techniques 36
Layout 35
Lists 26
Literary Heritage 129, 155–158
Literary non-fiction 42
Literary techniques 26
Lord of the Flies 88, 137, 138, 139

Macbeth 102–103, 107, 108, 110, 116
Magazine articles 33–36
Metaphors 76, 95, 112, 152
Mid-Term Break 150
Mood 149–151
Much Ado About Nothing 111
My Grandmother 158

Narrative viewpoint 87–89, 134–135
Newspapers 47–52
    Captions 47
    Comparing 49–52
    Headlines 47
    Illustrations 47
Non-fiction texts 32–44
Non-standard English 159–160
Notes from a Small Island 38–39
Novels 128–144
    Context 140–143
    Developing characters 135
    Openings 130–135
    Setting 140–143

Of Mice and Men 92
On My First Sonne 149
Onomatopoeia 95, 153
Opinion 35, 49, 66
Overlaps 24

Pauses 24
PEE technique 22
Personification 152
Persuasive writing 71–76
    Endings 75–76
    Openings 74–75
    Techniques 76
Phonological techniques 26
Planned speech 26–28
Play on words 71
Plot 89
Poetry 109–110, 147–162
    Comparing 160–162

Pole to Pole 43–44
Presenting 167–168, 172
Previews 57–58
Pride and Prejudice 131, 134
Prose 110–111
Puns 53
Purpose 9–10, 18, 21, 78

Questions 26

Repetition 24, 26, 53, 76, 153
Reviews 57–59
Rhetoric 26
Rhetorical questions 26, 70, 71, 76
Rhyme 53, 153–154
Rhythm 95, 154
Role play 170–171, 172
Romeo and Juliet 104–105, 114

Sentence structures 95
Setting 89, 123–125
Shakespeare 98–114
    Characters 106–108
    Endings 113–114
    Language 109–112
    Opening scenes 102–105
    Opening techniques 102–105
    Plot 100–101
    Structure 100–101
    Types of play 98–100
Short stories 128–144
Similes 76, 95, 112, 151
Slang 24
Slogans 54
Soliloquies 106–108
Speaking and listening 166–172
Spoken language 23–28
Spontaneous speech 23–25
Stage directions 123–125
Standard English 160
Stories 87
    Openings 90–91
Sunlight on the Grass 129
Superlatives 53
Symbols 135

Television 57–61
The Affliction of Margaret 156
The Eagle 162
The Perfect Storm 29–30
The Withered Arm 133
Thematic ideas 124–125
Themes 123–125, 143–144
Third person narration 88–89
To His Coy Mistress 157
To Kill a Mockingbird 88, 140
Tone 149–151
Topic 13–14
Travel writing 38–39
Turn-taking 24
Twelfth Night 109

Under Milk Wood 123
Use of three 26, 76

War Photographer 163
Wuthering Heights 132, 134, 141